THE FIRST A.I.F.

BY THE SAME AUTHOR

The Convict Settlers of Australia
(Melbourne University Press)

Australia and the Great War 1914-1918
(Macmillan of Australia)

The First A.I.F.

A STUDY OF ITS RECRUITMENT

1914–1918

L. L. ROBSON

Senior Lecturer in History
University of Melbourne

MELBOURNE UNIVERSITY PRESS

First published 1970

Printed in Australia by
Halstead Press Pty Ltd, Kingsgrove, N.S.W. 2208 for
Melbourne University Press, Carlton, Victoria 3053
Great Britain and Europe: ISBS Inc., London
USA and Canada: ISBS Inc., Zion, Illinois 60099

Registered in Australia for transmission by post as a book

ISBN 0 522 83981 9
Dewey Decimal Classification Number 994.04

Acknowledgments

During my research I sought and received hundreds of letters from veterans of the war. It was my intention to incorporate those reminiscences, together with the results of a statistical enquiry into the social origin of the A.I.F., into this book but my focus of interest changed and this became impossible. Reluctant to let the statistical findings and the letters slip through my fingers, I intend to incorporate them into a subsequent work.

Many other people helped me, sometimes because they held that I needed assistance, sometimes because they thought I was looking into the Anzac tradition, sometimes as a result of my steering the conversation around to World War I, and sometimes because they thought there had been enough written about the war on the Western Front. I was also helped, in a way, by some threatening letters, the authors of which were convinced that I was not going to be adulatory towards the A.I.F. But mostly the helpers were excellent State and Commonwealth civil servants.

I am, then, much indebted to Mr I. Maclean, the Commonwealth Archivist in Canberra, and in particular to his deputy, Dr Keith Penny, in both official and private capacity. At the Commonwealth Archives Office, Melbourne, I also met with unfailing courtesy and help from Miss Thea Exley. I am indebted to the Archives Officers and/or their deputies and staff in all States: H. W. Nunn and J. W. Wambeek in Melbourne, R. F. Doust in Sydney, R. C. Sharman in Brisbane, G. L. Fischer in Adelaide, Miss Mollie Lukis in Perth and Michael Saclier in Hobart. I was also helped by Miss Patricia Reynolds and the staff of the La Trobe Library, Melbourne; Mrs Pauline Fanning at the National Library of Australia, Canberra; W. R. Lancaster and Miss Blackwood at the Australian National War Memorial Library, Canberra; and the late Gavin Long.

I should also like to thank the staff of the Army Archives, Melbourne, and especially Messrs B. Stewart and H. C. Dowsett.

I have been helped by conversations with Professor K. S. Inglis, History Department, University of Papua and New Guinea; Dr F. B. Smith and Mr L. F. Fitzhardinge of the History Department in the Institute of Advanced Studies at the Australian National University, Canberra. Mr Fitzhardinge kindly let me examine certain of the Hughes Papers. I want also to thank Professor J. A. La Nauze, History Department, Institute of Advanced Studies at the Australian National University; Professor W. D. Borrie, Demography Department at the A.N.U., and Professor A. W. Martin, History Department, La Trobe University, who supported my work when it was only an idea.

Professor R. M. Crawford, Department of History, University of Melbourne, helped me in a particular matter and Mr P. A. Ryan, Director of the Melbourne University Press, gave me encouragement just at the right time.

For permission to cite documents among the Lloyd George Papers in the Beaverbrook Library, London, I thank Beaverbrook Newspapers and the First Beaverbrook Foundation. The Lord Birdwood and Mr Rupert Murdoch kindly gave me permission to use documents in the Beaverbrook Library written by Field-Marshal Sir William Birdwood and by Sir Keith Murdoch.

It was my good fortune to be assisted by two alert research assistants at different times, Helen Hunt and Patsy Hardy. I could not have done the work without them, and although the final result of their exertions may not bear much resemblance to what they or I had in mind at the time, I hereby record in print my sincere thanks.

Miss Gwenyth Williams's office staff in the History Department competently typed my draft.

This book was made possible by a grant from the Australian Research Grants Committee and I must thank that body for its help.

Contents

Illustrations

Introduction

Something eerie came over European civilization in the early twentieth century and led to a madness which was called 'the Great War'.

This book deals with the cause, course and effects of the recruitment of the Australian Imperial Force for that conflict. It is an analysis of the home front during the horrible four and a half years of the struggle in Europe and the Middle East and on the high seas, and seeks to show how Australia's effort to keep up the reinforcements said to be necessary to sustain and strengthen the A.I.F. led to the shattering of the spirit of optimism, virtual unanimity and cocky pride with which the new Commonwealth entered the war. The theme is the wrecking of Australian optimism and happiness, and the creation of a situation where negative thought and destructive criticism could flourish.

This capacity for destructive thinking may be observed in many areas but basically it was associated with the inability of the federal government and its agencies to induce enough men to enlist voluntarily. Government and people were reduced to the level of tell-tales, deceivers and liars in the consequent seeking out of scapegoats and in the paranoia about German spies; convinced that Australia, the British Empire and civilization were immediately endangered, the Prime Minister, William Morris Hughes, and his supporters were prepared to do anything to ensure that the Commonwealth strained all muscles to breaking-point so that the barbarians' invasion might be turned back.

At the outbreak of war and in the years leading up to it, there seems to have been almost a need for war: Australia was spoiling for a fight so that she could show the nations of the world what the new Commonwealth could do. The soldiers of the A.I.F. showed what they could do all right, but the cost of that demonstration was terrible. Wholesale slaughter on the Western Front was bad enough to a country whose population was barely five million people, but the downfall of the Labor Party, the great bitterness of sectarianism, and the splitting of the male population of the country into those who joined up and those who did not, led to a negation of civilized values and the elevation of expenditure of manpower into a virtue.

Perhaps there have been too many angry humanitarians who have cried out against stupid generals and the tactics employed on the battlefield, and failed to grasp that the war became not merely the grim result of man's aggression, but an entity in itself; it took on the character of an uncontrollable bushfire raging on till it burnt itself out. No man could control it, though all men together could have done so. Perhaps there have been too many critics, though certainly not in Australia, who have reappraised the war and blamed its stupefying shock for the rise of the totalitarians and the unleashing of total war on millions of people who never wore the uniform of a signed-up combatant.

Are there not some constructive effects of the war? It is hard to find any that may be sustained seriously as a counter-balance to millions of dead men, but in the case of Australia it is regarded as good that a nation was born amid the holly-scrub of Gallipoli and under the rain-clouds of France, a nation which was subsequently admitted to the councils of the world on a footing of equality.

There was a birth: the war had the clear effect of causing the inhabitants of the Australian continent to focus upon their unique nationality; it brought the soldiers of the A.I.F. to the realization that they were one and all Australians, and not primarily citizens of the various States. The A.I.F. apotheosized Australian nationality.

It was not just that; the awe-inspiring power of the Anzac legend is based on the great sigh of relief with which the Australian people discovered that their soldiers had not let them down on the long day and night of 25 April 1915. All the elements of legend were there: the landing at sunrise out of the sea on to the alien shore; the classical site; the high praise then and later heaped on the soldiers who fought with such superb insolence, competence, daring and nonchalance; the apparently overwhelming odds; the hand-to-hand fighting which dramatized a campaign where the machines of war had not yet taken over.

Added to all this was the fact which clinched the Anzac tradition and crystallized a sense of nationality—the blood sacrifice necessary for a deep stirring of the unsophisticated unconscious. In the following years this was reinforced by the very heavy casualties suffered on the Western Front.

The recruitment of the A.I.F. was the greatest effort Australia ever made as a nation, and the voluntary character of the army is the outstanding fact in explaining the effect of its enlistment, because every man who enlisted made his own decision.

This recruitment of the A.I.F. on a voluntary basis tore out Australia's heart, shattered the community and caused untold mental agony to those who appeared eligible but did not join the colours. Badges were available to men who were rejected on medical grounds but this served only further to isolate young Australians who did not join the army. They went through hell: some sincerely considered that the war was an unworthy and hypocritical one, and were disgusted and shocked by the hysterical conduct of their fellows, including those in uniform who became important for the first time in their lives; some trade unionists and others concluded that the war was a miserable conflict brought on by pre-war greed among conflicting economic interests. Some were under heavy parental pressure, complete with mother's tears, not to go to foreign places and desert the old folk, and reluctantly stayed, their decision a thousand times more agonizing than the impulsive and decisive enlistment of their mates, because for years those who stayed had to put up with social ostracism and the contempt of women; some who remained in Australia did not go because they were frightened of being shot; and others stayed for private and personal reasons which they thought they might have to divulge to the authorities if they went to the recruiting depot.

None of these reasons carried much weight with those in the community who actually revelled in the war and the sharpened purpose it gave to their lives as they terrorized prospective recruits, broke up meetings which protested against the war and conscription, shook collection boxes under people's noses, were most forward each 4 August in leading fervent prayers to crush the

Germans on the anniversary of the outbreak of war, wrote in to the Defence Department informing on neighbours, piously wished they were able to go to the war, and engaged in those thousand and one activities calculated to win the war for the forces of sweetness, light, reason and democracy.

The enlistment of the A.I.F., and the war, revealed both splendid and deplorable aspects of Australia: thoughtlessness, cruelty, unswerving devotion to the suppression of opposition; great courage, shining sincerity, high and proper ideals and mindful sacrifice.

Australia was wrung dry during these four and a half years. The procedures of democratic government, the rectifying of social injustice and the recognition of certain rights were all shelved on the grounds that the state was immediately threatened. I have sought to show the significant aspects of an episode which bites more deeply into the nation's psyche than anything else in its history. It should.

1

Australia on the Eve of the War

The Commonwealth of Australia was ushered into the world on 1 January 1901 to the tune of, among other things, 'O God Our Help in Ages Past', some of those in authority thus exhibiting the customary Australian ability to emphasize the obvious in lengthy platitudes. Though the seat of the new federal government was to be Melbourne, the ceremony was conducted in Sydney in the presence of the first Governor-General, Lord Hopetoun, a scion of the English aristocracy who symbolized that mystic union between Queen Victoria and her people in the Antipodes.

The event of Federation was wildly celebrated throughout Australia, and nearly every township had a procession of sorts, followed by a civic reception and a fireworks display. Sydney, the capital of the mother colony, outdid herself in ostentation, as the Melbourne newspapers observed. Undaunted by early morning rain, a grand procession of imperial troops, trade unionists, church dignitaries and national floats filed through vast crowds. The Italian allegorical car was possibly the finest. Its contents were two ladies classically garbed, representing Britannia and Australia, a bust of Sir Henry Parkes, four *bersaglieri* (Italian soldiers) of whom two were dressed as Garibaldians, much bunting in the Italian national colours, and a band of fifteen musicians.

Unobserved by Cardinal Moran, who stood aloof from all official functions because his precedence had been cancelled at the last minute, the procession passed beneath a large number of triumphal arches built by the French, Italian, American and German national groups in Sydney, together with others erected to represent the leading Australian industries of wool, wheat and coal. The coal arch fell down some days later because members of the public surreptitiously removed key pieces of fuel.

At Centennial Park the Governor-General took the oath of office. The new federal Cabinet led by Edmund Barton was then sworn in. Speeches were made, cheers were given and gun salutes fired. The jollifications, including magnificent fireworks displays on the harbour, continued for several days. J. Brunton Stephens, a poet, was moved to hail his country as 'a Pallas sprung/ Consummate from the brain of man', and further, to conclude that to Australians had been 'The Lordship of a continent assigned/ As God's own gift for service of mankind.' Though few of his countrymen would have put it quite that way, they were very proud of their new nation, knowing themselves to be, in the characteristically prosaic words of Sidney Webb, 'an adult Anglo-Saxon democracy'.[1]

The constitution of that democracy meant that there were now inflicted on the nation not twelve but fourteen Houses of Parliament, of which exactly half were essentially anti-democratic. But the Lower Houses of the States and the Commonwealth did at least theoretically reflect the principle of one man, one vote. The political scene remained peaceful between Federation and the outbreak of the war; even the emergence from the discontented classes of a full-fledged federal Labor Party did not exacerbate political tempers very much. Excitement was not lacking, but there was an absence of major issues which might have sharply divided the parties from each other.

At the federal level there were three political groups, the only one which could be termed a 'party' in the modern sense being Labor. Its organization was shiningly simple: in each federal electorate was a branch of the party, composed mainly of trade unionists but open to all comers. The branch chose the local party candidate and elected delegates to attend the State Labor League conference which drew up the party platform and imposed on candidates a pledge to accept the decisions of the parliamentary caucus on all issues affecting the party's political platform.[2]

Opposed to Labor were the conservative Free-traders who, like most conservatives, reacted rather than acted in the existing circumstances and supported the *status quo* when in doubt about anything, permitting society to make what way its members could according to the lawless laws of *laissez-faire*. Leader of this group was George Reid of New South Wales, a man of large stature and shrewd mind. Beatrice Webb thought his figure a caricature, the features of his face not more refined than his figure, and his clothes unkempt and dirty; with painless duty she recorded that his manner of speaking was rough and his repartee coarse. Reid was a larrikin politician and she was impressed by his pugnacity, humour and cunning; she remarked on the lack of any sign of statesmanship which she might recognize; she was intrigued by the phenomenon, up to a point.[3]

The other party of the Right was that of the Liberal Protectionists, led by Alfred Deakin and Victorian members of Parliament. They were closer to the Labor position than the Free-traders but their liberal consciences were affronted by the Labor 'pledge' which, it was thought, compelled members to obey the decisions of the annual Labor conference. To Liberals, this was a violation of conscience, which, of course, it was. Deakin was a rarity in Australian politics, a man of sensitivity and culture but essentially an enigma. Regarded by some as a smooth operator, in reality Deakin was a man racked with doubts and introspection which his colleagues had not the imagination to begin to imagine. Deakin was three times Prime Minister of the new nation before his mind slowly crumbled in the atmosphere of self-satisfied stupidity in which he found himself, because Melbourne from the beginning began to impose its rectitude, uprightness and philistinism on the new Commonwealth.[4]

From 1901 to 1910 none of the three groups was able to govern alone and unaided, the coalition of Deakin's Liberal Protectionists and the Labor Party conducting the affairs of the country under the banner of protection which, in various forms, was the keynote of early Commonwealth politics. One form was xenophobia; Delos of the coming sun-god's race[5] was not to be invaded by undesirable foreigners, and there was no disagreement in Parliament or up and down the country on the question of Australia for the white man. Its naked racism hidden by the fig-leaf of its euphemistic title, the Immigration Restriction Act was the first legislation passed by the Commonwealth Parliament, reflecting an antipathy to coloured labour that had a long history in Australia: as early as 1840 James Stephen at the Colonial Office in London had warned the governor

B

of New South Wales about the probable danger to a European society if it imported Asian coolies to replace the convict labour force, and in 1897 the colonies of the Empire had been asked by the imperial authorities to seek a form of words which would avoid hurting the feelings of any subjects of the Empire who might be denied entry.

Not only did the country fear the possible catastrophic results of injecting the cause of future disunity and tragedy (the American Civil War was only forty years in the past) but it also feared competition from such nations as Japan, possessed of inexhaustible energy and a low standard of living, it was stated. Manifestations of fear were not limited to coloured people; Italians were not altogether desirable, described as springing disease-laden from the malarial south and importing not only their miserably low standard of living but knives and razors as well. As one observer concluded with satisfaction as he contemplated the new Commonwealth reaching the economic take-off point from which it would surely overhaul the United States of America, Italians were not civilized in the Australian sense.[6] They were not.

The nation peered at the rest of the world like a frightened unarmed man looking through very thin bushes at marauding tigers. The bushes were made more protective by means other than manifestations of xenophobia: Australian Industries Preservation Acts provided penalties for intention to destroy or injure by means of unfair competition any Australian industry whose preservation was judged to be advantageous to the Commonwealth, and in 1908 emerged the 'new protection'. This involved the payment by local manufacturers of excise duties at the same rate as those on imports unless the local employers paid wages and provided working conditions that were held to be fair and reasonable. Though the High Court subsequently declared the Acts applying the 'new protection' *ultra vires* the Constitution, the principle of 'fair and reasonable' was so attractive to Australians of the Edwardian era that it got itself embedded in the country's brain like a fossil in living rock when, in 1906, the president of the Commonwealth Court of Conciliation and Arbitration, Mr Justice Higgins, decided in the Harvester judgment that the Sunshine Harvester Company should pay its employees a wage that was 'fair and reasonable'.

In a sentence so abstract and elegant that none could object to it with earnestness, Higgins concluded that such a wage must be sufficient to satisfy the normal needs of the average employee regarded as a human being living in a civilized community. The magic figure turned out to be seven shillings a day; the difficulty of awarding more for special skills was overcome by the award of marginal payments, but the touchstone was the welfare of the average man.[7] That principle was upheld when it came to paying the men of the Australian army.

The two parties of the Right joined forces under Deakin in May 1909 in opposition to Labor whose William Morris Hughes, one of the top-ranking men in the party at that time, but not leader, unleashed his unlimited imagination on Deakin: he likened the Prime Minister to Judas Iscariot and went on to say that at least Judas had had the decency to go out and hang himself after his betrayal.[8]

The remaining years of Commonwealth politics before the outbreak of war presented no fresh features that proved to be lasting, with the exception of defence arrangements. The imperial tie with Britain was no longer resented; the growth of a semi-independent defence policy had satisfied the 'Little Australian' and the absence of separatist movements contented the imperialist.

If anything, the self-congratulation of average Australians tended to make them isolationist, but the fact remained that they felt chilly in the shadow of the great powers to the north, whether asleep or awake, and slightly apprehensive about the growth of German naval power and its threat to the British navy which guarded Australia's trade routes.

Australian defence in the nineteenth century had been largely a matter for the imperial authorities. In 1870 Gladstone's ministry had withdrawn the last of the British troops stationed in Australia. Because the local colonial forces were sufficient in neither numbers nor strength to repel an invasion, British assistance would still have been essential in the event of an attack. By the eve of the war, Australian defence forces numbered more than 124,000[9] and there was a small navy.

The Commonwealth still was dependent on British might, however, and Australia saw this protection as an essential part of the mother country's imperial duties. Great Britain, while prepared to acknowledge responsibility for the self-governing countries within the Empire, was anxious that they shoulder some part of the burden of imperial defence,[10] even when it might not seem directly related to the defence of their own countries. The years between Australian Federation and the outbreak of the war saw conflict between, and gradual resolution of, these two opposed views.

The Australian Defence Act of 1903 was based on the Defence Bill of 1901 which had been withdrawn because it was inadequate. The revised Act, a substantial improvement, was essentially an amalgam of the existing mechanisms, a compilation of State Acts. It did not provide for naval defence, because that was regarded as an imperial responsibility and claimed by Britain as such, but it did lay down, *inter alia*, that all male inhabitants of the Commonwealth between the ages of eighteen and sixty were liable to be called upon to serve in time of war, but only within the Commonwealth. Those whose religion rendered them conscientious objectors were exempted from combatant duties.[11]

A new Naval Agreement was ratified in the same session. In 1887, at the first colonial conference, a Naval Agreement had been signed between the mother country and the Australasian colonies. The latter were to pay a subsidy of £126,000 a year towards the support of an auxiliary squadron to be maintained in Australian waters by the Royal Navy. The control of these ships was vested in their commander, and the squadron could not be moved from the waters of the station without the consent of the contributing governments.[12]

A new Agreement was affirmed by Barton at the 1902 colonial conference. In return for an increased Australian subsidy of £200,000 to the Royal Navy, there was to be a larger imperial squadron on the Australian station; there were also to be certain training facilities.[13] Severe criticism, however, was directed at a clause in the Agreement under which the sphere of operations was set out as the waters of the Australian, China and East Indies stations, where the Admiralty believed it could most effectively act against hostile vessels which threatened the trade or interests of Australia and New Zealand. This replaced the former stipulation that the squadron was not to leave the Australasian station without the proper consent of the contributing governments. This was not popular but then Australia could not afford an effective naval arm of its own.[14] No local enthusiasm could ever be expected in favour of a payment that looked suspiciously like a tribute and Australian pride was beginning to demand that the Commonwealth maintain its own fleet, as did all the great nations.[15] National *amour propre*, together with a growing hostility to foreign nations with interests in the Pacific, meant that Australia could not or would not see the Admiralty's point of view, defending its position by drawing attention to the grave danger of commerce-destroying raids by an enemy.[16]

The 1909 imperial conference solved most of the difficulties as a result of concessions made by the Admiralty. A plan was put forward for the construction of a number of fleet units to be maintained respectively by the United Kingdom in the East Indies and China (with the aid of the New Zealand contribution), by Australia in the south Pacific, and by Canada in the eastern Pacific. Although the scheme never came into full operation, the conference did lead to the foundation of the Royal Australian Navy, which by August 1914 consisted of one battle cruiser, four light cruisers, three destroyers and two submarines.[17] In time of war, the squadron was to come under the control of the Admiralty if and when the Commonwealth government agreed.

Australia was also to be defended on its own soil. From the early years of the new century there were advocates of compulsory training for a citizen military force, the name given to the militia and volunteers as distinct from permanent forces. Not all conscriptionists were crypto-conservatives or incipient militarists; among the leaders of the movement was W. M. Hughes who, in September 1905, was one of the founders of the New South Wales division of the Australian National Defence League. Among its influential supporters and office-bearers were Sir Normand Mac-Laurin, Sir Julian Salomons, J. C. Watson, Bruce Smith, Professors Mungo MacCallum and J. T. Wilson of the University of Sydney, the Bishop of North Queensland and A. W. Jose, Australian representative of *The Times*. A non-party organization, it had as its objects universal compulsory training, both naval and military, of the boyhood and manhood of Australia, and the establishment of an adequate and effective system of national defence.[18] The officers of the League were regarded as being in close contact with the National Service League in Britain, whose president was the national idol, Lord Roberts, and whose vice-president was Lord Milner.[19]

In 1906, the Australian organization began publication of the *Call*, a high-quality, well-produced magazine to which nearly all League funds were devoted.[20] Its articles were intended to awaken Australians to the need for compulsory military training and national preparedness. It asserted that as the conviction became general that Australia must one day endure its baptism of fire, then also spread the feeling in favour of an effective system of defence. One article by Colonel (later Major-General) W. T. Bridges, recently returned from manoeuvres and later to be first Commandant of Duntroon, Inspector-General, and leader of the Australian expeditionary force, deplored the lack of visible patriotism in Australia. He pointed out that the success of the Swiss military system depended on intense patriotic feeling which, if in existence, was certainly not apparent in the Commonwealth.[21]

The theme of disgraceful and shameful unpreparedness was reiterated. Cartoons likened the leisure of sports-loving Sydneysiders watching the All Blacks play New South Wales in 1906 to the fatal Roman inactivity when the Goths were at the gates in A.D. 408; or depicted Australia sleeping while evil orientals drilled assiduously (caption: 'In south China every school teaches physical and military drill'—Peking correspondent of *The Times*). Under the heading 'Apathy in Defence Matters', a correspondent 'J.D.B.' drew attention to the Northern Territory as a potential outlet for the surplus population of 'teeming Asia'. Noting that a few months before there had been a story that Japanese argonauts had landed and established a little colony, 'J.D.B.' concluded that if the story had no basis in fact, it had a lamentable basis in probability. He went on to deplore the relatively few rifle clubs in the nation and pronounced that it was a fallacy, fostered by the ignorant at home and abroad, that every young Australian could ride a horse. Perhaps the boys in the bush could, but of the youth living in the bloated cities that characterized the Commonwealth, it was ludicrously untrue. The *Call*'s correspondent concluded by drawing the most unfavourable comparisons with the Transvaal Boers.[22]

The *Call* never doubted that the danger and the enemy was there all right; exactly what danger and which enemy was not so clear. Sometimes there was a hint that the enemy was Germany; it was only a few years since Kaiser Wilhelm II had exhorted his troops in China to behave as the Huns of Attila when crushing the Boxer uprising.[23] More often it was the Kaiser's own bogey, the amorphous yellow peril. A military menace from the north was a natural corollary to the economically-based white Australia policy. But the educated Japanese[24] who had routed mighty Russia in 1904–5 were a more obvious danger than the dismembered giant, China.

Along with the League's call for national preparedness and alertness went an emphasis on the need for physical fitness, among women as well as men. Fit men not only made efficient soldiers, but also a morally upright community. Next to an advertisement for 'The British Australasian School of Physical Training ("For Country, for Empire")', was an article in which ladies were encouraged to take up rifle shooting, and the journal of the Defence League was heartened to note how gunnery was taking the place of archery, thus reflecting a change from national dilettantism to national diligence. There was nothing unbecoming to a lady in rifle-shooting, such ladies as read the *Call* were assured; it was perfectly safe, encouraged social intercourse and, by attracting the attention of men and boys to the subject, nurtured a spirit of patriotism. The League expressed the hope that as centuries earlier there had been a shooting place on the village green where the value was learnt of the cloth-yard shaft, so now there would be a rifle range in each centre throughout the Commonwealth.[25]

In succeeding issues the *Call* kept up its theme. It reported that in Britain the National Service League, established in 1902, was making great headway under the direction of Lord Roberts, and noted W. M. Hughes's speech at the Caxton Hall, London, on universal military training. Citing *Armed Australia* by Captain E. Digby, the magazine informed its readers that in that author's opinion the ultimate sanction of all human acts was the mailed fist, noted that the Minister for Defence, T. T. Ewing, was a member of the Australian National Defence League, and recorded that about 13,000 copies of the *Call* had so far been circulated or sold.[26] At the end of 1907 the League took pride in the drawing up by the Defence Department of a scheme of universal military training, and scolded modern Australians for their want of respect for constituted authority and their slackness and indiscipline. Warning that Australia was approaching the struggle that came in time to every country worth the taking, the *Call* invoked the spirit of the past, asserting that the men who struck out for Australia's shore half a century [*sic*] before were not the stock to breed the servitor type of citizen.[27]

But that type of citizen was too frequently to be found, and early in 1908 the *Call* appeared with a cartoon showing a Chinese about to bowl a smoking bomb at an apprehensive little boy defending his wicket with a tiny bat of '25,000 men'. This was followed by an article about 'the throat of Australia' which turned out to be the coastal strip from Port Stephens to Port Hacking: if once grasped by an enemy it would paralyse the Commonwealth, and in 1909 Arthur H. Adams weighed in with 'The Day the Big Shells Came', an anti-Japanese fantasy.[28]

The principle of compulsory military training introduced in 1907 was not finalized till 1909 because of a change of ministry, and by then an invitation had been extended to Lord Kitchener of Khartoum, Commander-in-Chief in India at the time, to visit Australia and report on its defences. His report was submitted early in 1910 and recommended a trained military force of not less than 80,000 fighting men. Boys between twelve and eighteen were to train as cadets. They would then pass into the citizen forces until the age of twenty-five, with an additional year in the reserves. The training would be done during brief annual encampments. The Commonwealth was to be divided into Military Districts in charge of area officers who were to supervise training. These Districts were almost identical with the areas of the six States except that part of northern New South Wales was counted as in the Queensland Military District (no. 1), and Broken Hill was included in Military District no. 4 (South Australia). Kitchener also envisaged a military college, on the lines of West Point, to train the career officers necessary for the scheme; in June 1911 the Royal Military College, Duntroon, was officially opened.[29]

Amending Defence Acts to give effect to these proposals were passed in 1910, 1911 and 1912. The growth of military expenditure in the decade more than trebled: in 1901–2 it was £780,260; by 1913–14 it had reached £2.7m.[30] Such expansion reflected more than concern with defence, although that was the primary reason; the Commonwealth of Australia was a prosperous nation, and the government had been freed from the financial limitations imposed by the Braddon clause which had provided that for the first ten years of the Commonwealth's existence three-quarters of the revenue from customs and excise was to be returned to the States.

Throughout the decade and a half before 1914, imperialists in England were worried by the Dominions' refusal to commit themselves to an explicit and organized system of imperial defence, in case the mother country was involved in a European war. When the leaders of the self-governing colonies were in London in 1902 for the coronation of Edward VII, a colonial conference was called. Joseph Chamberlain asked the assembled premiers what contingents they would supply in case of a European war. Australia had been eager to participate in the Sudan campaign, the Boer War and the suppression of the Boxer uprising, and the despatch of Australian contingents had been strongly supported, though the *Bulletin*, announcing that the British Empire was 'a nigger Empire run by Jews', dubbed them 'Cohentingents'.[31] Still, the Commonwealth was not prepared to offer a blank cheque and Australia and Canada would promise only to consider the matter when the need arose. Australian statesmen were wary of definite military commitment in advance. They shared the fear of Sir Wilfrid Laurier of Canada that they, too, might be drawn into that vortex of militarism which was the curse and blight of Europe.[32]

While evading the formal commitment, Australia and the other Dominions agreed to organize their respective defence forces with a view to possible, though not automatic, co-operation with Great Britain. In 1909 R. B. Haldane, Secretary of State for War, had managed to obtain the consent of the Dominions to the formation of an Imperial General Staff and some standardization on training and equipment and so on.

After the imperial conference of 1911, a separate meeting was held of the Committee of Imperial Defence. Sir Edward Grey, the Foreign Secretary, gave a long exposition of British foreign policy in relation to the European situation which greatly impressed the Dominion leaders.[33] Not only did they appreciate the seriousness of the situation but felt themselves admitted beyond the portals into the household itself. When Andrew Fisher (the Australian Labor leader), G. F. Pearce (later to be Minister for Defence) and E. L. Batchelor (Minister for External Affairs) left the gathering, they compared notes and unanimously came to the grave conclusion that a European war was inevitable and that it would probably come in 1915 when the preparations made by Germany would be complete. They thereupon determined to push on with all possible speed with Australia's defence programme.[34]

Flattered though Fisher obviously felt (not even the British Cabinet had been favoured with such an analysis, according to Lloyd George) he admitted that the United Kingdom could legally commit the Dominions to war, but insisted that any direct aid from Australia was a matter for the Australian Parliament to decide. His attitude was shared by the Canadians.[35]

The general impression given at this, the last imperial conference before the war, was that should there be a European conflict, Australia and Canada would come to the aid of the mother country, but somewhat grudgingly. True neutrality was out of the question; the Dominions had no standing in international law.[36] If war came, self-interest prescribed their participation, yet when the crisis of 1914 developed and the European powers gathered speed on the fatal collision courses they had chosen, both Englishmen and Australians were surprised at the surge of imperial feeling in Australia.[37] Sir Charles Dilke's words in 1868 that Australia would scarcely feel herself deeply interested in the guarantee of Luxemburg, or Canada in the affairs of Serbia, could not have been more wrong.[38] Although the realization of the true import of events was slow, when it came loyal fervour knew no bounds.

Great Britain had made Australians free, and she found them loyal. The crisis in Europe touched their hearts, and to some people loyalty to the British Empire was the supreme political duty. Imperialism had all the depth and comprehensiveness of religion. Its significance was moral even more than material, a question of preserving the unity of the British race and of enabling it, by maintaining that unity, to develop freely on its own lines and to continue to fulfil its distinctive mission in the world.[39]

This represented a change of view in Australia from the anti-British feeling voiced in the 1880s when 'Imperialist' was synonymous with 'Jingo' as a term of reproach, and a writer or speaker could count on a sympathetic audience when he spoke of Australia being dragged along behind England for her own greedy and selfish objects. Reasons for the remarkable change of sentiment which swept Australia in late July and early August 1914 are not readily to be found or neatly to be listed. Indeed, the official war historian, C. E. W. Bean, considered that when a threat to the 'old country' manifested itself, Australians were touched by deep feelings of loyalty which were not always apparent to the casual observer.[40]

The rapid rise of Germany and Japan compelled Australians to realize the value of the system of imperial defence. In addition, there had been fostered a spirit of unity and mutual interest among the different parts of the Empire. There were, for instance, the various 'imperial' leagues, the corresponding societies, the regular salute to the flag practised in schools, the interchange of flags and courtesies between schools in Australia and Great Britain, the circulation of standard British authors among the younger generations of Australians by means of state-aided school libraries, and the patriotic numbers of the school papers issued for Empire Day by the education departments.[41] The Poet Laureate, Alfred Austin, expressed in typical metre and quality the spirit which launched *United Empire*,[42] the journal of the Royal Colonial Institute:

> Each for all, and all for each,
> One in sceptre, sword and speech;
> With Imperial Flag unfurled,
> Greeting, peaceful, peaceful world.

Crossing that peaceful world of which the poet sang was a stream of British migrants bound for Australia, and this inflow was especially strong in the three or four years before the war.[43] Their significance lay in the reminder of their origin that they offered to the older Australians. Without a great history of their own, Australians could feel a pride of race, a sense of achievement in being British. In an increasingly hostile world it was encouraging to measure one's strength as part of the force of an Empire greater than Greece or Rome had known, and inspiring to feel that a colony's achievements were part of the historic mission of an imperialist power.[44]

That mission was enshrined in such books as the Reverend W. H. Fitchett's *Deeds that Won the Empire*, first published in

1897 from tales which saw the light of day in the Melbourne *Argus*. By 1898 the book had gone into its seventh edition, and in October 1914 was in its twenty-ninth impression. In his preface, Mr Fitchett, the headmaster of Melbourne's Methodist Ladies' College, wrote that the sketches were written not to glorify war but to nourish patriotism. They represented, he continued, an effort to renew in popular memory the great traditions of the British race and to exemplify not merely heroic daring but even finer qualities such as heroic fortitude, loyalty to duty stronger than the love of life, the temper which dreaded dishonour more than it feared death, and patriotism which made love of the fatherland [*sic*] a passion.

So were described some of the qualities which, it was said, had won the British Empire and by which it should be maintained. The notion of the greatness and merit of the Empire and the role of Australia in it was inculcated in Australian children by word of mouth and especially by schools. The achievements of the Empire were main points in the overall education of the child. The *Royal English Reader*, volume 1, for Grade IV, had various statements designed to make children proud of the imperial connection: 'Our Queen rules over one-sixth of all the land of the globe' (p. 12); 'British history shows us how the British Empire has become the largest and most powerful state the world has ever seen' (p. 15). Constant use of 'OUR ships', 'OUR great men', emphasized the common heritage and sense of pride in the achievements of 'OUR race'. History stories did more than hold up qualities of high character for emulation; many were concerned with deeds of courage and enterprise done for the love of country, and were included to stimulate patriotism.[45] All this, it was hoped, might lead to what the *Citizen Reader* emphasized, 'The great lesson of this book is—England expects that every man will do his duty.'[46]

Blood ran hot at times of crisis such as the Dreadnought hysteria in March-April 1909 or the Agadir crisis of November 1911[47] because basically the Australians had a deep attachment to the Empire. Once it became almost totally accepted, as it was by about 1900, that Australian nationalism was compatible with membership of the Empire, a form of imperialism became a component of that nationalism.[48] Vulgar feelings of spite, envy and even detestation for Britain and the Crown in some sections of the Australian community did not necessarily imply a disavowal of loyalty for the concept of the Empire. For many there was no distinction between loyalty to Britain and loyalty to the Empire but there was always available the option of the imperial connection to those who affected to distrust England's motives.[49]

The imperialists' view was a little later expressed by an Australian soldier on the Western Front. Correcting the impression that the British Empire was an aggregation of peoples in possession of vast territories and enormous wealth, he observed that the Empire, like the Kingdom of God, was invisible. The material things such as money and men were but the practical expression of great forces and unalterable principles such as freedom, democracy, justice and faith, which lay at the very basis of national life. He concluded: men went to the Great War for the cause of the British Empire, a cause synonymous with the cause of Christianity.[50]

2

The Formation of the A.I.F.

On 28 July 1914 the Australian public realized that its armed forces might be called upon: the Austrian ultimatum to Serbia was delivered and the Hapsburg Empire, threshing in its death throes, began a course of action which was fated to involve the rest of the world in its downfall. A series of telegrams from the Secretary of State in London to the Governor-General in Melbourne arrived daily with their increasingly ominous messages: 'Adopt precautionary stage'; 'Arrange for Australian ships to take up their preliminary station'; 'Enforce examination service'; 'Call out Royal Naval Reserves'; 'In view of strained relations with Germany, be on guard'; 'Advice as to course shipping should steer; premiers advised'; and finally and fatally, 'War has broken out with Germany'.[1]

The cablegram sent from London on 29 July was intended to read, when deciphered, 'See preface defence scheme. Adopt precautionary stage. Names of powers will be communicated later if necessary.' The message meant that a number of preliminary steps, laid down in a scheme prepared by the Committee of Imperial Defence in 1907, should be taken at once but, because it was incorrectly decoded, the message appeared to be only an answer to some request for information, and the Minister for Defence, Senator E. D. Millen, was unaware of its implications. The same message had also gone out all over the Empire and reached the commander of the Australian squadron, Rear-Admiral Sir George Patey, who deciphered it correctly and communicated the message to the government. Australia then offered to place the vessels of the Royal Australian Navy under the control of the Admiralty and further said that it would raise 20,000 soldiers to be sent anywhere they were needed.[2]

The first official statement of Australia's attitude in the European crisis was made on 31 July by Senator Millen. If the necessity arose, he declared, Australia would be no fair-weather partner of the Empire.[3] Andrew Fisher, the leader of the Labor Party, was in Colac taking part in the federal election when the news came through that war was imminent. Soon to become Prime Minister, he declared that should the worst happen, after everything had been done that honour would permit, Australia would stand beside the mother country to help and defend her to the last man and the last shilling. The same night, speaking at Horsham, the Liberal Prime Minister, Joseph Cook, was greeted with loud applause when he prophesied the arrival of Armageddon. Cheers followed his comment that should Australians have to leave their country's shore to fight on the other side of the world, then the response would be as spontaneous and complete as at any time in the history of the nation.[4]

Indeed it was. As the news filtered through from Europe, excited crowds gathered in the principal cities, awaiting the posting of the latest cables and greeting them as harbingers of the millennium. German bands and other groups of foreign instrumentalists switched to playing British and martial airs, at the same time increasing their takings as they played upon and to the enthusiastic feelings of crowds animatedly discussing the implications of the tremendous conflict now regarded as imminent.[5]

Australians had made up their minds and were ready and indeed terrifyingly willing to go to war. Their only anxiety was that Britain would not. Australians were all decked out, but what if there were no place to go? What if the Commonwealth were disappointed in her expectations?[6] She was not. On the Sunday morning in Berlin the Kaiser addressed 20,000 of his people at the Imperial Palace, stating that the sword had been forced into Germany's hand and that her adversaries would soon learn to their cost what it meant to attack the German Empire. He concluded by asking his subjects to go to church and ask the Almighty for His blessing on the German army. That army, the most formidable force in the history of the world, scarcely needed the help of the Supreme Being, but Belgium did: the same day she received the German ultimatum requesting a passage into France, the British Foreign Secretary, Sir Edward Grey, warned Germany not to send her fleet into the English Channel and at 9 a.m. Australian Eastern Time (4 August, 11 p.m. G.M.T.), Britain declared war, coming to the aid of Belgium and France.

Australians thrilled and shivered at the exciting course of events. For the first time since the Napoleonic Wars, the British fleet had put out to sea to defend the Empire against a serious threat, and at Melbourne, on that Tuesday morning, the first shot of the war by British forces was fired across the bows of the German cargo steamer *Pfalz* when she tried to leave Port Phillip at 7.45 a.m., an hour and a quarter before the actual declaration of war, and was stopped by a shell from Fort Nepean. Accounts differ as to whether the captain of the vessel was attempting to get clear before war formally broke out, or whether he was really totally unaware of the dangers of his situation.[7]

In charge of the Australian army forces to be raised was Brigadier-General W. T. Bridges, with Major (later Lieutenant-General Sir) Brudenell White his chief of staff, an officer who became one of the greatest soldiers of the A.I.F. and who, called up as Chief of the Australian General Staff, was killed at Canberra in an air crash in August 1940. A name for the expeditionary force of 20,000 men was canvassed and ultimately Bridges himself chose it: the Australian Imperial Force. It was deliberately designed to be national in character, because might not only the one contingent be sent abroad? The war was not expected to last long once the British navy and army came into action. New South Wales and Victoria were to supply four battalions each and the remaining States another four among them. So came into existence the 1st to the 12th battalions of the first A.I.F. which, together with the Light Horse and other units, were to make up the expeditionary force to be sent to Europe. Pay for the private soldier was fixed at six shillings a day when he was overseas, a sum which both the Governor-General and King George V thought excessive.[8] It was based on the pay received in the citizen forces. Arrangements were made for pensions, deferred pay and separation allowances; the widow of a private soldier was to receive an annuity of £50 and a quarter of that sum for each child.[9]

Apart from the Australian Naval and Military Expeditionary

Force which was sent to German New Guinea in August, the expeditionary force for overseas consisted of three brigades and divisional units composed of 624 officers and 17,351 other ranks, a total of 17,975. The Light Horse Brigade was planned to be three regiments comprising, with other units, 104 officers and 2,122 other ranks, a total of 2,226. The grand total was thus 728 officers and 19,473 other ranks, 20,201 men altogether, raised on a territorial basis roughly proportional to existing military establishments. The numbers suggested for the whole force were:

1st Military District	(Qld)	2,537
2nd	(N.S.W.)	7,076
3rd	(Vic.)	6,563
4th	(S.A.)	1,677
5th	(W.A.)	1,004
6th	(Tas.)	918
		19,775

The remainder, 153 officers and 272 other ranks, were specially chosen. The numbers for each State were subsequently altered, but the details of the alterations were not adhered to as more and more contingents were subsequently raised.[10]

The A.I.F. was designed to be a force of experienced and skilled soldiers; at least half the numbers of the rank and file were to be men in their twentieth year or over who were serving with the colours, and the remainder trained men specially enlisted who had served in the militia, in the imperial forces, or who had had war service. If any more men were needed, they were to be chosen from the best physical specimens offering. The standards of age, minimum height and minimum chest measurements for the A.I.F. were eighteen to thirty-five years, 5 ft. 6 in. and 34 in. respectively.[11]

When the recruiting depots opened they received an embarrassment of riches. Though complete unanimity is not attained among millions of people, the response of Australians at the beginning of August 1914 was close to it.[12] No wonder: the daily metropolitan newspapers were enthusiastically imperialist; there were no serious party political divisions on the issue of war; there was no organized opposition to Australia's entry into the conflict.

c

A spirit of enthusiasm for the Empire and the war was manifested openly and often. Outside the offices of the *Age* in Melbourne there was almost always a crowd reading the cables as they appeared. It needed only a single voice to give the opening bars of a patriotic song and thousands of throats took it up; hats and coats were waved, and those who possessed even the smallest of Union Jacks were the heroes of the moment and were raised shoulder-high by the surging, singing crowd. 'Rule Britannia', 'Soldiers of the King' and 'Sons of the Sea' were sung over and over again. The National Anthem had a sobering effect from time to time and people who failed to take off their hats were abused.[13] Down at the wharf a fight between Australians and stevedores of German descent developed when a German alleged favouritism had been shown in picking the gangs and said he would trample the British flag. A Union Jack 10 ft by 4 ft was thereupon put on a pole over the club of the Victorian Stevedoring Association and every member entering compelled to salute the flag and raise his hat. During this incident a large crowd gathered and two men marched up and down in front of the club premises playing patriotic airs on an accordion and bagpipes. Two policemen were posted to maintain order.[14]

The leaders of the various churches supported the cause of the Empire whilst decrying the necessity for war. The Church of England's view, as expressed in a Pastoral Letter, was that the war was just, but it hoped for ultimate abandonment by all nations of the spirit of aggressive military despotism. A sermon at St Paul's, Melbourne, did not mince matters and recorded bluntly that it was the strife of commerce that had caused the war.[15]

The *Spectator*, speaking for Methodists, declared that Britain's participation in the war was a call to loyalty and prayer on the part of all her people, and the president of the General Conference of the Methodist Churches of Australia commended the cause for which the Empire had taken up arms, rejoicing in the ready response of all sections of the community to the call for help in personal military service and in providing succour and help in many ways.[16] The Roman Catholic Archbishop of Melbourne, T. J. Carr, came out in favour of the Empire and laid great stress on the justice of its cause, but Dr Daniel Mannix, Coadjutor Archbishop of the same diocese, said in the course of an address that he believed Great Britain had been dragged into the war possibly because she had not taken a stronger hand in dealing with the troubles in Ireland. Britain's inactivity was known to the nations of Europe, pursued Dr Mannix, and though men talked about peace conferences and Hague tribunals, all excellent in their way, he was one who believed that so long as human nature existed as at present, war would be the final arbiter.[17]

The Presbyterian Assembly expressed its unfailing loyalty to the King, its confidence in the wisdom of the policy of the imperial government, its admiration of the wonderful and self-sacrificing gallantry of British soldiers and sailors and its hearty forwardness in sharing the national burdens of giving and suffering in an unparalleled time of the Empire's needs. The president of the Evangelical Lutheran Synod in Australia expressed the loyalty of his church.[18]

The labour press regarded the outbreak of the war with more sorrow than enthusiasm. The *Worker* concluded that not a single extenuating reason could be given for the war: there was no great principle behind it, no vital issue on which two high-spirited and intelligent people might earnestly differ and deem it not unworthy to shed their blood. Certainly Australia must be defended, went on this journal, but it hoped that no wave of jingo lunacy would sweep over the land, unbalancing the judgment of its leaders and inciting the population to wild measures. It ended its reflections in the tone of one foreseeing the worst: 'God help Australia; God help England; God help Germany; God help us!'; basically the paper's attitude was one of helplessness and sorrow but final loyalty to the Empire.[19]

The voice of labour in Victoria was not wildly enthusiastic but it too was not disloyal; the *Labor Call* emphasized that the labour leaders and indeed the Labor Party were no whit behind the Liberals when it came to patriotism: 'The murmuring of some workers gathering against war in some distant part of the world will be quoted as the voice of Labor in Australia. Chance words will be misinterpreted, mostly wilfully, sometimes stupidly, for there are people too stupid to understand that it is possible bitterly to denounce war as a barbarous, brutal, and uncivilized expedient, and yet be willing to fight to the death when one's country is threatened.'[20]

Socialists denounced the war. Although the *Socialist* asserted that it was Australia's duty to protect herself, it also stated that it was the duty of patriotic Australians to protest against the inflammatory utterances of armchair firebrands who sat at their ease in suburbia yelling for ships and men to be sent on murdering expeditions abroad. But in the publication there was little suggestion of any practical opposition to the war, and there were not many who listened to or took notice of such effusions; in the working-class electorate of Cook, the lone socialist in the general election of 1914 won only 509 votes in a poll of 27,272.[21]

Also opposed to the war was Miss Adela Pankhurst, a daughter of the British suffragette leader Emmeline. In March 1914 she set about organizing the Women's Political Association of Victoria, with headquarters at 213-215 La Trobe Street, Melbourne; Vida Goldstein was the president. Later this association became the Women's Peace Army, the president of which was again Vida Goldstein who had stood for the Senate in 1903 and was editor of *The Woman Voter*; its secretary was Adela Pankhurst and the organizer Cecilia John.[22]

One of Adela's speeches against war occurred, strangely enough, on a date none other than 25 April 1915 when she spoke at the Bijou Theatre, 225 Bourke Street, Melbourne, in a manner calculated to cause a breach of the peace, thought the Women's Recruiting Committee in Toowoomba when news of her views came to its attention; Miss Pankhurst's remarks were clearly disloyal and she should be interned, thought the Queensland ladies.[23]

At the end of 1915 Adela was opposing recruitment, and when she addressed one meeting on the subject 'Shall men enlist?', soldiers of the A.I.F. took it over. Recruits in the gallery interrupted Miss Pankhurst with cat-calls and yells, singing 'Boys of the Bulldog Breed', 'Australia Will be There', and similar sorts of songs. They stamped their disapproval of utterances which the *Daily Telegraph*'s reporter considered were not of the type to persuade men to enlist or fight, and when Miss Pankhurst finally started to say that people had been dragged into a war of conquest upon instructions from the imperial government, the soldiers mobbed the stage and refused to permit the address to continue. Pandemonium reigned and for a moment it appeared as if there would be a free fight.

There was not a free fight with the ladies, however, the soldiers merely crowding around Miss Pankhurst and Miss John, who had been singing 'I Didn't Raise my Son to be a Soldier'. It was a fine entertainment for those whose sense of humour permitted them to enjoy such moments. More popular songs by the men of the A.I.F. followed and then someone in the wings dropped the fire curtain. The soldiers propped it up with chairs, and a discussion followed between Adela, Miss John and the men, while the chairman tried to get the audience to sing 'The Red Flag' and the 'Socialist Hymn'. There was some 'rough-and-tumble fight' but after holding the stage for about half an hour while one of the soldiers at the piano thumped out popular songs, the soldiers called for order. Miss Pankhurst was allowed to speak for about five minutes, one of the men even standing with his arms around her in a protective manner while she addressed the audience. Then a Major McInerney arrived and ordered the men to clear out. 'There was very little heat displayed on either side, the only instance being when one irate woman pushed a soldier off the stage into the orchestra stalls.'[24]

Complaints were made about the conduct of Adela, and, as a result, on 16 April 1915 a police constable and an officer of the Crown Law Department found themselves in the audience at the Oddfellows Hall, Victoria Street, Melbourne, on the occasion of Miss Pankhurst's lecture to the Melbourne Spiritualists' Society on the subject 'War and civilization from a woman's point of view'. The policeman reported that about 150 people were there and that they were orderly. He summed up her observations—she blamed all countries alike and the capitalists in particular for the war, and was as thorough in condemnation of Germany as she was of England. The Commissioner of Police reported that her address contained nothing whatever on which the police could take action.[25]

This could not be said about the later activities of the Industrial Workers of the World (I.W.W.), a group which wanted to bring down the existing capitalistic structure of society by such direct action as sabotage, who were quite clear where they stood: let those who own Australia do the fighting, was their philosophy; the wealthiest should be put in the front ranks, the middle class next, and then the politicians, lawyers, sky pilots and judges in that order. The declaration of war, thundered the I.W.W., should be answered with a call for a general strike: 'Don't go to Hell in order to give piratical, plutocratic parasites a bigger slice of Heaven . . . DON'T BECOME HIRED MURDERERS. DON'T JOIN THE ARMY OR NAVY.' Later the I.W.W. developed the point a little more by way of little labels which they stuck to telegraph posts: 'Don't scab upon the unemployed by working hard. Slow work means more jobs. More jobs means less unemployed, and less competition means higher wages—less work, more pay. Slow down, slow down. Don't be a slave. Be a man and join the I.W.W.'[26]

No one of any importance listened to the 'Wobblies'. Early in the morning of the day recruiting opened there was gathered at the Victoria Barracks in Melbourne a large crowd of young volunteers and a great many South African veterans as well as some with more remote war honours pinned on their breasts. In Sydney more than 2,000 men applied to join the expeditionary force, including nearly 200 officers, in addition to large numbers of militia, light horsemen, infantry and artillerymen who volunteered at regimental headquarters. Here, as in Western Australia,[27] many applications came from the veterans of the South African war and, in Sydney, from the Legion of Frontiersmen, a civilian, self-supporting and self-governing association which, although it had no official recognition in Australian military circles, was regarded in the Empire as a means of securing for the service of the state men of good education who had been trained in savage countries, at sea or in war.[28]

Two weeks after the declaration of war, 7,000 men were assured in Victoria and more than 10,000 had applied in Sydney where, as elsewhere, only picked men were accepted for the quota. Australians were heart and soul behind the recruitment of the A.I.F., and in at least one case the excitement proved too much: Gunner Bellchambers, an ex-member of the Royal Australian Garrison Artillery, visited the Sydney Barracks and, hearing the war news, dropped dead; and a bank manager from Quambatook begged the military authorities to cancel his brother's application as a volunteer in the A.I.F. because the shock would kill his mother.[29]

The war led to other forms of shock as well; at Broken Hill several mines were already reported to be closing down, and a representative of one of the leading tin-producing companies told

the Chief Secretary in New South Wales that buyers had refused
to take any more tin. It was feared also that the Mount Bischoff
mine in Tasmania might have to cease production, and at Lithgow
the mills at the ironworks almost all came to a standstill in the
temporary uncertainty concerning the future of the industry. At
Emmaville, about twenty miles from Glen Innes in New South
Wales, it was reckoned that the war would put an end to the
demand for tin, and large numbers of workers, after 'swag drill',
shouldered their belongings and headed for Sydney to enlist in the
A.I.F.[30]

By the end of August, as the first contingent was being completed, many men from the countryside were still enlisting, after
the first rush from city-dwellers living near the recruiting depots.
Regarded as excellent material, some were none the less rejected because of their lack of previous military training. There
were complaints in New South Wales about the centralization
of recruiting which involved volunteers from the backblocks in
long expensive journeys and the possibility of eventual rejection, a
factor which it was thought hampered applications to enlist.[31] Not
until public complaints were made about the injustice of inducing
men to wind up their affairs and travel perhaps hundreds of miles
only to be disappointed, was it determined to establish recruiting
depots at country centres.[32]

There was really no need for the federal government to do
anything but watch the flood of volunteers in 1914, so widespread
was enthusiasm for the war. It was evinced in various ways: in
South Australia Scoutmaster A. E. Flavel of the 1st Glen Osmond
Troop offered the services of his lads on the lines being used in
London, stating that four of his scouts aged between sixteen and
eighteen owned their own bikes;[33] a patriotic Perth business man
who had fought in the South African war offered personally to
organize a force of 120 men or one complete mounted squadron
for overseas or other services; several men who had deserted from
the British army appeared at the drill hall in Perth to offer their
experienced services;[34] and at the heart of the Empire Hugh D.
McIntosh, an Australian theatrical manager and entrepreneur who
had arranged the world title fight in Sydney between Tommy
Burns and Jack Johnson, and who was to make and lose several
fortunes before dying in poverty in 1942, cabled the Prime Minister

offering to raise a corps of motor cyclists to act in conjunction with any Australian contingent.[35]

At home, there was a similar move for the raising of a specialized unit of ex-public school boys. Delegates from old boys' associations offered every encouragement to members to join the forces, but in their capacity as Australians and not as representative of any special section of the community. By the beginning of September, when the second contingent was being enrolled, seventy-one 'Old Scotchies' in Melbourne were receiving an enthusiastic send-off by the Old Scotch Collegians' Association, and a kindred organization called the Victorian Union of Scottish Societies had already held a meeting to consider raising a Scottish unit to form part of the expeditionary force.[36]

Citizens enthusiastically offered what they thought best to prosecute the war most effectively: there was an interesting suggestion concerning the use of stockwhips against the enemy, a correspondent in Hobart wrote to the Defence Department offering an idea about the use of boomerang-shaped bayonets, and a lady from Epping in Tasmania insisted that she be sent to Europe to help the wounded.[37]

Other forms of help were also offered to the A.I.F. The Australian branch of the Red Cross Society in New South Wales advertised at the end of the year, 'You smoke because you like it? So do the soldiers who are fighting for you! We try to supply men with tobacco when wounded. WILL EVERY MAN HELP?'[38] Farmer and Co., Sydney, sent a large gift-parcel of underclothing to be distributed to destitute Belgians in destroyed cities and undertook to continue to send more, and Professor Frank Stuart, carrying on business as 'Examiner and Member of the National Society of Physical Education etc. etc.' offered to instruct members of the A.I.F. in bayonet fighting because he was a fencing expert. His offer was declined.[39]

So everyone expressed his enthusiasm and offered to do his duty as he saw it. The writer Ethel Turner rejoiced that the iron hand of war had suddenly clutched at the crumpled silly scroll of women's lives and begun mercifully to straighten it out. Women's duty was now splendidly clear. Miss Turner looked back to the decadence exemplified by the *fin de siècle*, at the mincing female figures in Louis Quatorze heels and narrow hobble skirts, teeteringly absorbed in bargain sales of litter, occupying their too-ample time in playing cards and indulging in the mindless dance of the tango. Were those ludicrous people real, she reflected seriously?: they were not, because now the real women had appeared, quiet-faced and placing no detaining hand on husbands, sons and fathers, at peace with themselves as they epitomized the feminine role, dry-eyed and smiling bravely in spite of it all as they sent their men off to the wars, hastening to pour out their boundless passion for service in ambulance work and eager sewing and knitting.[40]

Other Australians offered to the war effort the fruits of their inventive genius, and some were particularly active in suggesting ways and means to win the war from the air: an aerial Dread-nought was said to have been invented, and countless people sought financial assistance from the federal government in order to complete prototypes of inventions whose full powers of destruc-tion would be revealed when the money was forthcoming. Others offered a means of finding out the exact position of an aircraft by means of a balloon and electric wires; an automatic parachute was offered to the government for money; a gentleman said he had invented a new type of aeroplane and sought tuition in flying; another placed in the government's hands a set of plans to show how the rear of an aircraft might be depressed and raised without the front stays of the machine being affected; there was an inven-tion for flying machines which would effectively prevent them from turning over in windy weather; an automatic aeroplane; an invention for raising an aeroplane straight up and down; an aerial torpedo; an automatic balancing plane; aero rafts; and details of an invention to be opened and read in the presence of experts.[41]

More spiritual assistance was offered by other Australians to assist the A.I.F. One wrote a patriotic piece of music entitled 'The Dead March for the Federal Troops' but it was not considered to be of sufficient merit by the military bandmaster, who concluded that the piece would never replace the funeral marches currently in use.[42]

A duplicated letter to the Minister for Defence enclosed a correspondent's 'Grand German Concert Humorous Programme', together with a copy of his latest and best production, an 'In Memoriam' piece of verse entitled 'Drunken Jim' which might be useful in the war effort. The Governor of Victoria, said the writer, had sent him £1 as an appreciation of his talent, and he had received complimentary letters from prominent citizens. Disclosing that he was an incurable neurasthenic invalid of fifty-four, who had been attending the Melbourne Hospital for twenty years taking medicine, the writer asked the Minister to buy a few copies of his work for two shillings, though he now had few to spare. 'Drunken Jim' was an affecting tale of 'Melbourne's soldier hero, Founded on Fact':

> ONLY A DRUNKARD—he loved Ale;
> He lounged each day near 'The Daily Mail'
> Only a 'Boozer', and people said
> 'Twere better far if he were dead;
>
> He never worked, did 'DRUNKEN JIM'
> He lacked all energy, go and vim
> No worry ever crossed his mind
> And yet his heart was mighty kind . . .

Jim gave up the drink, joined the A.I.F. and was shot by the enemy. His dying words were of his mother.[43]

Another loyal citizen wrote to the Minister for Defence that he presumed to send certain lines which he had written in a spirit of patriotism which was always rising within him. He thought that such lines, being put into the hand of the young citizen soldier, would find their way into his heart and thus inculcate a spirit which, the writer felt sure the Minister would agree, it was desirable to cultivate.[44]

In the meantime, a general election was held on Saturday 5 September. The Liberals had gone to the country after a double dissolution because the Senate, dominated by Labor men, frustrated Cook's government. The outbreak of war hampered Liberal electioneering, and the Labor campaign was dominated by the exertions of W. M. Hughes who pledged the party to a vigorous prosecution of the war. In the opinion of the Governor-General, the attitude of the Labor opposition was quite correct, despite a speech by one of their members, in the outback of Queensland where, alluding to the change effected in the design of postage stamps by the Liberals, he expressed a preference to licking the backside of a kangaroo to that of his sovereign, and promised to send the Governor-General home as soon as a couple of cruisers were available for escort.[45] Labor won a decisive victory and on 17 September the new Cabinet was being led by Andrew Fisher as Prime Minister and Treasurer, Hughes as Attorney-General and Senator G. F. Pearce as Minister for Defence.[46]

On 3 September Australia offered to Britain another 6,000 men over and above the reinforcements for the first units. Command of this extra brigade was given to Colonel (later Lieutenant-General Sir) John Monash.[47] The age range was from nineteen to forty-five but each applicant under twenty had to take to the recruiting office the written authority of his parent or guardian before his case would be considered by the enrolling officer. In reality the age was reduced to eighteen.[48] In addition, the raising of the age limit to forty-five made eligible many men who had fought in the Boer War; in the opinion of the Governor-General, this admixture of older men and recruits from the country improved the quality of men enlisting.[49]

But in spring 1914 there were still plenty of lines being drawn for recruitment in the A.I.F.: a man who claimed to have been a cook in the Boer War spoilt his chance of selection by saying rashly that he had never seen a shot fired. Though he then tried to explain that he had not been in the danger zone anyway, his confidence was enough to cause his rejection.[50]

Such picking and choosing was characteristic of the early days of recruiting. Defective teeth as well as cooking without shooting prevented men from fighting for their country, but from September 1914 this did not deter applicants who were in other respects suitable for enlistment, provided they received attention at the United Dental Hospital, Chalmers Street, Sydney, or approved places elsewhere before final acceptance.[51] High standards could become ridiculous: one man from the Tweed River district of New South Wales, anxious to get overseas with the troops, showed signs of being a cigarette smoker, whereupon the officiating colonel told him that smokers were not needed to fight for the Empire, and enquired whether the recruit would give up cigarettes. 'I will when I get my teeth to hold a pipe,' was the steady reply. The man had lost his false teeth when suffering from sea-sickness on the Tweed. Being in other respects a suitable candidate for the A.I.F., he was advised to go to the dentist as soon as he was sworn in.[52]

Despite the high standards, there was no difficulty in filling the second contingent and the high quality of men offering from the country areas was noticed: not one of an incoming batch of circus riders, horse-breakers and wallaby hunters was rejected in Sydney in early September, and at Ballarat only three of eighty-five recruits coming forward were turned back. Recruits from the rural areas became particularly noticeable in September 1914 and, indeed, were reported to be the majority of those men in camp in Victoria, their enthusiasm, determination and fitness reflected in the case of Ernest Charles Pepper, a resident of the Elaine district who walked twenty-five miles to Geelong on a Sunday evening in order to enlist. Arriving at his destination on the following morning, he was promptly accepted.[53]

On 25 September thousands of people lined the streets of Melbourne to watch the parade of the First Victorian Regiment. In the early morning, as the crowds gathered, dark and heavy clouds hung over the city. Against this sombre background the long lines of troops appeared, a drab khaki column spiked with the gleaming steel of bayonets. Led by the Light Horse, the column wound along the wet and shining streets from Spencer Street station, marching briskly against the cold south wind.

The densely packed spectators, at this first sight of the A.I.F. in full parade, were strangely quiet, their voices silenced by a baffled perplexity of mind natural to people in the presence of incredible events. Here and there a white handkerchief fluttered and a tiny Union Jack waved, but there were few cheers as the troops marched down the hill of Collins Street. Perhaps the hush reflected a sense of awe at the solemnity of the occasion or perhaps it was, as one observer declared, yet another instance of the stoical self-repression which the public had exhibited ever since the tremendous struggle had begun. Perhaps no one knew what to do.

At the steps of Parliament House the scene was more emotional. Drizzling rain had deepened the red and purple stains of the bunting, and transformed the seats of chairs placed in the official reserve into miniature reservoirs. The arrival of the Governor of Victoria and the Governor-General had been announced by the military band playing the National Anthem, and the Empire and Commonwealth flags had been unfurled. These preliminary ceremonies over, the Governor-General was standing at the flag ready to receive the salute as the column of troops drew near. Suddenly, thousands of little Union Jacks appeared and, as the tramping ranks approached, the volume of sound grew until a thunder of cheers welcomed the leading line into Spring Street.

The enthusiasm of the crowd was then demonstrated. Cheers drowned the bands, and flags and handkerchiefs waved above the heads of the crowd and from the upper windows and roofs of verandahs where groups of women were clustered. One enthusiast had climbed a pole and managed to cling there for an hour and a quarter. Close upon the finish he lost his grip, felling two men and a stout matron. 'Be a sport,' he admonished an irate and mud-covered victim. 'Make a little allowance for a bloke's patriotism. If I 'adn' o' le' go to wave me 'at I wouldn't 've fallen.'

If there were some spectators who lamented the substitution of loose, dull-buttoned khaki uniforms for the traditional tight-stuffed, gold-braided and brass-buttoned ones, and who were pessimistic about the capabilities of the infantry, there were many more for whom the soldiers in their colourless uniforms displayed both military bearing and something characteristically Australian: there was a freedom and ease underlying the disciplined order of the ranks. Even the short, nuggety horses, an ungroomed lot compared with the mounts of the crack regiments of England, were seen as the sort that looked as if they could be depended on to do a good deal on very little.

Many observers noted with pride the contrast between the raw recruits who had gone into camp only a few weeks earlier and the ranks who now marched before them. Gone were the slouching gait and unseemly laughter and chattering in the ranks. These men looked fitter, stronger, even taller; a hard-bitten, warrior group they looked, said one report with enthusiasm.

They would be a grand advertisement for Australia, declared the spectator who was clinging to the pole, even if they got there too late to do any fighting (at which a patriotic listener protested, 'God forbid!'); they would let the world see the kind of men Australia could turn out.

After marching through the city, the ranks halted at Royal Park where they were given a light lunch ration of bread and jam. Private citizens selling hot rolls and frankfurters were enthusiastically patronized by the soldiers, who were apparently untroubled by the scruples which prompted a reporter to complain that one could have wished for something with fewer Teutonic associations than the frankfurter.[54]

On 1 November the men of the first contingent were on board transport vessels steaming from their anchorages in Western Australia out into the Indian Ocean where on 9 November escorts of the troop-ships, principally H.M.A.S. *Sydney*, engaged and caused to run aground the German light cruiser *Emden*.[55]

It was a grand start to Australia's participation in the war. The Commonwealth government was inundated with telegrams and messages of congratulation on having drawn first blood; they came from the Secretary of State in London, the merchants of Jamaica, the Governor-General, the president of the Chamber of Commerce in Bundaberg, the *Express* of Cooma ('Congratulations on success of so-called toy boats of Australia'), the Toronto Board of Trade, the Governor of Madras and the Prime Minister of New Zealand, who expressed his appreciation of the protection afforded his country by the Australian fleet. The citizens of Wonthaggi congratulated the Prime Minister for initiating the Royal Australian Navy, and Lord Derby on behalf of a large and representative meeting of Liverpool merchants also offered his congratulations; the secretary of the Boulder branch of the Australian Natives' Association said that this one action justified Australia's defence policy; five hundred Australians on the Rand in South Africa cabled their thanks; Lord Tennyson pointed out how hard he had worked that Australia should have a fleet of her own; and the French consul at Kharkov in Russia expressed his congratulations on Australia's achievements. The Granville Political Labor League tempered its congratulations by deploring the loss of killed and wounded.[56]

Meanwhile recruiting continued, and the numbers and calibre of the recruits from the Australian countryside continued to impress observers: when on 10 November 1,000 men marched through the streets of Melbourne, it was noted that at least three-quarters of the troops who attracted so much attention from the crowds came from rural areas. Bigger than the men in the first contingent, they were reckoned to be more hardy as well as more freckled.[57] They had other characteristics, too, because they did not want to pick positions and seek instant commissions but went cheerfully into the

ranks, believing that the officers knew best where their services
would assist the Empire.[58]

Everyone had a good word to say for such volunteers; they were
well-knit and though they sometimes made mistakes and were not
quite as quick as the city men in making out their application
forms, there was no doubt as to their fitness for military service,
concluded a report.[59] Some of the credit for the quality of such
recruits was attributed to the country police in New South Wales
who were empowered to issue to them second-class orders for
railway and steamer fares to Sydney.[60]

The police were offered inducements other than the satisfaction
of helping their country: three weeks after the outbreak of the war
the Premier of New South Wales, W. A. Holman, suggested to
Senator Millen that the police be used to aid recruiting. The
Minister agreed and there was issued a booklet entitled *Instructions
for Officers of Police acting as Recruiting Agents*. It promised that
for every candidate finally accepted by the central military authorities a fee of ten shillings would be paid by the government of New
South Wales to the police officer responsible for the enrolment.
This sum was arrived at after deliberation by the State Cabinet.

The scheme was not without its critics. In October there was a
press report that some country police were sending their friends
down to Sydney, or people who were coming anyway. In December
the metropolitan area and Newcastle were excluded from the
scheme, though Newcastle was later re-included, but by the end of
June 3,814 recruits had been directed to Sydney by the police
recruiters; by June 1915 this figure had increased to 7,469. Seeking
the purely voluntary system, however, Muswellbrook council protested in February against the capitation fee as a waste of money,
and two months later the federal Prime Minister told Holman
that the method of recruiting used in New South Wales should be
in the hands of mayors and shire presidents. The Military Commandant of the 2nd Military District, Major-General E. T. Wal-
lack, disagreed with this and asked the State to continue the system
because the men were needed to keep up the total District quota
of 1,600 men expected each month.

By mid-1915 the Inspector-General of Police, James Mitchell,
wanted the scheme looked into because in many instances the
police were declining to accept their ten shillings a head, or else

gave it to patriotic funds, though some were prepared to continue to act as recruiting agents. When Holman caused a memorandum to be sent to police, some said they did not want the money. Dubbo Political Labor League told the Premier that it thought the payment was unjust and that the authority to enrol volunteers should be in the hands of military officers: no body of men without effort on their own behalf should be permitted to reap monetary advantages at the expense of another's patriotism. In July, New South Wales finally abandoned the fee when a fresh recruiting drive was introduced.[61]

Holman's scheme undoubtedly drew attention to those country men who enlisted and may have increased their numbers, but praise for them, and implicit criticism of city-dwellers, could be overdone. A military officer, stating that he had not seen finer types of men (a phrase which occurred at least once every three days in the press reports) did not wish it to be inferred that any special favour was being bestowed on country applicants; he simply wanted suitable men. Be that as it may, emphasis on the country recruits continued in newspaper accounts of the raising of the A.I.F.; scarcely 2 per cent of those men who came from the country districts failed to pass the medical examination, it was held.[62] Perhaps this was due to the work done by police in pre-sorting the men offering their services.

At the end of 1914 the Chief of the General Staff, Colonel (later Major-General) J. G. Legge, announced that arrangements had been made under which more than 3,000 reinforcements a month would be sent from Australia. The basis of contribution to these units was fixed:[63]

1st Military District	(Qld)	406
2nd	(N.S.W.)	1,021
3rd	(Vic.)	970
4th	(S.A.)	330
5th	(W.A.)	357
6th	(Tas.)	153
		3,237

The new year opened in New South Wales with nearly 1,000 men being recruited in the first week[64] and the military authorities

were so sure of getting all the men they wanted that they did not
bother enlisting after midday, in order to have all the examinations
finished in time for the volunteers to catch the early afternoon train
to Liverpool camp.[65]

In this period of the war the recruitment of the A.I.F. was
voluntary to the highest degree, except perhaps for Holman's use
of the police. But some encouragement was offered in the form of
little newspaper advertisements. An item, 'Volunteers wanted',
appeared in the press at the end of 1914, giving the age range as
eighteen to forty-five, the minimum height as 5 ft 4 in and the
minimum chest measurement as 33 in.[66]

More sophisticated techniques were used for the first time in
Melbourne early in 1915 when at each picture theatre in that city
Miss Beatrice Day recited the recruiting verse 'You?'. This was the
work of 'Oriel', a columnist on the *Argus*:

> You sit in your camp this New Year's Eve
>   And you sing the whole night long
> To the windy words and the tum-tum tune
>   Of the latest panto. song,
> Your coat is gay in its ribboned pride,
>   Flaunting the red, white and blue,
> But we want a hundred thousand men
>   Can't you see that this means YOU?
>
> You stand all day in the sunny street,
>   Watching the cable board,
> Gloomy or glad as the case may be if the
>   Allies have suffered or scored,
> And perhaps 'we made progress yesterday',
>   And perhaps we advanced anew,
> But we want a hundred thousand men—
>   Can't you see that this means YOU?
>
> You left your seat in that Bourke Street bar
>   Where you'd drowned the foe in beer,
> To watch the brown battalions pass—
>   Perhaps you gave them a cheer,
> But a year from now, if you don't wake up,
>   You'll be drinking bitter brew,
> We want a hundred thousand men—
>   Can't you see that this means YOU?

D

You have carried your bat for a hard-won
  Score, you have played the game like a man,
You have cursed your luck for backing the horse
  That starred with the also-ran,
But what, I ask, of the other game—that
  Game we will have to see through—
We want a hundred thousand men—
  Can't you see that this means YOU?

Not for glory and not for gain have we
  Drawn our sword to the strife,
It's a fight for our homes, a fight for our
  Freedom—a fight for our very life.
Your king is calling, your country's calling,
  Your women are calling, too—
We Want a Hundred Thousand Men
  And the First they want, is YOU!

The last stanza of these verses was then thrown on the screen, followed by the King's message, and finally a portrait of His Majesty himself. Audiences everywhere were thought to react well to this form of cinema recruiting, an inducement to enlist which had worked very well in London and in the English provinces where recruiting sergeants waited outside the cinemas for the young men as they came thoughtfully away.[67] But this seemed as far as the government was prepared to go; although in the Defence Minister's room at the Victoria Barracks in Melbourne there were on display a number of striking recruiting posters which had been placarded throughout the British Isles, Senator Pearce said that there was no intention of using them, though the Department might decide otherwise later on.[68]

In March 1915, 9,000 men joined the A.I.F. and there was evidence that enthusiasm still ran high: scores of men rejected because their chests were too small took courses at physical culture schools; short men tried all known methods, and others invented hitherto unknown ones, to increase their height, and the number of men who had disqualifying defects removed by operation was 'legion'.[69]

Despite this, the figures showed that recruiting was declining. No one seemed very sure how many men were needed every month but a number of steps were taken to try to keep up the figures. For instance, the enrolling depot in Melbourne was kept open all day Saturday[70] and, second, the Australian Natives' Association started a recruiting campaign of its own in March by issuing a pamphlet entitled *Messages to the Young Men of Australia* from the Governor-General, the Governor of Victoria, the Premier of Victoria and the Chief President of the A.N.A.[71]

Third, recruiting meetings began to be held. Frank Tudor, M.H.R., was on the platform at one and urged the enlistment of everyone who had no pressing reason for hanging back. There was an interruption: 'A voice: Sack them if they won't go. Tudor: No . . . let them alone at present. The Allies are fighting for honour and liberty.'[72]

The fact of the matter was that although all was not quiet on the Western Front, the A.I.F. had not been in battle and hence the need for large reinforcements was not apparent.

During these first months of 1915 while the number of recruits diminished in Australia, the Australian soldiers were being trained in Egypt. It had been expected that the expeditionary force would go to England to complete training but accommodation there was unsuitable, as well as restricted, and so the A.I.F. disembarked in Egypt. When Turkey entered the war against the Allies, Russia suffered attacks in the Caucasus and sought from the Western powers a campaign which would relieve pressure on her. It was decided to try to capture or effectively threaten Constantinople. A British naval expedition failed in this and Winston Churchill, then First Lord of the Admiralty, eagerly took up a project for an amphibious attack: troops were to be landed at a number of points on the Gallipoli Peninsula. Among the units which were planned to make this attack was the A.I.F. and the soldiers from New Zealand, who became known as the Australian and New Zealand Army Corps, or 'Anzacs'.

At 4.30 a.m. on Sunday 25 April the soldiers of the A.I.F.'s 3rd Brigade began going ashore at a spot later to become known as Anzac Cove. Landed too far north, the Australian troops found themselves in unrecognizable country; as the light became better, there developed the Battle of the Landing. Units were split up by the razor-back ridges and lost contact with each other. Individuals fought hand to hand with the Turkish defenders. Some men got far enough inland to see the shining waters of the Narrows. All was confusion. Everything was wrong, but within some twenty-four hours or so it appeared that the Anzac forces had stabilized a precarious front line about half a mile inland. At some points only yards separated the invaders from their enemies. There had begun the extraordinary campaign of Gallipoli.[73]

In a sense Australians at home had suffered more from a drought which threatened to reach the dimensions of a national calamity than from the war when, in the middle of the lull in recruiting, the Prime Minister rose in the House of Representatives on 29 April and officially informed a hushed audience that a few days previously the government had been told that the bulk of the Australian expeditionary force sent to Egypt had left that country for the Dardanelles. Its members had been transported without loss, landed on the Gallipoli Peninsula and had been engaged in active fighting against the Turkish forces. The action, concluded the Prime Minister, had proceeded and was proceeding satisfactorily. In the Senate, the Minister for Defence made a similar statement.[74]

The federal government had known early in March that Australian and New Zealand troops were destined for the Dardanelles but the first tantalizingly brief information that they were actually in action came in the form of a cable from the Secretary of State to the Governor-General. In it the British government congratulated the Australian contingent on the successful progress of operations at the Dardanelles. This was followed by a similar telegram from the King and on 30 April by official War Office news that Australian and New Zealand troops were established on the peninsula to the north of Gaba Tepe. On 11 May came a message from the commander of the Mediterranean forces, General Sir Ian Hamilton:

May I, speaking out of a full heart, be permitted to say how gloriously the Australian and New Zealand contingents have upheld the finest traditions of our race during the struggle still in progress, at first with audacity and dash, since then with sleepless valour and untiring resource. They have already created for their country an imperishable record of military virtue.[75]

It was a measure of the confused way in which the Commonwealth learnt that its sons were in battle that on the same day as the announcements were made in Parliament, the Premier of

Western Australia, John Scaddan, cabled the Prime Minister
saying he had not been informed officially what was going on.
Pointing out that the local newspaper knew that the Governor-
General had received congratulations, but that he did not, Scaddan angrily demanded information. He was right to do so: the
11th (Western Australian) Battalion had been one of the first
ashore.[76]

What was really happening at the Dardanelles? Though the
Commonwealth government received congratulatory messages
from such as the Governor-General of New Zealand, the First
Lord of the Admiralty, Lord Tennyson, the secretary of the Kalgoorlie branch of the Australian Natives' Association, and the city
of Ballarat (which sent a draft of a cable for the General Officer in
Command of the A.I.F.),[77] it was only on 3 May 1915 that the
people of Australia had an intimation of the facts: on that day
arrived the first of a series of lists of casualties which were to continue with ghastly regularity for three and a half years. As next of
kin of Australian soldiers certainly knew, a deathly struggle was
being waged at Gaba Tepe, a hill on the coast of a peninsula which
probably not one citizen of the Commonwealth had heard of, let
alone seen; but it was not until 8 May that a despatch from Ellis
Ashmead-Bartlett, a British war correspondent, was printed in
Australian newspapers and thereby informed the people what had
apparently happened at the Hellespont on the morning and day
of 25 April.

The despatch was a vivid piece of reportage. It noted that the
Turks were hurled back when the Australians went at them with
fixed bayonets; it described the men of the A.I.F. at the landing as
a race of athletes; it concluded that there had been no finer feat in
the war than the storming of the heights of Gallipoli by the men of
the Australian Imperial Force. The heart of every Australian filled
with pride: their boys had not been found wanting. The despatch
and the subsequent news from the embattled Australian soldiers at
Gallipoli excited Australians to more strenuous exertions in recruiting, especially because the despatch was brought to the attention
of schoolchildren all over the nation at the suggestion of the Prime
Minister: it was either read out to wide-eyed boys and girls or
printed in the State education publications.[78]

Australians were more than ever impressed with the gravity of the war when they learned that friends and neighbours had fallen at the Dardanelles. One of three recruits questioned about motives replied, 'I should have gone long ago but somehow I didn't like to leave home. On Sunday, George, my cousin [evidently returned wounded] came out to see us and he talked to me and Dick (indicating his brother) so that we both decided that we hadn't done the right thing. Then when Bob, my mate, heard we were going, why, he said he would come too. That's all.'[79]

Not only Gallipoli jolted the Australian people: on 10 May they read in the paper the horrifying news that the unarmed liner *Lusitania* had been torpedoed without warning by a German submarine off the southern coast of Ireland. No fewer than 1,457 people had been drowned,[80] and even lukewarm supporters of the war were shocked and shaken by this evidence of German cold-blooded murder and piracy. If any one in Australia had thought that the war might be waged according to some sort of rules, the sinking of the *Lusitania* and Germany's U-boat campaign were unmistakable evidence that total war was now being waged for the first time.

Imperial sentiment led to greater national involvement in the European conflict. Revenge was in the air. A man from the back-blocks declared that he was going to the war because his brother had been killed at Gallipoli,[81] it was reported, and by June 1915 the enlistments in the A.I.F. had doubled from the April figure to 12,000 men for the month.[82]

The effect of the constant casualties at Gallipoli was illustrated by a dramatic incident at the St Kilda Town Hall when, at the end of a recruiting meeting conducted by the mayor, a man climbed on to the platform and informed the crowd that he had four sons away at the front, three in the 6th Battalion. To cheers, a woman called out, 'The glorious 6th Battalion!' and the speaker warmed to his subject: 'One of them was wounded the other day and I ask you ladies who have brothers to let them go, those who have lovers to let them go. When my youngest enlisted I said to him, "You never got my consent." "No," he said, "but I got mother's." That's the sort of mother. If anything should happen to them, it is the sort of death to die.' The speaker then left the platform amidst great applause and a minute or two later returned to deliver his punch-line. 'I forgot to say my eldest son was killed. When I got down to the railway station the morning after the news came through, everyone gripped me by the hand. One man said, "I am going to avenge Ossie". (Cheers)'. The meeting ended with the singing of the National Anthem.[83]

3

The Recruiting Drives of 1915

In mid-June 1915, following the substantial increase in recruitment after the landing at Gallipoli and the sinking of the *Lusitania*, the Australians asked the British government whether it would accept as many men as could be recruited in Australia. On 18 June the British government replied that it wanted every available Australian who could be recruited.[1] Clearly the position was grave, and less than a week later a State parliamentary recruiting campaign was launched in Victoria, where enlistment was said to have been especially backward.

This accusation was made by Senator Pearce at a recruiting meeting at the Melbourne Town Hall on 21 June. The Minister quoted figures which showed that in the four weeks up to 12 June, New South Wales had enlisted 2,788 men, Victoria 1,180 and South Australia 1,210.[2] He scarcely needed to point out to his uneasy audience that the State of Victoria should not be third in that list. The Premier of Victoria, Sir Alexander Peacock, asked all members of Parliament in the State to help in convening meetings for the appointment of local recruiting committees.

A Victorian Parliamentary Recruiting Committee was formed as a result of informal meetings of members of both Houses. Three men on the committee were to arrange recruiting drives: F. Clarke, M.L.C., J. W. Billson, M.L.A., representing the Labor opposition, and Donald Mackinnon, the Attorney-General.[3] On this basis, the campaign got under way to restore Victoria's fair name. Motor-car owners offered to put calico posters on cars reading, 'O.H.M.S. Your country needs you. Hail us for recruiting depot'; the minimum height required for recruits was reduced to 5 ft 2 in, dental health not being quite so relevant as previously;[4] moving pleas to

don khaki and join their countrymen at the greatest war in human
history were made to men who had so far held back. As the Premier
of New South Wales urged all Australians, 'Your comrades at
Gallipoli are calling you. This is not the time for football and tennis
matches. We are at death grips with the greatest and most unre-
lenting military power the world has ever seen. It is serious. Show
that you realize this by enlisting at once.'[5]

This campaign in Victoria was a great success. The Parliamentary Committee conducted the central recruiting depot for a
fortnight, after which the Defence Department took it over. The
depot was situated at the Town Hall, the most convenient point in
the city, thus focusing attention on one spot alone and avoiding
fragmentation of efforts. This centre was open to the would-be
recruit day and night till 10 p.m., bands played patriotic and
martial music, and a great variety of recruiting posters was displayed: in front of these advertisements stirring speeches were
made by men in public life and by soldiers in khaki who spoke from
a raised platform at the entrance to the depot.

These inducements to join up were accompanied by personal
persuasion from soldiers in uniform who moved among the crowds
of young men gathered there. Women helpers handed out refresh-
ments and further influenced the prospective recruit, the depot
had a wooden floor and was made comfortable and attractive,
there were efficient arrangements for dealing rapidly with volunteers, and there were facilities for posting up results of recruiting
several times during the day and night. Prahran and Malvern
Tramways Trust played its part by sending out every evening a
specially illuminated open tramcar to go through the shopping
centres. This carried a brass band and displayed a tableau showing
Britannia, supported by her sea and land forces, represented by
senior and naval cadets; the driver was dressed up as John Bull
and accompanied by a bulldog.[6]

Recruiting committees were also active in all boroughs, shires
and towns, with country depots at the chief provincial centres.
Thought-provoking posters were put up on railway stations in the
suburbs and country, the 'Will they never come?' one, donated by
private citizens, judged to be the best of all; the dials of public
clocks showed the words 'Enlist now' twenty-four hours a day, a
slogan on Victorian railway stations, thought to have had a

splendid effect, at which the standard recruiting posters also appeared.[7] But the principal reasons for the success of the State's campaign for recruits was the centralization of the drive on one depot, with the result that the recruiting at the Melbourne Town Hall far exceeded that at the barracks in St Kilda Road, the only depot previously used.[8]

On 5 July 813 Victorians flocked to the colours in twenty-four hours, and two days later 934 Melbourne men and 137 from the country, 1,071 men in all, enlisted in the A.I.F. The next day 962 more joined up. The grand total for the week was no less than 6,222 men, and the press proudly and properly congratulated the State on its patent and overwhelming loyalty: men of British blood needed only to have brought home to them that they were really wanted in the firing line for them to rally to the cause of the Empire, nodded the _Argus_, understanding that it was not now a question of 'business as usual', but that every fit man was wanted.[9]

On the night the Victorian campaign opened there was a stormy meeting at Williamstown when the Premier sketched the events of the last eleven months for the edification of his audience and dilated on the great part played by the British and Australian navies. At this point the voice of a wharf-labourer interjected, 'A tin-pot navy!' There was complete uproar, the hall resounding with angry shouts and cries of 'Put him out!' The Rev. F. Lynch, M.A., of Williamstown, sitting in the front row, rushed on the interjector and exclaiming angrily, 'A tin-pot navy, is it?', punched him on the nose.

That might have been that, but a week later the man he had struck enlisted in the A.I.F. Mr Lynch, hearing of this, at once sought him out. Roberts, the new recruit, had ever since the meeting denied that he had used the words in the sense in which they were interpreted by the crowd, but had simply repeated in an ironical way the catch-phrase of two or three years previously. The clergyman, at this revelation, shook hands with Roberts and expressed his regret at having misunderstood him at the meeting. The crowd of recruits having their names and particulars taken down gave the actors in this scene a hearty cheer. It was later learned, concluded the newspaper report of this transaction, that Mr Lynch had promised his late victim a wristlet watch if he was accepted for active service. He was.[10]

Early in June the Minister for Defence amended an earlier list of required reinforcements. He pointed out that Australia was pledged to provide 5,300 men a month to keep up the forces fighting at Gallipoli. Monthly requirements were:

N.S.W.	1,700
Vic.	1,700
Qld	700
S.A.	500
W.A.	500
Tas.	200

This meant a rate of sixty men a day in Victoria and New South Wales.[11]

So successful was the Victorian recruiting campaign that a week after it started, the State Premier proudly asked the Prime Minister, Andrew Fisher, to send a cable to General (later Field-Marshal Sir William) Birdwood, commanding the Australians, to inform him that during the special Victorian recruiting week, men had enlisted at the rate of 1,000 a day. The cable was sent. By the end of the month, 21,698 men had enlisted in Victoria, the largest number in any State in any month during the war.[12]

Such was one result of appealing to Victorians' pride in their State; local mayors had appealed to householders in terms which included, 'I desire to point out that the number of enlistments in Victoria compares very unfavourably with other States, and greater numbers are necessary from every State', and in an address to the people of Victoria, the three members of the State Recruiting Committee made the same point: 'Victoria is falling behind even in her supply of reinforcements to keep up the strength at the front'.

In an endeavour to help, none other than John Wren enlisted in August 1915. He was a very well known promoter of sport and a racecourse proprietor with interests in Melbourne, Brisbane and Perth. He owned the horse Murmur, winner of the Caulfield Cup, and Garlin, winner of the Australian Jockey Club Doncaster Handicap, Sydney. He had offered £500 to the first Australian to win the Victoria Cross, and subsequently handed over that sum to the relatives of Private Albert Jacka. Described as forty-three years old and father of six children, Wren told a reporter that he was prepared to do any duty that might be allotted to him; he was in good health and had slept out for years, so should not be worried by army life.

But he was; in November Corporal Wren was discharged from the A.I.F. in consequence of an ear infection and declared unfit for active service. Wren had been in Royal Park camp since September, and a month after his discharge commemorated his army career by giving £500 as a loan fund to men in that camp who might be in temporary financial difficulties. The money was to be lent out in sums of up to £5 at a time, to be repaid at such rates as an appointed board might determine, without interest. Wren nominated his board to be Captain E. H. Sugden, Father John Norris and Sergeant F. B. Collins, of the 24th Battalion.[13]

In federal Parliament Senator Millen reported with pleasure that the Victorian campaign led to more volunteers enlisting in one week than had previously offered in five or six weeks, and he foreshadowed a similar drive in New South Wales.[14]

Indeed, so successful was the recruiting that the same day the Minister for Defence approved a suggestion by the Adjutant-General, Colonel (later Major-General) T. H. Dodds, that an offer be made to the imperial authorities to double the October and November reinforcements, making now 10,526 men a month. He also suggested that the Commonwealth should send one infantry brigade, a signalling section, a brigade train and a field ambulance. If the double reinforcements were considered necessary, he offered as an alternative three infantry brigades, equipped with rifles and bayonets, to leave in November.

Six days later the first alternative was accepted by the Secretary of State, but in September, after the attempt in August to break out of the Gallipoli perimeter had failed with heavy casualties, the War Office cabled the Defence Department that as long as the Australian Light Horse was employed as infantry, reinforcements of 15 per cent a month were needed; so heavy was the 'wastage' in the A.I.F. that it urged reinforcements be hastened. Australia replied that reinforcements would be increased from and including the October drafts. A month later, the War Department consulted Sir Ian Hamilton and General Birdwood, and calculated that reinforcements would be required monthly in advance to replace the normal losses in 1916 at the rate of 20 per cent for infantry,

Light Horse, artillery gunners, and engineers, and 7 per cent for medical units. To meet further exceptional demands which were liable to occur, another 10 per cent reserve of trained men in Australia was thought to be of great value, but in view of the substantial assistance already given by the Commonwealth, the War Department hesitated to put this forward as a definite request.

It need not have been so diffident. The Australian government cabled an immediate reply that the War Department's request would be met from December onwards, and Senator Pearce told W. M. Hughes (who succeeded Fisher as Prime Minister on 26 October 1915) that monthly reinforcements from 15 to 20 per cent would now be necessary and would mean about 9,000 men a month. At that time, about 10,000 men were being recruited each month.[15]

A month after Victoria's recruiting campaign, New South Wales opened one, but the results were disappointing: on the first Saturday in August, only 212 men were accepted as fit and, although the results got better, there was nothing to come up to the July rush in the southern State. It was characteristic of New South Wales throughout the war, indeed, that enlistments continued at a much steadier rate than in Victoria. This was realized in New South Wales, one recruiting sergeant there pointing out in July that although there had been an enormous increase in Victorian enlistments, recruits in New South Wales still appeared at a steady rate. No bands and campaigns were used but the men simply came in on their own.[16]

The recruiting drive in Australia's most populous State coincided with the first anniversary of the outbreak of the war and a commemoration ceremony was conducted at the instigation of the New South Wales government on 5 August at 10 a.m. to correspond with midnight G.M.T. Government departments were ordered to stop work for five minutes to mark an occasion which, it was hoped, would help bring home to people the seriousness of the struggle with the Central powers, and lead to more men joining the forces. Local authorities were told of the government's wishes and leading churchmen were also asked for their co-operation. Michael Kelly, the Roman Catholic Archbishop of Sydney, replied in careful terms that it was ever the purpose of himself and his clergy to co-operate in their own sphere with every undertaking of the government, and to continue their special prayers and functions in order to obtain from on high the repression of the fierce militarism by whose unjustifiable aggression Australia's higher interests were endangered. 'God bless every Volunteer Defender of Australia's native land! In their bravery we shall claim a share,' was the sentiment of the Archbishop.

The Anglican Archbishop of Sydney, Dr J. C. Wright, accounted it a privilege to assist the government to arouse the public conscience to a yet fuller sense of the demand made by the needs of the Empire for men and means. He concluded by wishing the day had been appointed one of Special Humiliation.

In association with the anniversary of the outbreak of war, Holman arranged for a large recruiting meeting at the Exhibition Building on 31 July although Senator Pearce objected to a military parade because it interfered with the training of the troops. At civil services to commemorate the solemn anniversary, the following resolution (repeated in later years almost word for word on the same occasion) was proposed: 'That on this first anniversary of the declaration of a righteous war, this meeting of citizens of ——— records its inflexible determination to continue to a victorious end the struggle to maintain that ideal of Liberty and Justice which is the common and sacred cause of the Allies.'[17]

The Premier of New South Wales and his colleagues were disappointed with the fruits of the August campaign, but recognized that many factors told against them. In Holman's opinion, men were rejected on frivolous grounds and this was a great deterrent to others in their native town; again, the military authorities were unready to accept recruits the moment they offered and sometimes told them to come back later, and did not make appropriate displays of recruiting or give prominence to new recruits; he also stated that the federal government should clearly say, difficult though it might be, how many men it contemplated raising.[18] The fact that conditions at Liverpool camp had been found to be not up to standard was also thought to have had a deterrent effect but the government was confident that a second campaign would find them on sounder ground.[19] It did not. This time the *Sydney Morning Herald* comforted itself by noting that the campaign had coincided with harvesting and shearing which had necessarily employed thousands of men in work almost as

essential as the work of the men at the front.[20] The Minister for
Defence was not so sure about that ranking order: not 20,000 men
had been added to the ranks during the campaign in the largest
State, he sorrowfully reported.[21]

The government of New South Wales determined to play its part
by other means. One of these was the production early in 1916 of
a weekly magazine entitled the *Call to Arms*, printed and published
by the New South Wales government printer and issued to get
publicity for the recruiting campaign. It was in the charge of J. H.
Catts, organizing secretary of the New South Wales recruiting
campaign, and W. A. Holman, and cost £163 a week. It was
calculated that advertisements would bring in the £63 and that
the loss would be £100 an issue. It was sold for a penny a copy, and
the first number was issued on 3 March 1916 from Challis House,
Sydney.

The sixteen-page issue of 10 March was typical. The front page
was a cartoon showing men placing their tools of trade into a heap,
taking up rifles with fixed bayonets and joining a unit of marching
soldiers. The caption read, 'Downing tools—the right way to
strike.' The *Call to Arms* listed about 300 municipalities, gave the
name and address of the local secretary of the War Service Committee and the name of the recruiting sergeant, and was full of
news and information concerning the recruiting campaign. Among
the items reported was a notice that fifty-six men from Resch's
Brewery, Waterloo, had already enlisted, and that the directors
were keeping open the jobs of those men as well as making up the
difference between their civil and military pay; that the Baulkham
Hills War Service Committee had voted ten guineas from the
council funds to provide Recruiting Sergeant Thurgar with a
'turn-out' for six weeks; that nearly 500 men had enlisted from
Forbes, and more than £5,000 been subscribed to various patriotic
funds there.

The editorial appealed for a total Australian army of 500,000
men, and beneath the heading 'Compulsory Enlistment' took to
task the advocates of compulsion who were criticizing the alleged
failure of the voluntary system. Rebutting these people, the leading
article cited Senator Pearce's statement that the voluntary system
would suffice, but added that if the imperial authorities considered
the Empire could only be saved by compulsory enlistment in the

overseas Dominions, then they would say so. The paper noted with great approval the fate of one Edgerton Gaynor at Hay who was sentenced to six months in Goulburn Gaol for saying, 'We are dragged by the heels of Britain, and Britain will go under. I don't care, but we have no right to go under with her. We will be better under the German flag.'[22]

Encouraged by Victoria's mighty efforts in early July 1915, the Premier of South Australia, Crawford Vaughan, subsequently tried the same method when he presided at a meeting of 19 July and formed a recruiting executive consisting of the Premier, the leader of the opposition, Sir Richard Butler, and five others. The Military Commandant of South Australia helped by sending out recruiting posters to corporations and district councils.[23]

Tasmania also conducted a vigorous recruiting campaign in mid-1915 and sought from Sydney copies of the recruiting poster 'The Call from the Dardanelles', which had appeared in the *Bulletin* and then been issued by the government of New South Wales. Daily open air meetings were held in front of Hobart Town Hall at 12.30 p.m. each day after 9 August, and recruiting centres were extended to include Sandy Bay, Lansdowne Crescent, New Town and the A.M.P. Society's corner. Recruiting posters were put up on railway stations; at Zeehan on the west coast the local military band offered to aid a recruiting meeting by playing in the main street and arranging for a few patriotic songs from the platform.[24]

All the Australian States made such concerted efforts to persuade men to join the A.I.F. in mid-1915 that, although there was in the other States no such amazing increase of numbers as in Victoria, the number of enlistments in the whole of Australia increased very greatly.[25]

1915	N.S.W.	Vic.	Qld	S.A.	W.A.	Tas.	Total
May	5,654	1,735	1,069	1,062	689	317	10,526
June	5,279	3,381	1,267	1,394	806	378	12,505
July	8,961	21,698	2,197	1,453	1,485	781	36,575
August	12,991	3,983	3,013	2,705	1,903	1,119	25,714
September	6,911	2,331	3,569	1,651	1,385	724	16,571

SOURCE: *Official History*, vol. 11, p. 871.

Recruiting Office, Melbourne Town Hall

Diggers of the First A.I.F. marching through Melbourne

Men came from everywhere and from all occupations in the campaigns which were launched in mid-1915 and continued into 1916: twenty-two men of the Ballendella Progress Association had joined the forces by July 1915, the Association proudly informed the Defence Department,[26] and by April 1916 well over 20,000 members of the Australian Workers' Union had enlisted.[27]

By the beginning of September 1915 nearly 2,000 employees of the Victorian Railways Department had also enlisted for active service, as well as 306 schoolteachers, a fact which led to the closure of small country schools.[28] By April 1916 the implications of this led Senator Pearce, then acting Prime Minister while Hughes was in England, to address the Premiers on the shortage: because State Education Departments were feeling the loss of enlisted technical teachers and because the State War Councils were preparing to train returned soldiers, the Minister sought opinions on whether any more teachers should be permitted to join the A.I.F.

In answer, the Victorian Minister for Public Instruction, H. S. W. Lawson, reported the alarming fact that Victorian technical schools had lost more than one-third of their teachers, and many more were going because public opinion in favour of enlistment was so strong. The Minister stated that the federal government should not permit irreplaceable teachers to enlist, and in May the Commonwealth instructed the recruiting authorities not to accept anyone who said he was a technical teacher.[29] The same month, instructions were issued in New South Wales by the Chief Commissioner of Railways that the enlistment of mechanics and machine workers should also be prevented because of their possible value for the manufacture of munitions. Such workers, it was explained, would first have to resign if they wished to enlist, in which case they would waive their claim to the difference between military and railway pay.[30]

Another difficulty emerged in Western Australia as the Commonwealth's manpower was drained away. In that State large numbers of miners and fitters enlisted when they might have been kept back for munition work, and expert and irreplaceable gold miners also joined up.[31]

There was involved in all these cases a problem of priorities which the government refused to face and, indeed, could not unless it introduced a rational system of mobilization, i.e. conscription.

E

Other people aimed to assist recruiting and the war effort in other ways. In Queensland a gentleman from Stonehenge wrote to the Premier seeking his help as a lawyer and patent attorney to share the joy of making a gift of a patriotic parlour game called 'Southern Cross' secure and substantial for dedication of the proceeds of its sale to the Disabled Soldiers Fund. Another game called 'Little Jack' was also offered to the Premier, T. J. Ryan, who regretted his inability to accept his correspondent's invitation to bless the venture. In the same State a station owner had another idea to encourage recruiting: he informed the Premier about arrangements for a bushmen's carnival for October 1915. The principal events were to be a camp-drafting competition and an exhibition of trotting. The money so raised was to go to the Red Cross and to help sick and wounded soldiers, and he asked that the Brisbane Recruiting Committee send a good speaker and a few returned men with whose help an appeal to enlist would be made.[32]

The pressures to enlist which had really started in July continued to have their effect. These included a riot in Melbourne on Saturday night 6 November 1915 when a number of returned soldiers tried to help recruiting. During the early part of the evening men who had returned from the Middle East accosted male civilians in several of the principal streets of the city and asked them why they had not enlisted. In this work they were eagerly assisted by drunk members of the A.I.F. still in camp who, while not so sure of their own steps, tried to direct those of the civilians they had fixed upon towards the recruiting office at the Town Hall. Resentment was occasionally shown by the men so addressed, but the majority, it was reported, treated the matter as a joke. Perhaps these were the sorts of returned soldiers whom the Governor-General noted when he recorded that Australia was being flooded with soldiers who had been restored to such robust health as to give a good deal of trouble and who, if they increased in numbers, would become a troublesome and dangerous element in the community, like the men from the Seven Years War who were the subject of Robert Burns's poem 'The Jolly Beggars'.[33]

It was no joke to everybody who was asked impertinently why he had not joined the A.I.F. There was in Australia a shrieking sisterhood who wanted to get everyone to enlist, females who sent white feathers to men they thought were eligible to join the A.I.F.

It was pressure of this sort that led the Returned Soldiers' Association, 12 Spring Street, Sydney, to seek the formation of a Rejected Volunteers' Association of New South Wales. The object was to assist generally all patriotic movements and safeguard the interests of those who had tried to enlist but had been rejected. They were told that the Commonwealth would issue an official badge for medically unfit volunteers very soon, and that therefore it would not be suitable for a private body to do so.[34]

The pressure to recruit had earlier induced a Senator to ask whether or not it was really essential that a man should have a rifle placed in his hands before he should be drilled; Senator Bakhap (Tasmania) considered that recruits could take their place in the battle line within a week or two after actual rifles were placed at their disposal. When Senator Newland implied that such men might shoot themselves or their comrades by mistake, Senator Bakhap retorted that any Australian country-bred lad, if given a military rifle, would, after two days' tuition, hit a target more frequently than he missed it. He added the encouraging story of the Australian boy who was being pressed to join a rifle club and who pleaded that, although accustomed to a sporting rifle, he had no experience of shooting with military rifles. But the captain of the club, who was also a Justice of the Peace, gave him a rifle and supply of cartridges, undertaking to swear him in when they reached the township. The boy then took the rifle and scored four bull's-eyes in succession, thus demonstrating the sort of material which made the Australian soldier so resourceful.[35]

Another effect and result of making people aware of their duty in this hour of danger was the organization of 'snowball' recruiting marches in New South Wales. The object of these was to encourage men to enlist by example: a few men would start marching towards Sydney from the country and would, it was hoped, induce more and more to join the group as they went along. In mid-November 1915, for instance, there was a snowball army of recruits marching from Gilgandra to the capital to enlist, a distance of 320 miles. This march of the 'Cooees' was a manifestation of local enthusiasm, twenty or so men deciding to make a start for Sydney.[36]

The military authorities were not too happy about these marches (Should the men march with rifles? When did their pay start? Who should supply their clothes?) but people along the way were indeed generous to the prospective recruits to the A.I.F. At Eumungerie the marchers were given a turkey dinner, entertained at a social and given a harvest hat each by Mr Wheaton. There was no need for 'Cooees' to kiss themselves goodbye, a report said archly, 'the girls attended to that, and set an example that many hope will be followed right along the line.' Later, by following a track instead of the road, it was possible to reduce the day's march. The only obstacle was a fine wheat-field owned by a Mr Taylor. He got his wire-cutters to work on the fence. 'Drive right through,' he told the transports which carried the recruits' gear. 'Never mind the crops; you'll save a few miles, and that's what counts.' At Dubbo fifty overcoats were issued, and the 'Cooees', after being welcomed by the mayor, were given afternoon tea by the ladies, and rump steak and eggs for their evening meal.

At the start there were only thirty 'Cooees', but their number had swelled to a satisfying 263 by the time they reached Sydney. The metropolitan press reported them as hardy, sun-browned men of the west, with manner somewhat rough and uncouth, marching not exactly as the Grenadiers would march, wearing blue dungarees which did not always fit them, and somewhat travel-stained, slouching and weary in appearance after their five weeks on the road. They had been joined out west by a swaggie, humping his bluey. He tossed it down and joined the marchers. They asked him whether he knew anything of soldiering, whereupon he untied his swag and produced his South African medals, asserting that he had not suffered from 'Mauseritis' or 'Pom-pom debility', whereupon he was roped in, commenting, 'I was "out" yesterday, but I'm a man today.'[37]

Seven other enterprises were conducted along similar lines in New South Wales and, including the Gilgandra 'Cooees', 1,436 men entered camp. The numbers enlisted at the appeals made along the line of the march probably led to two or three times more than those who ultimately enlisted. These marches were made from November 1915 to February 1916 and included the South-West 'Waratahs' (117 men), Wagga 'Kangaroos' (213), North-West 'Wallabies' (180), 'Men from the Snowy River' (142), Tooraweenah 'Kookaburras' (100), the 'North Coasters' (220), and the Middle West 'Boomerangs' (201).[38]

Recruits were also encouraged by other means such as special

days during which attention was concentrated on the war effort.
In New South Wales such a day was 30 July 1915, called 'Australia
Day', which sought also to raise money for sick and wounded
Australian soldiers. There were all kinds of ways of raising money,
focusing attention on the war, and trying to get men to enlist in the
army; for instance, there was a boxing contest at Bungwahl Flat
and at Gunnedah, concerts at Randwick and Ultimo, and horse-
racing everywhere. The scheduled bouts at Bungwahl Flat created
a problem, according to the local policeman. He reported that
contests were to be in the form of four-rounders and a knock-out
for a prize of ten shillings, and he warned that in those cases where
a K.O. occurred, especially for money prizes, a brawl generally
ended the evening's entertainment. The New South Wales under-
secretary thought the risk worth it and directed that the contests
be conducted subject to the usual police conditions.[39]

The 'Day' in New South Wales raised £400,000[40] but the
donors would not have been pleased to learn that the Governor-
General of the Commonwealth reported to King George V's
private secretary that the carnivals in the State for the various
'Days' had the ulterior motive of advertising the wealth of the
State, and that Holman's government consisted of political adven-
turers. Still, they would have been pacified a little to know that
Sir Ronald Munro Ferguson a week or two later reported that on
his tour of the forest and wheat areas of southern New South
Wales he had been received with extraordinary respect and cordi-
ality: 'the loyalty of this democracy to the Crown is almost unique
in its touching simplicity'.[41]

These individual efforts were all very well, but early in November steps were taken to organize recruiting more effectively. A
memorandum from the Adjutant-General, Colonel Dodds, suggested that the Military Commandants of the six Military Districts,
together with another officer, be appointed members of the State
War Councils and, where appropriate, to the State Recruiting
Committees so that the military and the civilian recruiting agencies
might keep in touch with each other.[42]

This was approved by the Minister, and appropriate action
taken by all States. Yet recruiting continued to decline (though it
always did at the end of the year). A still more disquieting feature
was the high percentage of unfit men now noted among the Vic-

torian volunteers: on one day in December only ten out of thirty-two townsmen were passed fit at the Town Hall.[43] This lent more point to an appeal to footballers in New South Wales made in a letter written by the captain of the Wallaby Rugby Union team which toured Great Britain, Dr H. M. Morgan. It was typical of many references to the war that he should refer to the conflict raging in Europe and the Middle East as a 'game' for which Australians were particularly suited: 'Send us men, men, men and more men. It is the best game in history. There are no rules, and the only referee—posterity—has a whistle that cannot be heard. Yes, they're in our twenty-five at present, but when we heel out our ammunition more cleanly we shall move forward.'[44]

When W. M. Hughes succeeded Andrew Fisher as Prime Minister, the Commonwealth government's attitude to recruiting and the war in general changed radically. During his period of office Fisher had done practically nothing to organize recruiting on a national basis, limiting himself to a proposal made in August 1915 that the Commonwealth Parliamentary War Committee be the central body to control and lead recruiting, and that the States be asked to act in conjunction with it without prejudice to their own arrangements.[45] The state of the war did not of course demand imperatively that Fisher do much more, and his shrewdness told him that hard-line tactics would lead to trouble with a Labor Party whose policy, programme, philosophy and general outlook could not deal with the unpleasant implications of total war without shelving social objectives.

It is not clear why Fisher resigned at the point he did, nor precisely how Hughes came to power, though he was obviously the dynamo in the labour machine. In the same month that Hughes became Prime Minister, the Australian government and people had brought home to them the importance of nationally organized and centralized recruitment when in Great Britain Lord Derby was appointed to the position of Director-General of Recruiting; but so satisfactory was the campaign of mid-1915 that the Australian government did not put enlistment on such a centralized basis.

Yet the war was going far from well for the Allies, and on the morning of 23 December 1915 the Australian public read in their newspapers a significant piece of information. This was a report of a speech made by the Prime Minister of Great Britain to a House of Commons which heard him in grave silence. Mr Asquith asked Parliament to sanction the addition of no less than 1,000,000 more men to the imperial military forces, and further asserted that every eligible man should now be enrolled in the armed forces of Britain.[46] The greatest Empire since Rome was going to call home its armies and ask every citizen of the Empire to rally to its defence.

Could Australia, out on the fringes of that Empire, do more? Hughes believed it could, and at the end of November 1915 had announced that in addition to the 9,500 men a month currently being raised, a further 50,000 were sought for the A.I.F. before June 1916.[47] One reason why the new Prime Minister felt confident that the Commonwealth would find those men was information that he now had from a war census.[48] It led to the conclusion that there were tens of thousands of eligible men in the nation who had not yet volunteered. That war census, the manner in which Hughes tried to persuade 50,000 more men to enlist, a certain decision he took shortly after replacing Fisher, and a decision by Field-Marshal (later Earl) Haig in July 1916, were tragically to divide Australia and lead the ruling Labor Party to destruction.

4

The Decline of the Voluntary System

When the Labor Party won the general election of 1914 it did so on a policy which included putting to the electorate a referendum to seek federal power to curb monopolies and protect the people from extortion by big business. Such powers had been sought in 1911 and 1913 and rejected on both occasions. Despite this, Andrew Fisher had determined to ask the people again,[1] but W. M. Hughes now decided otherwise, securing instead an undertaking from the States that they would pass the appropriate legislation and consequently avoid turning people's attention from the war effort by a political campaign.[2] Hughes's name became mud to some of the labour journals when he did this,[3] and from then on every step he took inexorably led to his parting company with the principles of the labour movement. One such step was a series of four questions associated with the Australian war census.

Like every political and military leader during the war, Hughes became a creature of the stupendous war of attrition being waged on the Western Front. In Britain a national register of all persons between fifteen and sixty-five was made in mid-August 1915, the intention being that every member of the community should bear not merely a part in the war but the part which he or she was best qualified to take.[4] A similar measure was adopted in Australia when a Bill was introduced in the federal Parliament on 15 July and passed eight days later. It required certain information to be supplied by all males aged between eighteen and sixty. There were also questions about income.[5]

Introducing the Bill, Hughes said that its object was to ascertain the resources of the country in men and wealth and not to foreshadow conscription. Hughes's speech was characteristic of his attitude to the war:

At present we are drawing from the vitals of society our best men, without regard to their usefulness, and putting them into the firing line, without any regard to anything except the sublime spirit that led them to offer their services. The country is being deprived of its financial resources at a rate which makes all preconceived methods of supply totally inadequate . . . We are proceeding in the wrong way at present. We call for the services of anybody without considering whether they can be spared or not. What we should do is to ascertain what men should go and then call them to go.[6]

This census was taken between 6 and 15 September 1915.[7] All males aged between eighteen and sixty years were asked their name, address, age, marital status, dependents, general health and debilities, current occupation and any other occupation they could undertake, military training (if any), numbers and descriptions of firearms and ammunition in their possession, place of birth (and place of birth of father and mother) and, if born in a foreign country of foreign parentage, particulars of naturalization. Following this on 22 December, a regulation under the War Precautions Act made mandatory the answers to certain other enquiries including willingness or unwillingness to enlist for active service abroad, either then or later. There were four demands in particular which led the Prime Minister into trouble. They were:

Are you willing to enlist now? Reply 'Yes' or 'No'.
If you reply 'Yes' you will be given a fortnight's notice before being called up.
If not willing to enlist now, are you willing to enlist at a later date? Reply 'Yes' or 'No' and if willing, state when.
If not willing to enlist, state the reason why, as explicitly as possible.

In addition, a special personal message from the Prime Minister was enclosed. This was the 'Call to Arms':

The present state of war imperatively demands that the exercise of the full strength of the Empire and its Allies should be put forth. In this way only can speedy victory be achieved and lasting peace secured.

If those rights and privileges for which Australian democracy has struggled long and values dearer than life itself are to be preserved, Prussian military despotism must be crushed once and for all.

The resources of the Allies are more than adequate for this task, but they must be marshalled. To wage this war with less than our full strength is to commit national suicide by slowly bleeding to death.

Our soldiers have done great things in this war. They have carved for Australia a niche in the Temple of the Immortals. Those who died fell gloriously, but had the number of our forces been doubled, many brave lives would have been spared, the Australian armies would long ago have been camping in Constantinople, and the world war would have been practically over.

We must put forth all our strength. The more men Australia sends to the front the less the danger will be to each man. Not only victory but safety belongs to the big battalions.

Australia turns to you for help. We want more men. Fifty thousand (50,000) additional troops are to be raised to form new units of the Expeditionary Forces. Sixteen thousand (16,000) men are required each month for reinforcements at the front.

This Australia of ours, the freest and best country on God's earth, calls to her sons for aid. Destiny has given to you a great opportunity. Now is the hour when you can strike a blow on her behalf. If you love your country, if you love freedom, then take your place alongside your fellow Australians at the front and help them to achieve a speedy and glorious victory.

On behalf of the Commonwealth government and in the name of the people of Australia I ask you to answer 'yes' to this appeal, and to do your part in this greatest war of all time.

This 'Call to Arms', and the questions about willingness to enlist, were sent out to men aged between eighteen and forty-five, other than enemy subjects, who had replied to the war census personal card. The total number of appeals so distributed was 990,000. Because some people did not answer, further enquiries by registered mail were sent to approximately 173,000 people.

This census revealed that there were in the Commonwealth 215,770 men who were single, without dependents, and aged between eighteen and forty-five, together with 91,380 single men in that age-range with dependents, making a grand total of 307,150 single men between eighteen and forty-five. There were calculated to be 600,000 'fit' men altogether, 'fit' meaning every man describing himself as in good health, not having lost a limb, and being neither blind nor deaf.[8]

So it was that the Commonwealth government tried to equip itself with some of the information needed to prosecute the war, and in trying to secure complete returns, it ran into trouble.

One of these difficulties arose from suspicions by the industrial wing of the labour movement that Hughes was a militarist now revealed in his true colours: not content with shelving the proposals for the referendum, they said suspiciously, he asked questions about enlistment which were not only impertinent but which showed the impatience of a man who was really only waiting for a suitable chance to introduce conscription.[9] The secretary of the Federated Clerks' Union in Melbourne, F. Katz, was active in persuading the Trades Hall Council there to pass a resolution which recommended that unions affiliated to the Council ignore the questions. News of this leaked out, and on 21 December 1915 some returned soldiers tarred and feathered him. The Minister called for a report on the incident and Katz claimed £250 compensation for himself and his wife. He had already been scrutinized by someone, because two weeks before this incident the Commonwealth Statistician had informed the Prime Minister that, according to the confidential census card filled in by Katz, his address was 362 St Kilda Road, Melbourne, he was aged thirty-eight and born in Australia of a father born in Germany. Hughes was further told that Katz was assistant secretary of the Trades Hall, and had been very active in opposing the scheme for enlistment.[10]

The recruiting drive continued and, at the same time as Katz was being attacked by returned soldiers, it was announced that the new 50,000-man army would be organized in thirty-six battalions. Queensland recruits would form four battalions, those from New South Wales and Victoria twelve each, four would be formed from the South Australian volunteers, three from Western Australia and one from Tasmania. The numbers were to be raised from thirty-six territorial recruiting areas which would contribute 1,400 men each. These areas, it was planned, were to provide reinforcements for the new battalions together with extra men for one of the existing battalions. The actual numbers to be raised in each State were: Queensland 5,600, New South Wales 16,600, Victoria 16,000, South Australia 5,600, Western Australia 4,200, Tasmania 1,400. In the same order, approximate monthly reinforcements were 2,000, 5,400, 5,100, 1,700, 1,400, 400.[11]

To help in this work, recruiting committees were formed in all centres of population throughout the Commonwealth, and recruiting sergeants were instructed to exert every effort to enlist the required number of men. On 13 January 1916 there was an official opening of the campaign at the Melbourne Town Hall under the auspices of the Melbourne City Recruiting Committee; both the Prime Minister and the Minister for Defence, G. F. Pearce, were present as well as the Lord Mayor of Melbourne, Sir David Hennessy. Hughes had evidently been stung, or recognized a threat, from those labour publicists who had accused him of defecting to the capitalists, because he made two interesting statements: he said that no one could accuse W. M. Hughes of couching a lance for property-owners, and further observed that the gap between the syndicalists and unionists was as wide as hell[12]—all of which meant that the gap between Hughes and the labour rank and file was also widening.

Meanwhile recruiting sergeants were asked to follow up those men who had not replied to the enlistment cards, and were further asked to send in the delinquents' names to the local recruiting committees which were told to transmit them to the Military Commandants with a view to prosecution.[13]

The point was that the Australian body politic was not unanimously behind the government. As the police reported concerning the premises at 221 Castlereagh Street, Sydney, the owner had refused to accept a census card, saying that there was no law to compel anyone to fill it in. The police added that the lady who had thus refused to make a return was not only twice married, but her first husband was a German. The report added that a number of men, mostly socialists, resided at the place.[14]

That sort of thing occurred elsewhere. The organizing secretary of the New South Wales Recruiting Committee advised the Minister for Defence that many men of military age had destroyed their cards and that some had deliberately changed their boarding-houses to avoid communication from the authorities. To overcome this inconvenient difficulty, he arranged that shire and municipal war service committees be given extra copies of the Prime Minister's appeal and the form, each form issued in a given area to have a stamp indicating that area, together with a progressive number. He further asked for an appeal to be made calling on eligible men to collect the appeal and the form.

Pearce agreed with this in part, but felt moved to seek the view of the Crown Solicitor as to whether the method adopted should provide for penalties up to £500 or one year in gaol if the cards were not filled in and returned by 1 March 1916. At the end of February, Pearce finally gave instructions that recruiting sergeants be told to send in the names of all persons who had not complied with the proclamation. A memorandum along these lines was sent to State War Councils and followed up a week later: action was to be taken against all persons who made false declarations, influenced others to reply in the negative, abused recruiting sergeants, refused to reply at all, or who submitted evasive replies. Such awkward customers were to be reported by State War Councils to the Military Commandants.

All this was a lot easier written down than done because the instructions placed the recruiting committees, and everyone concerned with recruiting, in a difficult position. At once, in a letter typical of those received by the Department of Defence, the local recruiting committee at Scottsdale, Tasmania, pointed out that recruiting sergeants could not be expected to know who had made or not made a proper reply to the questions in the census; the Tasmanian body could only assume that a house-to-house canvass would have to be conducted. The Department considered this difficulty in reply to many such letters and drafted a circular which said that by comparing the lists of replies received with the electoral rolls and other such information, it should be possible to find out whether any person had not sent back his form. But again the Tasmanian War Council found itself in difficulties in following this, and sought from the Defence Department a list of those people who had made their returns, so that defaulters could promptly be detected and brought to book, public comment having been made on the delay in dealing with these cases. But as the Crown Solicitor ruefully pointed out, there were many difficulties in the way of prosecuting, especially in regard to proving an offence.

The municipality of Beaconsfield in Tasmania was one in which such difficulties were reported in early 1916. Asked by the recruiting sergeant whether they would enlist, men gave replies such as 'When all the single men have gone', 'When conscription comes' and 'I do not care to go to foreign lands to fight.' Others replied to Hughes's 'Call to Arms' with 'I am not prepared to go while the big bugs remain behind', 'I don't believe in being bluffed into enlisting' and (from a man who answered that he would go 'later') 'I am not prepared to argue the point.'

What was to be done with such people? The Crown Solicitor's conclusion was the inconvenient one that, if the matter were to be taken further, legislation was needed because the onus was wholly on the prosecution (the Crown) which would have to prove that any defendant was a male aged between eighteen and forty-five, was in the Commonwealth between 22 December 1915 and 29 February 1916, and had failed to send in his form. Any proceedings against men who had not lodged a return were consequently bound to fail unless the defendant admitted all these things. The Crown Solicitor could only suggest the passage of legislation that assumed the men charged were between eighteen and forty-five and resident in the Commonwealth, and that the Statistician should certify that no form had been received.[15]

Although the Commonwealth Statistician computed that certainly no more than 83,000 men failed to return an answer, and probably substantially fewer,[16] the number is uncertain. So is the number of men who said they would not enlist, though in May E. D. Millen told the Senate that 120,000 single men had written 'no' on their census cards in answer to the question of whether or not they would join up, and thus deliberately stated that they were not prepared to offer their services to their country.[17]

The town clerk of Balmain recorded an example of what was going on. He said that in the case of 1,412 enlistment cards received, 94 men were willing to enlist at once, 126 had already enlisted, and 54 undertook to enlist later. He classified the excuses of those who refused to enlist: because all German and alien subjects were not interned; because not all single men had gone to the front; because there was no conscription; because parental consent had not been given; because of engagement in the iron trades at Cockatoo and Garden Islands; and because of physical

defects. As in the case of the Tasmanian men at Beaconsfield, there
had been a number of evasive and impertinent replies at Balmain
too.[18]

So there were emerging various reasons why the Defence Department could not enlist the number of men it thought it should.
Relations with the public were not good and they got worse when
early in 1916 there was a mutiny at Casula Camp in New South
Wales.

There had earlier been trouble at this camp outside Liverpool:
at the end of the preceding November the Minister for Defence
had asked for a report into the alleged absenteeism of 1,780 soldiers
who had overstayed their leave one week-end. Conditions in
general were said to be bad and this led to the appointment of a
reluctant Royal Commissioner, Mr Justice Rich of the High
Court.[19]

Despite changes in the condition of the camp, on Monday 14
February 1916 about 2,500 disgruntled men marched out of
Casula to Liverpool. Here they rushed the bar at the Railway
Hotel and took more than £100 worth of liquor. Windows were
broken and looted casks of beer rolled into the street where the
contents were consumed. Other hotels were then entered and
extensive damage done, after which a large number of men, most
of them half drunk, went to the train. Some hundreds went on to
Sydney where they continued to riot. A military picket was sent to
the Central railway station and soldiers turned a fire hose on the
pickets who were being called 'scabs' and 'blacklegs' by some
civilians. The pickets were finally given the order to fire revolvers,
and Trooper Ernest William Keefe died of gunshot wounds. He
had been one of the three rioters wielding the fire hose. This riot
was so hushed up by the censorship that it assumed fearsome
proportions in the popular imagination; reports of it went all over
the world.[20]

In Parliament various reasons were offered for the decline in
enlistment. J. Mathews, Labor member for Melbourne Ports, complained about the condition of, and treatment meted out to, the
soldiers invalided from Egypt to Australia, and considered that the
decline would continue if returned soldiers were carelessly treated
on the way back home. Another member of Parliament, complaining about the shortage of rifles for rifle clubs, informed the House

that he had been assured that thirty or forty men in one district had gone to the front without ever having handled a rifle in their lives. He thought that was a nice state of affairs.[21] And of course there was the perennial excuse that Australians would not enlist while Germans or people of German descent stayed back: as 'Ready to Fight' informed the government, he would certainly go to the war when the government took charge of all the Germans in his home State of New South Wales, so that those who joined up would be sure that during their absence wives and daughters would not meet the same fate the women and children of Belgium and France had met at the hands of the enemy.[22]

Enthusiasm for the war was on the wane, and so was the number of recruits who were being raised by the voluntary system. What could be done? Some people knew what was to be done and gave public expression to their opinions when, on 11 September 1915, there was published in the daily papers the manifesto of the Universal Service League. This body included some of the most influential members of the Australian community. Archbishop Kelly of Sydney was in it and so was Archbishop Wright; Professor T. W. David was a prominent member of the New South Wales branch and so was W. A. Holman, the Labor Premier. The objects of the League were three: 1. to advocate the adoption for the period of the war of the principle of universal compulsory service at home or abroad, and to support the government in providing such organization as was necessary to secure the application of this principle; 2. to secure the passage of legislation for universal compulsory service and to assure the federal government that such legislation would command the loyal support of the people of the Commonwealth; 3. to adopt any other measure calculated to promote the objects of the League.[23]

It was, then, clear to some that conscription was the only way to keep up reinforcements and to distribute the burdens of the war equitably. England had adopted conscription, and early in April 1916 the *Argus* began publishing a number of letters from readers who demanded compulsory overseas service.

The newspaper was not completely satisfied with the existing system of recruitment. Gallantly, even eagerly, it observed, men of the British navy had gone to their death in thousands at the Battle of Jutland to maintain the flag and safety of the Empire. The

The children's war effort

Horse-drawn ambulances in Melbourne

German hordes continued to dash themselves to pieces against the invincible French lines at Verdun, the sons of Canada had once more faced and beaten back a deadly German onset, gallant Italy was being sorely pressed but the Russian steamroller was in forward motion along almost the whole of the Eastern Front. In Australia, however, asked the newspaper more in sorrow than anger, what was happening? Strikes were on, race-meetings were crowded with punters, picture theatres bursting at the seams. Were the eligibles perhaps so interested in the dramatic events in Europe that they forgot to enlist?, pondered the *Argus*. Or if they did think about joining the army, perhaps these eligible young men gave themselves the benefit of the doubt and enjoyed themselves at home. The paper said that it dared not quote figures about probable requirements and the prospects of meeting them. Australia had now emblazoned its name on an ever-enduring roll of fame. There was unlimited scope for advancement in the A.I.F., urged the paper; what other walk of life offered the same advantages as the army?

However, there were other more deep-seated reasons for the failure of the Commonwealth to keep up the stream of volunteers at the rate its government had chosen. The first casualty of the war in 1914 was truth: on 4 August there began the strictest censorship by the military authorities of all cable messages, both press and private, received in and sent from Australia.[24] The struggle in Europe was the best example to that time of the suppression of facts which might conceivably be useful to the enemy, and of the feeding to the public of half-truths and, sometimes, utter lies. This was recognized early in the war: in June 1915 Lieutenant-Colonel Sir Albert Gould told the Senate that one of the great troubles the nation had to contend with was the erroneous belief that the Allies were doing well. Unfavourable news had been carefully suppressed, he asserted, and that fact had led Australians to fail to realize fully the grave position in which the Commonwealth stood.[25]

The government's censors thought that the people could not be told the truth, and in turn this led to the government being distrusted by the people, perhaps when it should not have been. An example of this occurred in August 1915 and involved the Gallipoli campaign and the fierce attempt to break out of the perimeter in that month. On 26 August the Defence Department received a telegram from the Premier of Western Australia which read that a

F

statement had been published in Perth that units of the Light Horse
had been practically wiped out on 7 August. This was the day on
which the Nek was attacked by units which included many
Western Australians. John Scaddan said that he was receiving
anxious enquiries, and he wanted the report confirmed or denied,
together with an official comment on statements that the disaster
was largely due to the Australian Light Horse being fired upon by
allied artillery. Pearce noted that a similar report had been in the
Melbourne *Herald* of 25 August and minuted an angry 'How did
such a cable escape censorship?'

He at once communicated with the A.I.F. headquarters in
Egypt, and in reply to Scaddan said that heavy casualties had been
reported but that there was no official news. The Minister for
Defence two days later agreed that his reply to the Premier of
Western Australia might be published: Scaddan said that it would
alleviate enormous anxiety in the West because many people believed that official information had been received and suppressed
for some reason.

On 3 September A.I.F. headquarters in Egypt reported total
casualties of the 3rd Light Horse Brigade as 13 officers and 310 men.
On 19 September the Perth *Daily News* carried a stop press item:

Grave news received from Gallipoli. Disaster to Light Horse. Today grave news was received by officers of the —th Light Horse,
now serving at the front. The news conveyed was that a number
of officers had been killed in action. The names mentioned but not
officially available yet are those of M'Masters, Jackson, Proctor,
Huxham, Piesse.

This drew a demand from the censor asking why the *Daily News*
had published unofficial information. In reply, the paper retorted
that the loss of ten officers had been common knowledge in the
city for two or three days, and that the paper had carefully omitted
five names it was not sure of. The Crown Solicitor's opinion was
sought as to whether the *Daily News* might be prosecuted under
the War Precautions Act (a piece of legislation based on Britain's
Defence of the Realm Act and delegating very wide powers to the
Governor-General in Council), but it was thought that such a
charge would not stand up. The censors were furious, especially at
the attitude of the Perth paper, which announced that it could not

submit to a restraint which served no useful purpose. The matter ended with the *Daily News* being told to be more careful in future.[26]

Thus was the public cushioned and, in a way, misled by the perverted way in which war news appeared—or did not appear. The inevitable slow dawning of the truth led only to cynicism. It was unfair to blame the Defence Department for such incidents all the time, but Joseph Cook, the Liberal leader, noted how interesting it was that whenever there was special trouble at the front, whenever anything happened to cause a shock to the public mind because of the horrors of war, it proved the best recruiting agent.[27] This suppression of news was complemented by overfulsome praise; exaggeration of minor victories into triumphs, and skirmishes into battles was deprecated at the front where the members of the A.I.F. were annoyed and made to feel foolish at hearing false news crediting them with deeds of valour they had not performed at all.[28]

Censorship of news and suppression of views thought by some censor to be prejudicial to the recruiting only inflamed those who had their doubts about Australia's role in the war and the motives of Britain. As the feelings of some hardened in favour of conscription, so others became more and more suspicious of Hughes and the enormous powers he was making use of under the War Precautions Act and its multifarious regulations. They would have been a lot more alarmed had they known what was thought to be prejudicial to recruiting.

One example of statements so thought to be disloyal occurred in early 1916 when there fell under notice an article in the official organ of the Labor Party in Victoria, *Labor Call*, a journal which made up in spite and crudeness what it lacked in polish. Headed 'The Verbosity of William Morris Hughes M.P.' and signed by W. Wallis, it reviled the Prime Minister for associating with such 'toffs' as William Irvine, Baillieu, Hagelthorn, Peacock and Hutchinson, poured scorn on the Prime Minister's repetitive stories of the German menace and delusive spies, and jeered that Hughes the apostate was now significantly fêted and eulogized by every trust-monger and moneybag in the nation.

Giving an opinion on these comments, the Crown Solicitor held out little chance of a prosecution leading to a conviction under the common law, but under sections 10 (1914) and 2 (1915) of the

War Precautions Act, which forbade people to make false statements likely to cause disaffection to the King and likely to prejudice
recruiting, he suggested that the Commonwealth might act. The
Victorian government proceeded no further.[29]

Another example of what was held likely to prejudice recruiting
occurred in New South Wales in January 1916. This involved a
report in the *Sydney Morning Herald* headed 'Anti-Conscription
League', and it was said not to have been submitted to the censor
before publication. One of the speakers at this meeting of the
League was reported to have stated that he considered no country
in the world was worth the sacrifice of a working man's life; he was
cheered to the echo. H. Ostler, of the Socialist Labor Party, also
caustically criticized the Prime Minister, and stated that he
(Ostler) had returned his recruiting card with the comment that
'if the commonwealth looked to him in its hour of trial, then it was
"God help the commonwealth".' In March, Pearce gave instructions that the *Sydney Morning Herald* was to be prosecuted, but
on 25 April he decided that a warning would do. The reaction of
the paper was one of surprise; it commented that after its report
on the meeting showed what sort of body the Anti-Conscription
League was, it had collapsed. The newspaper added that a too
rigid suppression of news might defeat its own object.[30]

Opposition to the prospect of conscription was also manifested
by the Political Labor League executive of New South Wales in a
circular to all branches and candidates, but Holman replied that
Germany must be crushed and that therefore he favoured compulsory service during the war.[31]

A lot of people did not agree with the Premier of New South
Wales and many incidents reflected badly on the army and were
thought to deter men from recruiting. For example, while 30,000
people were at a recruiting rally at the Exhibition Oval in Adelaide
in April 1916, an exhibition of bomb-throwing led to the removal
of one eye of a young male spectator after he was struck by bomb
fragments.[32] 'For King and country' was still a powerful slogan,
but not quite as good as it had been.

Following the Prime Minister's 'Call to Arms' there was initially
a substantial increase in the number of recruits: from 9,000 in
December 1915 the numbers went to 22,000 in January 1916,
18,500 in February and 15,500 in March. In Victoria by the

beginning of February about 6,700 men had enlisted for the 'new army' but this was far short of that State's quota of 16,000.[33]

In June the Victorian State Parliamentary Recruiting Committee, 451 Collins Street, advised that the voluntary system had reached its limit, and suggested that all eligibles be called up. Recruiting diminished considerably; the number of enlistment depots was reduced from fifteen to five and at the beginning of July only the Central Depot in Melbourne remained open; many local committees considered, and several reported, that it was impossible to get any more volunteers in their districts; recruiting sergeants reported that they had met with little or no encouragement; some recruiting committees had asked for the removal of recruiting sergeants because they could do no good; it appeared that the great public interest in what Hughes would do on his return from overseas (he had gone to England from Sydney on 16 January at the invitation of the imperial authorities) had affected adversely the rate of recruiting. In view of all these circumstances, the Victorian State Committee wound up its affairs.[34]

In June the secretary of the New South Wales Recruiting Committee, J. H. Catts, resigned on the grounds that the Prime Minister's appeal had been tried and found wanting:[35] recruiting was just about exhausted and the War Council of the State considered that little more could be done to bring the numbers up to the quota. At the end of July there was a report from Professor R. G. Macintyre, a member of the State Recruiting Committee, and a statement by the Military Commandant of the District, Major-General G. Ramaciotti, in which both men confessed that they knew of no further means of pursuing the recruiting campaign with advantage; they added that the cost of getting recruits was now prohibitive.[36]

Not only the States of Victoria and New South Wales were having trouble; when it was decided to raise a wholly Tasmanian battalion (the 40th) to infuse new spirit and please the Tasmanian public, the Chief of the General Staff, Brigadier-General H. J. Foster, noted that two companies of this unit had already partially been raised not in Tasmania but in Victoria. The Adjutant-General, Colonel Dodds, considered that Tasmania could not keep up the necessary reinforcements, and suggested that only half the battalion be raised in the island. This disappointed the Tasmanians because young men had been induced to enlist on the grounds that they would be in an all-Tasmanian battalion. To that date, 6,000 Tasmanians had gone to the front, and 1,500 were in camp. The Chief of the General Staff was adamant, stating that the numbers Tasmania had put together for this battalion had only been made possible by relieving her of the State's obligation for reinforcements, which were being supplied by Queensland. Foster urged that his comments be released to the press because they were a severe indictment of Tasmania and would encourage rather than discourage enlistment. The Minister for Defence agreed to this, but three days later Foster told the Tasmanian Military Commandant in Hobart that now the whole of the battalion would be raised in the island, but it was expected that Tasmania would raise other reinforcements as well.[37]

Australia was falling further and further behind both the promise of Hughes and what were held to be the needs of the situation; by May 1916 it was clear that recruiting could no longer continue at the required rate. How far short of its quota Australia had fallen is shown by Table 1.

Should there not be conscription? Australia's experience of compulsory military service at home had been significant in terms of the wave of indifference with which it was greeted. In 1909 the Australian federal Labor Party at its Brisbane conference had been persuaded to place the plank of compulsory military training in the platform because it was regarded as desirable citizen service and because there was a powerful group of people who thought that Australia should be prepared in this way to defend the new Commonwealth. It was alleged that the Brisbane conference fell into the hands of jingoistic labour leaders who were closely in touch with the War Office in Great Britain and with the National Service League whose ideal was a pan-Britannic militia.

In 1910 the term of compulsory military training service was raised to seven years: boys aged between twelve and fourteen were made junior cadets and required to drill for a total of 120 hours a year; youths between fourteen and eighteen drilled for four whole days, twelve half-days and twenty-four night drills. Between the ages of eighteen and twenty-five, such males were members of the citizen forces with the liability of sixteen whole-day drills, eight of which were to be in camp.

TABLE 1

Enlistments in the A.I.F. from
1 December 1915 to 13 May 1916

State	Quota of new army	Reinforcements for existing and new units	Total number required	Weekly quota 1 Dec. 1915 to 30 June 1916
N.S.W.	16,800	36,400	53,200	1,773
Vic.	16,800	36,260	53,060	1,768
Qld	5,600	13,200	18,800	679
S.A.	5,632	11,872	17,504	583
W.A.	5,000	8,701	13,701	456
Tas.	1,429	3,577	5,006	167

	Number required 1 Dec. 1915 to 13 May 1916	Actual enlistments 1 Dec. 1915 to 13 May 1916	Difference
N.S.W.	41,765	27,479	14,286
Vic.	41,548	23,951	17,597
Qld	16,203	13,604	2,599
S.A.	13,700	6,740	6,960
W.A.	10,488	6,892*	3,596
Tas.	3,927	2,188	1,739

*Enlistments in Western Australia not available after week ending 6 May 1916.
SOURCE: Premier's Dept, 16/3785, A.A.N.S.W. (totals corrected).

Thus was the youth of Australia to be prepared. The reality was different. Boys or their parents often did not obey the government, and between 1 January 1912 and 30 June 1914 there were 28,000 prosecutions, ranging from 11,000 in New South Wales to 1,500 in Tasmania, including 5,732 cases of boys and youths being imprisoned for evading their responsibilities. Although efforts were made to induce schoolteachers to register their pupils, at the end of June 1912 it was announced that 17,000 cadets were liable to prosecution.[38]

There was, then, a record of avoidance of compulsory national service, but as it became clearer to Australians that the war was going to be long drawn out, so it became correspondingly clear to some that the federal government should have power to conscript men in order to use them in the most effective way. Indeed, if the conflict was one to the death, then it was obvious that the country must equip itself to wage total war; this could not be done properly on a piecemeal please-yourself basis.

Hughes's views in July 1915 were opposed to conscription for overseas service and, in discussing the War Census Bill, he made a statement which was later thrown back in his face many times, 'The Bill is not for the purpose of conscription for service either in Australia or abroad. In no circumstances would I agree to send men out of this country to fight against their will.'[39] Four months later, on the eve of his visit to the United Kingdom, he said the same thing again, though with an interesting addendum: the government had no intention of departing from the policy of voluntary enlistment, but it did propose to consider very seriously the position concerning the forces needed to bring the war to a satisfactory conclusion.[40]

Hughes left for England in January 1916 through submarine-infested seas, not even telling his wife which route the ship was taking to Europe.[41] Exactly when the Prime Minister changed his mind on the question of conscription is not clear, but he was in England during stirring times: the Battle of Jutland was fought, the disaffected Irish presented with martyrs by the British authorities, and conscription adopted by the imperial government. Hughes, speaking after Lloyd George when the latter commented on conscription, was quoted as talking in terms of victory being dependent on 'organization'. With a characteristic metaphor, he concluded: 'We must make a final blow, and the greater it is the more quickly the tide will turn. If we fail now to make the maximum effort, then as surely as the Saviour lives, we will go down to hell.'[42]

The Australian Prime Minister was lionized in England. He dined with the King, was awarded the freedom of a number of cities and generally made much of.[43] It might have turned his head. Why was Hughes featured so prominently? Perhaps because of his undoubted energy and vigour when contrasted with the exertions of the Asquith government, his patently clear determination to crush for ever the military might of the German Empire, or because for a time he was the only Dominion leader in the United Kingdom. Different reasons were offered by the New South Wales Agent-General in London, B. R. Wise: he considered that the prominence given to Hughes was due to the accident of the Melbourne journalist and war correspondent Keith Murdoch being in London. Murdoch, concluded Wise, had gained the confidence of the newspaper magnate Lord Northcliffe by returning from Gallipoli with the first news of what was really going on at the Peninsula. Ashmead-Bartlett, the war correspondent whose descriptions of the Gallipoli landing had so stirred Australia, had been deprived of his notes and documents (reported Wise cryptically), while Murdoch, 'not being suspected', got through. He then printed his documents privately and circulated them to members of the Cabinet. Northcliffe had taken a fancy to Murdoch, declared Wise, and allowed him to have his own way with Hughes in writing up his pronouncements.[44]

At home, the labour movement in Australia began to split as the land was pervaded by war weariness, frustration and a lack of enthusiasm made more apparent by the contrast with the high hopes of 1914. The depth of feeling evoked by the war led men to take up extreme positions and over-state their cases. Recruiting meetings led to highly emotional scenes: at Tallangatta a wounded returned soldier appealing for recruits concluded his pleas with an affecting, 'Won't someone take my place, I'm done'; Sergeant A. Ball, blind in both eyes and with his right arm shattered, made a pathetic appeal to send reinforcements to 'the boys out there': women and girls rushed forward to shake his good hand, but there was little response from the large gathering he addressed on this occasion at the corner of Victoria and Shelley Streets, Richmond, Victoria.[45]

One reason why enthusiasm for the war had waned so markedly was the continuing polarization of the community into those who became more and more certain that conscription was not only just but inevitable, and those who feared what conscription might lead to. As a notice pasted over a recruiting poster read, 'Workers, as you are giving your lives, insist on the rich giving their wealth. Demand the surrender to the state of incomes over £300 per annum.' This was signed on behalf of the Women's Socialist League by A. Warburton, Honorary Secretary.[46]

The Australian Natives' Association agreed in a way with the League, demanding the conscription of men, money and material. It was significant that such a staunchly conscriptionist body had its Collingwood chairman, Councillor McNamara, assert that men were not enlisting because the capitalists were exploiting the people, so that wives and children of soldiers had to pay twice as much for necessities as before the war. But 35,885 electors signed a petition circulated by the A.N.A. favouring conscription.[47]

Violence began. A deputation to Senator Pearce by the Australian Peace Alliance and F. J. Riley, its secretary, spoke of meetings being smashed up, and wanted to know whether in Australia there was civil law or military mob law. This was a reference to men, said to be soldiers, breaking up meetings of anti-conscriptionists at such places as the Yarra Bank. The Melbourne City Council refused the use of the Town Hall to the Trades Hall for a public meeting on the matter of conscription, correctly anticipating which side of the question the Trades Hall would favour. The Guild Hall had earlier been hired for an anti-conscription meeting at which Maurice Blackburn, the prominent Labor M.P. for Essendon, spoke powerfully, asserting that the existing system was one of moral and economic pressure and that men were not enlisting because there was not enough provision for their dependents: whereas both rich and poor recruits risked their lives, the poor risked the future security of their dependents as well. Blackburn concluded that where there was conscription, as in France, it was applied so that women and children were overworked. E. J. Holloway, secretary of the Melbourne Trades Hall Council, agreed. Conscription was opposed because it was repugnant to the Australian people, he said, because there was no necessity for it, and because the motive of some of its most ardent supporters was to break the trade unions.[48]

Whether or not the last statements were true or not, it was clear that conscription, if applied logically, would lead to a serious weakening of the trade union movement. The attitude of the labour movement in New South Wales was emphasized by the passage of a resolution by the central executive on 15 October 1915. This regretted that members had permitted its name to be associated with their membership of the Universal Service League, and considered that labour men should not associate publicly with controversial issues on which the labour movement might have to express an opinion.

During Easter 1916 that opinion was expressed at the annual conference of the labour movement held in Sydney; from Wagga Wagga emanated a fateful motion. This pledged labour to oppose conscription abroad by all lawful means, and directed Labor

Leagues and affiliated trade unions to oppose all Labor members who voted for or who supported such conscription. Second, where unions or Leagues failed to take such action, the central executive was instructed to refuse endorsement of conscriptionist candidates. Third, New South Wales delegates on the interstate executive were instructed to oppose at all costs the policy of conscription.[49]

Meanwhile the conduct of the Prime Minister in England continued to shock some labour men in Australia. Senator Ferricks spoke of Hughes's association with the King and Queen, and of the Prime Minister's cavorting with duchesses, commented that the tories of Australia were awaiting the Prime Minister's return with no little interest, and said with disgust that Joseph Cook or Sir William Irvine would have represented Australian labour just as well as Hughes was doing.[50] The next day there was another indication that Hughes was parting company with a certain element of his party: addressing 3,000 Australian soldiers at Weymouth Camp, he stated that he had stood more than any other man for compulsory military service because there was no other way whereby a free people could strike a blow for liberty.[51]

All Australia was waiting for the Prime Minister's return so that its inhabitants might find out just how W. M. Hughes intended to strike that blow. Certainly the war was not going well: even the drowning of Lord Kitchener had no stimulating effect on recruiting.[52] Though a recruiting sergeant asserted that this death would lead to his getting fifty men a day off his own bat,[53] 'Loyal Australian' complained that the standard on the military building was not even flown at half-mast. It was a year of tragedy: the national flag was shown reversed on some recruiting posters and objections were lodged about another one because it featured a picture of a half-naked woman.[54] Most important of all, on 27 April 1916, Australia's people read that there had been a serious rebellion in Dublin. The Easter Rising had occurred; the shots being fired in the streets of the Irish capital were to ring around the world and help to cause the most savage sectarian and political battle in Australia's history.

5

Opposition to the Conscription Proposals in 1916

On the last day of July 1916, W. M. Hughes returned to Australia
(some said spitefully that he had travelled on a hospital ship),[1] and
on 8 August, anniversary of the battle at Lone Pine, Gallipoli, the
Prime Minister arrived back in Melbourne. At the Spencer Street
railway station, Mrs Hughes was presented with floral sprays and
a basket of wattle, and the Prime Minister with a model in flowers
of the battle cruiser *Australia*. Hughes turned and spoke to the
returned soldiers of the A.I.F. who were in the surging crowd,
saying that there seemed hardly a spot on earth where one might
not now meet an Australian soldier. He spoke of their behaviour
and of how they who had set the standard of Gallipoli had uplifted
Australia in the eyes of the world.

At the Town Hall Hughes was given a civic reception and, just
before his arrival, fifty returned soldiers filed in to take their places
at the back of the platform to the strains of 'Australia will be
There', played by the city organist, Dr W. G. Price.[2]

It was two weeks after the A.I.F. had been thrown into the
battles of the Somme. This onset, launched in part to relieve
German pressure on the French at Verdun, had begun on 1 July
after a five-day artillery bombardment so intense that it was heard
in England. But it had not destroyed the German defences when
the British advanced that morning: they walked into a hell of
machine-gun fire and by nightfall had lost 60,000 men, of whom
20,000 were killed.[3] It was the most shocking slaughter of the war
on the Western Front.

In the first seven weeks from mid-July in which they too were engaged on the Somme, the A.I.F. sustained 27,000 casualties[4] and Australia was flooded by telegrams informing next of kin that men had been wounded; thousands of families received solemn visits from clergymen who broke the news that a man had made the supreme sacrifice, a duty so harrowing that some clergy vowed that they would never again undertake it. The sheer concentration of casualties was far greater than at Gallipoli: Australia had no experience of war on this scale; there were no precedents, and misleading newspaper accounts of the terrible battle raging in Picardy further served to confuse and, perhaps, frighten.

The casualty rates in the A.I.F. on the Somme were so high that normal reinforcements and recruiting in Australia could not hope to fill up the gaps if such carnage continued. In this predicament, General W. R. Birdwood and General C. B. B. White urged that the Australian government frankly be told the number of reinforcements necessary if its five infantry divisions were to continue to take a full and active part in the war. Accordingly, they made some calculations and told the War Office how many men were needed. These conclusions were based on an estimate of the fighting probably ahead of the force: the two officers arrived at a huge total which was accepted by the War Office and sent to the Australian government as the recommendation of the Army Council.[5]

This intimation was foreshadowed on 16 August in a cable from A.I.F. headquarters, London. It read that the lack of recruits was especially pressing because of the recent severe casualties, and that the War Office had decided to borrow the shortage from the 3rd Division, then training in England. An alternative proposal discussed by the War Council involved the disbandment of this Division and the dispersal of its members among the shot-up units. This news was followed within twenty-four hours by a communication from Birdwood in which he expressed the hope that it might not be necessary to interfere with the threatened Division, and he subsequently suggested that Australia seek permission from the War Office to send to England from the Middle East the 11th and 12th Light Horse, and all excess reinforcements beyond 6 per cent in the Light Horse division, to meet the requirements of infantry reinforcements for the divisions in France. A cable was thereupon sent to the War Office, but received the reply that these troops were fully employed in Egypt and that the Australian and New Zealand forces were the keystone of that defence.

Finally, on 24 August came a fateful cable from the Secretary of State: because of the heavy casualties recently suffered by the Australian forces in France, it would be necessary to draw upon the 3rd Division for reinforcements. The Army Council had recommended that a special draft of 20,000 infantry, in addition to the normal monthly reinforcements, be sent as soon as possible to make good the current deficit and so enable the 3rd Division to be brought up to strength again. The Council suggested that for three months following the despatch of this special draft, the monthly reinforcement of infantry sent should be calculated at 25 per cent of the establishment, that is to say, about 16,500 men a month. The Council admitted that these steps might greatly inconvenience the Commonwealth government in training and other arrangements, but could see no other way of keeping the 3rd Division for service in the field.

It certainly was greatly to inconvenience the Commonwealth government. No one had bargained for the Somme blood-bath. Four days later on 28 August the Chief of the Australian General Staff, Brigadier-General H. J. Foster, minuted on the cable: 'I fear we are not in a position to meet either of these two demands. As I have reported, we shall have very few men to send after October even for our normal reinforcements.' Despite these views, he put together a decisive answer which was then amended by the Minister for Defence (amendments in square brackets):

The position as to reinforcements is not understood. Last state furnished by Stralis dated 21 August shows in England 38,553 other ranks of whom probably 13,000 of 3rd Division. Are they absorbed in field force? In addition, at least 15,000 are now at sea on passage [Normal reinforcements are being despatched in September and October] Australian government prepared to provide the 20,000 desired and hope they will begin to embark middle November [Uncertain at present whether full] normal reinforcements can be despatched that month [but they will be in] December. In January the 16,500 reinforcements desired will be sent, and also in February and March.[6]

So the Commonwealth was committed. On the same day as the

agreement so heavily to reinforce the A.I.F. was transmitted to London, Senator Pearce announced in Parliament that the voluntary recruiting system could no longer be relied on. In the Lower House, Hughes explained the position: the number of reinforcements needed for the next month was the special draft of 32,500 and subsequently 16,500 a month. On the other hand, the number of recruits for June was 6,375; July 6,170; and up to 23 August 4,144, making a total of only 16,689. The most recent figures showed casualties to have been 6,743. It was not intended, continued Hughes, to apply compulsion to married men, men under twenty-one, to single men with dependents, or the remaining sons of families in which one or more of the members had already volunteered, until the supply of single men without dependents was exhausted. Taxed with his earlier inconveniently clear statement that he would under no circumstances introduce conscription for overseas service, the Prime Minister said all that could be said: 'What does it matter what we thought yesterday? We have to consider now what is the best and quickest way of doing the thing that has to be done.'[7]

Conscription was not imposed as a regulation gazetted under the War Precautions Act, as it could have been with the consent of both Houses, because Hughes did not wish irrevocably to split the party he had done so much to build: with Liberal support he might have secured approval for such a regulation in the House of Representatives, but in the Senate he had no such prospect. A plebiscite was to be held, an agreement between Hughes and those of his followers in Parliament who did not want conscription but had agreed, democrats as they were, to put the matter to the people.

In New South Wales there followed, at the request of the Prime Minister, a special meeting of the State Labor executive at which he put the case for the Conscription Referendum Bill. That was on Monday 4 September. After a long debate, Hughes's proposals were rejected by twenty-one votes to five. He continued to flout the will of the conference and, with E. S. Carr, member of Parliament for Macquarie, was expelled from the New South Wales labour movement. The endorsements by the movement of other conscriptionist Labor candidates were similarly withdrawn, and W. M. Hughes was on his own except for the Liberals and those members of his own party who were supporters of conscription. The destruction of the Labor Party had begun.

Labour opposition in New South Wales to the proposed referendum on conscription was based on the grounds that the fundamental right of every man to his bodily freedom could not be taken away by a majority who would be largely composed of persons not liable for the service they would enforce on others, and that matters of conscience were not fit subjects for decision by majority rule. Furthermore, ran the official Labor view, the Defence Act passed by the federal Labor government, providing for compulsory military service in Australia, but making specific safeguards against compulsion for service outside Australia, correctly interpreted the spirit and intention of the labour movement. A referendum was therefore intolerable because it destroyed a vital principle of the Act. Finally it was held by Labor in Hughes's home State that the War Precautions Act permitted the government to exercise the widest powers to prevent free discussion of the question at issue.[8]

Two days after Hughes had confronted his party and been defeated by the 'Star Chamber' or 'secret junta' of which he had himself been the creator,[9] ironically enough, the Commonwealth evidently had uneasy second thoughts about its recent undertaking to the War Office: it cabled the imperial authority pointing out that there were 27,000 soldiers of the A.I.F. in England, not counting the 3rd Division, many of whom had had three months' training in Australia and many more weeks in England. The Commonwealth government begged to suggest that those with longer training go for reinforcements and that the 3rd Division on no account be broken up. It added that there were 204 officers and 5,337 men unallotted to units in Egypt who could be sent to England as reinforcements.[10]

But the federal government had no luck, and eight days later, on 14 September, the Referendum Bill was announced in Parliament. The voters of Australia were to be asked on 28 October 1916, 'Are you in favour of the government having, in this grave emergency, the same compulsory power over citizens in regard to requiring their military service, for the term of this war, outside the Commonwealth, as it now has in regard to military service within the Commonwealth?' The Bill was readily passed. To succeed, the referendum had to be approved by a majority of the people and a majority of the States. Voting was to be compulsory, under the Compulsory Voting Act of 1915 applying to constitutional referenda, and the procedure for such referenda was adopted. The Act of 1915 had introduced the principle of compulsory voting in relation to referenda held under section 128 of the Constitution to approve amendments to the Constitution.[11]

The storm clouds thickened over an angry Australia, and in the months of September and October 1916, that optimism and basic unanimity which had characterized the Edwardian era in Australia shrank and disappeared against a backdrop of shattering war in western Europe. What did conscription really involve? No one knew, no more than any man could comprehend the outcome of the war. Men seemed perfectly helpless in the hurricane which Austria had unleashed; as the war exploded onwards, man's inhumanity to man reached the level of unbelievable nightmare; the artillery and the machine-guns took over their operators.

The wording of the government's conscription proposal was a model of prolixity but there were thousands of people only too anxious to explain its implications to the innocent. J. Mullan, a Labor Senator from Queensland, in the manner of many a puzzled man before him, claimed that it was all a plot, and expressed what he termed the truth of the matter: the authorities wanted industrial conscription. Nobody, the Senator announced, was so foolish as to think that the men of Great Britain were conscripted for the trenches. No; the powerful Northcliffe press, supported by the capitalistic influences of Britain, had determined that the workers be brought under military control in the interests of capitalism. The Senator stated that at the last conference of the Chamber of Manufactures in Australia, it had been said that if there were national service or conscription, there would be no strikes, and the difference of opinion in government workshops would be wiped out while the war was on. Senator Mullan concluded that national service would also be extended to the women of Australia as well as to the men, and further pressed his point: in view of the fact that the government had found the greatest difficulty in finding transport to send away 13,000 men a month, and that in 1916 the average had not been more than 9,000 or 10,000 a month, how could 16,500 men a month be embarked?[12]

Such a practical question was not typical of those placed before the Australian people by individuals and organizations who opposed conscription for overseas service in the war. These arguments varied from the hysterical to the cunning, and, against the background of the Irish troubles and the role of Australian Catholics, four themes ran through them: the danger to the labouring classes inherent in permitting the federal government to use such vast powers as it sought; whether or not it was possible to enlist the required number of men given Australia's demographic composition; an appeal to the women of Australia to protect from death the children they had borne and the men they loved, and not to condemn other women's children to death; and the general proposition that it was not right to kill and certainly not right for one section of the community to compel another to take life.

Six months before the conscription campaign and two months before the A.I.F. saw action on the Somme, there occurred the Irish Easter Rising. Hughes was in England at the time of this typically inept rebellion by the Irish. About 21 per cent of Australians were Catholics when the census of 1911 was taken, and of these 921,000 people, no fewer than 784,000 lived in the three principal States: there were 375,000 Catholics in New South Wales, 271,754 in Victoria and 137,000 in Queensland.

Newspaper accounts of the Irish rising of Easter 1916 were first read in Australia on 27 April, and generally deplored by Catholics, although Archbishop Mannix, Coadjutor Archbishop of Melbourne, had little sympathy with the British and considered that they had reaped what they had sown.[13] Perhaps the rising would have faded from the public consciousness, but in May the British authorities, apparently beyond the reach of reason and argument, began executing those held to be the ringleaders of the rebellion. This action staggered the public in Britain as well as in Ireland, and in Australia too was widely condemned. Archbishop Duhig was 'dazed' by the news and Archbishop Carr deprecated the executions in the strongest terms: 'In no other country has punishment more ruthlessly been resorted to, and in no other country has it produced more unexpected and more undesirable effects.'[14]

The effect on Australia is impossible neatly to determine. The rising was thought to have handicapped recruiting but there is, of course, no way of knowing whether men who might have enlisted were deterred by the thought that they might find themselves part of an army of occupation in the land of their fathers. The importance of the rising lay in the focus it gave to Archbishop Mannix's view that the war was an unworthy one, and in the influence it had in splitting the Australian community between Protestants and Catholics, although, as it happened, the number of Catholic recruits remained steady throughout this period of sectarian strife.[15]

There had for long been smouldering animosity between some Catholics and extreme Protestants, based on centuries of distrust. Ireland had traditionally, and rightly, been feared as the springboard from which the invader might launch himself upon the British Isles. In the 1916 rebellion there was perceived a repetition of history. Associated with this was the anger and, in some cases, genuine puzzlement of some Australian Protestants at the great importance Catholics attached to their school system and its strengthening, particularly in Victoria by the exertions of Mannix.

Characteristic of extreme views were those aired in the Melbourne Town Hall in mid-July 1916 in connection with the Loyal Orange Institution. There the Grand Master, O. R. Snowball, member for Brighton in the Victorian Legislative Assembly, chose to announce that although Ireland had not given much joy to the Empire, its destinies were safe in the hands of Sir Edward Carson; he added that Dr Mannix was a kind of cross between a Tipperary man and a Spaniard, and that the Catholic separate schools were a greater menace than the German schools in Australia.[16] In Parliament Snowball continued his savage attacks on Catholic schools, accusing them of disloyalty, asserting that they kept up no such holidays as the King's Birthday and Empire Day, speaking of their divisive character, and urging the internment of Mannix, a rebel to the core,[17] even according to the Governor-General.[18]

These comments were partly caused by Mannix's observations on Sunday 20 August 1916 when laying the foundation stone of a new Catholic church at Northcote. On that occasion the Archbishop expressed sympathy with Lutherans because, he said, like the Catholics, they too maintained schools for the religious education of their children and had had no charge of disloyalty proved against them. The Archbishop, with characteristic directness, told his audience that the bigots who were out to put down the Lutheran schools would probably try to suppress the Catholic schools as well, and Mannix did not heal the breach between Catholics and Protestants by observing provocatively that the Catholic religion was the only true religion. He concluded by deploring that there was no fund for relief of distress in Dublin, and announced that he would send a donation directly to the Irish capital.[19]

Coadjutor Archbishop of Melbourne, Dr Daniel Mannix was born at Charleville in County Cork in 1864. He arrived in Melbourne in 1913, having been president of Maynooth College and professor of philosophy and later professor of theology there. He had a deep love for his church and the Irish people, and a distrust of British motives in the war. He perceived the conflict as really a trade war, and continually criticized those people of capital who were gaining from the war at the expense of members of the working class laying down their lives. Mannix took up a position which was unconciliatory, uncompromising, implacable and remorseless. He was a gifted speaker and could hold audiences transfixed with his brilliantly pellucid, simple prose and directness of argument. He had a commanding appearance. He was a terrible problem to the censors.

After the speech at Northcote, the censor demanded to know whether action was necessary in the case of that speech as reported in the *Age*.[20] But Mannix was really impossible to censor, he was far too important—and clever. His views strengthened by the rising and the fate of the martyrs, the events of Easter 1916 were almost certainly a great turning point in his public life. When he read the news, he is reported to have wept.[21] From that time on, Mannix's public statements had a biting edge to them that challenged the assumptions on which the conscriptionists based their case. The conscriptionists were livid and religious animosity deepened.

The Minister for Defence declined to censor Mannix's speech of 20 August 1916[22] and the Archbishop continued in his task to destroy the case for conscription. He aroused enormous opposition, including that of Dr Alexander Leeper, the Warden of Trinity College, University of Melbourne.[23]

Mannix, then, exacerbated sectarianism in Victoria. There was a Liberal government there, but not in Australia's largest State: what is more, in New South Wales the ruling Labor Party was closely associated with the Catholic working class vote. It was therefore not unexpected that the executive of the Political Labor League appealed for mercy for those it termed 'the Sinn Fein rebels', asking that its view be transmitted to Mr Asquith. This was done, the League footing a bill for £3 1s 9d. The Federated Clerks' Union of Australia also urged the Commonwealth government to ask Britain to have the spirit of mercy and justice meted out to the Irish rebels, as did the Toorak State Electoral Council.

As the British continued to clamp down on the Irish, so did Australians become more and more divided among themselves. The real significance of the rebellion was further loss of solidarity among Australians, as in mid-June the Commonwealth was informed that martial law was in operation in Ireland. But whatever was happening in perennially troubled Ireland, at least one body had faith in the British government: the Ulster and Loyal Irishmen's Association of Victoria deplored the fact that anyone should interfere with, and indeed question, the conduct of the British Parliament.[24]

The Irish rising was thought in New South Wales to militate against the passage of the referendum, and therefore the Premier of New South Wales, under the ban of the labour movement because he was a conscriptionist, sought the aid of the British government itself in inducing the people of New South Wales, and the rest of Australia, to vote 'Yes'. He did this because of his conviction that the Irish troubles would be critical in the campaign: in a communication to the New South Wales Agent-General in London, B. R. Wise, Holman confided that it was universally believed in the State that martial law was prevalent in Ireland and that Home Rule had been suspended. It followed from this belief, he continued, that one section of ordinarily trustworthy followers of the Premier was alienated and anti-conscriptionist; the Premier expressed the hope that, during the following fortnight, a statement might be made in Britain that martial law had definitely ended and that Home Rule was to be the firm policy of Britain. Holman was sure, he told Wise, that such an announcement would favourably affect voting in Australia.

In reply to this, the government of New South Wales received an official communication from Britain that there was no shooting in Ireland and that although martial law was still in force, it was not being applied.[25] Holman rightly concluded that this extra-ordinary message would not satisfy the Irish-Australians who inhabited New South Wales, and in September 1916 certain of them held a meeting to raise money to relieve Irish distress (though in fact Ireland was doing well economically from the war). This gathering in the Sydney Town Hall had two objects: to succour the unfortunate people of Ireland, and to assist Ireland to become a self-governing part of the Empire. Among those present were the Lord Mayor, Alderman R. D. Meagher; Archbishop Kelly; the Chief Secretary, George Black; the vice-president of the Executive Council, J. D. Fitzgerald; a large gathering of Catholic clergy, and several members of the Legislative Assembly.

In an opening statement that would have done credit to anyone bearing an Irish surname in Sydney in 1916, Alderman Meagher said that the meeting was a splendid demonstration of the un-quenchable love of country in the hearts of the Irish race; the masses of the Irish people were in a desperate plight; they were without the necessities of life such as food, clothing and shelter. People should keep for Ireland some of the tears they were shedding for the small nations, because the blood of Ireland's sons, shed on every battlefield in every country and clime, had cemented the cornerstones of the British Empire. The Lord Mayor went on for some time like this, mentioning martial law, bread-winners dragged from their families purely on suspicion, the horror of the Dublin slums, and the great response of the United States to Ireland's appeal.

Archbishop Kelly then rose to address the enthusiastic audience. Moving that an appeal for funds be made, he said that every shilling they gave would further condemn the misgovernment of Ireland under actual and partial British rule. Ireland was an ancient race and her sons prospered everywhere (a voice: 'Except in Ireland!'), he continued, protesting against the suspension of all liberty in Ireland. If England went on acting the way she was, the Archbishop informed his audience, England could not be blessed by God.

Subscriptions promised totalled nearly £1,700, including £20 from Archbishop Kelly, £200 from Mrs F. B. Freehill, £100 from the Hibernian Society, £100 from John Meagher, M.L.C., and £100 from the St Vincent de Paul Society.[26]

Holman, then, had good reason to worry and, after hearing from Wise in London that the Agent-General had now gone to see Walter Long, the Secretary of State for the Colonies (he had drafted the British Conscription Acts) in a continuing attempt to get some good news out of Ireland for the people of New South Wales, the Premier decided to see Kelly to ask him whether he would come out in favour of conscription.

While the Archbishop was thus being wooed, Holman heard from Wise that the views of the Premier of New South Wales had been pressed on the British Cabinet but without any effect, partly because of the optimistic Australian reports about the probable outcome of the plebiscite. What could Wise do now? He did not have to take any decisions or obey any further directions from Sydney because he suddenly died. He was temporarily replaced as Agent-General by Timothy Coghlan, an author and sometime New South Wales Government Statistician, who went to Ireland to see J. E. Redmond, the Irish member of Parliament who led the Irish Nationalists and who actively supported enlistment. Redmond, however, was unable to send a message to Australia supporting conscription, he informed Coghlan, because he and his colleagues were busily opposing it in Ireland. Coghlan then went to see Lloyd George, who agreed that Australia should have conscription, and promised to bring up Holman's problem in Cabinet. It was a case of round and round the mulberry bush for the Australian: the Welsh wizard advised Coghlan to see Walter Long because the Secretary of State was influencing Lord Lansdowne and Lord Cecil and the Unionist Party generally. Off went Coghlan. Long listened to him and agreed that a win for the anti-conscriptionists in the Commonwealth would have a bad effect on the Allies and the neutral powers and only encourage German efforts. He promised to try to get martial law lifted in Ireland, but he did not succeed.[27] Thus it was that the British Cabinet helped to defeat the conscription proposals of W. M. Hughes.

Some of the most virulent attacks on the anti-conscriptionists were directed at the alleged disloyalty of Catholics. One such was launched by Critchley Parker in *The Slippery Way*, a booklet aimed at the International Workers of the World (I.W.W.) as well as Catholics. It was a despicable work. On page 3 was a list of German-sounding surnames headed, 'A few members of the

I.W.W. who have so far kept out of gaol'. 'Australians,' the author asked venomously, 'why not celebrate our conscription victory with a deportation day as early as possible.' The Commonwealth of Australia was, rightly or wrongly, likened to a beautiful mosaic. 'You who lay claim to the mosaic as a heritage must take care the enemies of our country do not destroy it.' The anti-conscriptionist, whatever his motives might be, was a destructionist, said Critchley Parker, and his pamphlet went on to call up every useful prejudice: 'Remember that those who vote "no" are not only against Australia, but England. They want to stop sending help in any form to fight against Roman Catholic Germany and Austria.' The ever-smouldering embers of sixteenth-century Smithfield were blown into hateful flames: 'I refuse to be silenced by some mumbo jumbo party who, for interested reasons, says, "Don't stir up the sectarian question". I will stir up any question that is directed against my country. This referendum will at least disclose the voting power of the Roman Catholics within the Commonwealth, and that is no small achievement.'[28] Indeed it was not.

In this way the tensions between Britain and Ireland were revived 10,000 miles away from the bullet-marked buildings and barricaded streets of Dublin. An Australian poster screamed that one Father O'Keefe threatened to fight in the civil war. Preaching in Bowen, Queensland, Father O'Keefe was said to have expressed the hope that the hand would wither of all those who voted for conscription. If compulsory recruiting for overseas service were agreed to, the priest was alleged to have prophesied, there would be a civil war in Australia as well as in Ireland, and he would fight with the rebels to the last drop of his blood.

The decent Irishmen fighting in Irish regiments on the Western Front called in vain for help from their treacherous countrymen, cried the conscriptionists: the appeal for assistance sent in October from the front by Major W. H. K. Redmond, brother of the Nationalist leader whom Holman's agents had begged to intercede, fell on deaf ears, for had he not said that it would be a thousand pities and almost a betrayal of Ireland's heroic dead if the divisions which brought so much honour to the Irish name ceased to be Irish? This poster went on to offer deadly conclusive figures of Irish enlistment in Ireland between April and October 1916 which showed that less than 1,400 men a month had joined the colours.

The list was headed, naturally, by Ulster (3,556 men) and ended by Connaught (469). What was more, the Irish, typically ungrateful for the blessings showered down on them by England, had offered only 105,000 recruits all told. And what did those Irish who remained behind do? They took the loyal Briton's job; the Aberavon Military Tribunal was quoted as protesting against men coming over from Ireland to do the jobs of British workers gone to the war. And in a final weird twist, the poster quoted with triumphant inscrutability the editor of the I.W.W. journal *Direct Action*: 'The crucifixion of a religious fanatic 2,000 years ago seems of more importance to the religiously susceptible than the crucifixion of millions of wage slaves right now.'[29]

Men and women of Irish extraction were stirred by the rising of Easter week in Dublin and the cold-blooded executions of the rebel survivors. The dormant distrust of the English government had awakened again in Irish-Australians. Catholics who in 1915 would have given their last man and last shilling became overnight the eager and resolute opponents of conscription, though this gain to the anti-conscription cause was thought to have been offset by the defection of those Protestants who thought that conscription was needed to save Australia from becoming a Catholic country.[30] Australia in September and October 1916 could be described as paranoic.

Another theme running through the conscription campaign concerned the fears of labour spokesmen that the government would, if the referendum were passed, suppress the unions, compel people to work for low wages, and generally stifle freedom of speech and contract. Hughes had undertaken that censorship would not interfere with freedom of speech during the campaign: by word of mouth or through the press, everyone was to be permitted to say what he liked. Well, nearly what he liked, because the Prime Minister added that this freedom was to be in accordance with the law of the land and would not be extended to permit any Tom, Dick or Harry to say things which might discourage voluntary recruiting, insult the Allies or incite anyone to commit a breach of the law.[31] But what did these phrases mean? The Crown Solicitor's opinion was sought on the likely effect of one card headed 'Women vote "No" and guard against cheap black labour now landing.'[32]

This was a reference to the spectacularly untimely arrival in September 1916 of Maltese, largely of military age, who were thought to have been imported secretly under contract; the Premier of Tasmania, for example, sought a denial of Senator O'Keefe's statement at Beaconsfield during the campaign that there was cruising in Australian waters a vessel with eight hundred Maltese on it ready to land the moment the referendum was passed.[33] There were in fact only ninety-eight Maltese, but two hundred more were on the high seas, and when the Minister for External Affairs, Hugh Mahon, himself suspected that they were being secretly imported under contract,[34] it was no wonder that the anti-conscriptionists thought they held a trump card. If the government considered that censorship would help the case for conscription, they were in this instance probably wrong because such suppression only served to encourage the rumour and exaggeration that surrounded the Maltese incident. Indeed, the Premier of South Australia protested to Hughes that only relaxation of censorship, not more of it, could help the case of compulsion.[35] Hughes evidently did not think so and hence continued to give the impression that the government had something to hide.

Published in Geelong in September 1916, the *Distributing Trades Gazette* (vol. 2 no. 12) appealed to the working classes, asserting that though in principle conscription was an instrument of national defence, in reality and practice it was an instrument of working-class subjugation. Conscription was the idol of the capitalists, it emphasized, and concluded an appeal to the forces of light and reason on the earnest Victorian note that the seeds of liberty, sown in the blood-stained soil of Eureka, had created an Australian environment which was responsible for the bold, courageous and self-sacrificing characteristics which had made her sons the admiration of the world: conscription was the very foundation and cornerstone of the servile state.[36]

Fear of industrial conscription, and the destruction of organized labour by an erstwhile labourite seduced by cavorting duchesses, had been expressed earlier by the Australian Trade Union Congress meeting in Melbourne in May 1916. In its manifesto, the Congress declared that in the cases of both Britain and France, conscription had been used to reduce the achievements of the trade unions to nothing, to destroy customs, rights and practices, and to put unskilled men in the place of skilled, and women and children in the place of grown men. In other words, conscription had been used not only as an instrument of national defence but as a bludgeon to break down the stand of the industrial classes. The Congress feared that the same thing would happen in Australia because there was already 'a slavish imitation of the laws, regulations, verbiage and practices of the imperial government'. The working classes should act before the clock of trickery struck the hour of doom; in both France and Britain 'the industrial magnates, the controllers of oceanic transportation, and the great financiers have been permitted to wax fat on the blood of slaughter.'

These were stirring words. They were too stirring: the manifesto was seized by the military authorities in a raid on the Melbourne Trades Hall and the *Labor Call* office at midnight on Saturday 29 July. Excised by the censor were the passages about a slavish imitation of the laws and practices of the imperial government, and the Congress's statement that industrial magnates and big business had been permitted to grow fat on the blood of slaughter.[37]

The T.U.C. which thus got itself into hot water with this forthright manifesto represented 280,000 unionists in all States. The Congress was initiated by the Melbourne Trades Hall Council to discuss conscription and to determine the official stand of the industrial movement thereon. It was agreed that if conscription appeared imminent, members should conduct a referendum themselves on whether to strike or not, and it was further agreed to co-operate in opposing political candidates speaking or voting for conscription.[38]

The forces for and against conscription in 1916 produced a vast pamphlet and poster literature associated with recruitment to the A.I.F. They also produced badges; J. H. Catts, a Labor member of Parliament in charge of recruiting in New South Wales, subsequently charging that a soldier wearing a 'No Conscription' button on parade had been arrested whereas other soldiers sporting 'Conscription' badges had not been detained.[39]

Badges on parade could be dealt with, but meetings in other places and in the open air were another matter. Here much more sinister action was taken: whether or not it was true, some people became uneasy at what appeared to be officially condoned and systematic breaking up of meetings by military personnel. The secretary of the Women's Socialist League in March 1916 had already lodged a protest against what was termed the federal government's 'allowing' uniformed soldiers to disrupt peace meetings. The Trades Hall Council sought a deputation concerning the breaking up by military men of meetings on the Yarra Bank, and the Socialist Party of Victoria objected to the Yarra Bank being closed on Sundays, protesting at the same time against the prosecution and conviction of F. J. Riley, the secretary of the Australian Peace Alliance and prominent labour activist. A week later the Defence Department informed the Prime Minister that everything possible had been done to prevent riotous conduct by soldiers.[40]

Adela Pankhurst continued to be a focal point for anti-conscriptionists. The Political Labor League at Ballarat and the Socialist Party of Victoria had both complained early in January 1916 about soldiers at the Bijou Theatre, and sent in their bills for the damage done. In March the secretary of the No Conscription League reported that soldiers would attempt to break up an anti-conscription meeting on the Yarra Bank, and the Socialist Party of Victoria yet again complained that the Defence Department just did not seem to have its heart in dealing with men in uniform who continued to disrupt socialist meetings. The I.W.W. Club agreed: whichever Department was established to look into the defence of the Commonwealth should take steps to prevent soldiers denying free speech by smashing up meetings. The Minister for Defence then alerted the military police to be on guard at the Yarra Bank on 2 April 1916 to prevent trouble. But it still occurred, F. J. Riley, the Women's Socialist League and the Australian Peace Alliance all continuing to complain about soldiers' disorderly conduct on the Yarra Bank.[41] In May the Minister laid it down that soldiers were not to be permitted to remove civilians from meetings; troops evidently did not understand the gravity of the offence of mutiny and were to be instructed on this point once a month.[42]

Throughout the conscription campaign of 1916 the undercurrent of ugliness and dangerous intolerance strengthened into a main stream. But those who were pacifists and those who were not, yet opposed to conscription, found it hard to conduct meetings peacefully. In Adelaide, for instance, larrikins disturbed meetings of the Peace Alliance at the Botanic Park, and at the end of 1915 the Adelaide *Advertiser* and the military were alleged to have

worked up an organized opposition to meetings at Victoria Square
and the Botanic Park. Every speaker had to get a permit from the
military, and the jarrah posts through which the public passed
from Frome Road on their way into the park were wrenched out
of the ground by a mob trying to get at F. J. Riley and J. F. Hills,
the latter a prominent anti-conscriptionist. In reply to a communication from the Premier of South Australia, Hughes said that the
printer and honorary secretary of the Alliance had been warned.[43]

The anti-conscriptionists also appealed to sources of feeling
similar to those voiced by Adela Pankhurst: the female voter's
desire to protect her son and save her husband from death, a desire
sharpened and made poignant by the daily columns of casualties
as the Somme campaign tore to pieces the earth of Picardy and
the men fighting in that nightmare landscape. Sometimes this
appeal was associated with the class struggle. At a protest meeting
in the Sydney Domain, a Mrs Lorimer demanded to know why
Hughes had exempted only sons of families, and answered her own
question: it was not from kindness of heart for the poor woman
with only one son, because the Prime Minister knew too well that
mothers of the working class had three or four sons, but it was to
save the only sons of the rich, 'it was to spare the only son of Mrs
Love-by-Night of Rose Bay.'

Perhaps because the conscriptionists feared how women would
vote, a most effective weapon in the hands of the anti-conscriptionists was said to be a piece of verse entitled 'The Blood Vote' by
W. R. Winspear, a member of the Australian Socialist Party, whose
members were pledged never to vote Labor. This verse was distributed on a leaflet illustrated by Claude Marquet. It showed a
thoughtful and fearful woman about to place a 'Yes' vote in the
ballot-box. In the background was fiendish, cloven-hoofed and
evil W. M. Hughes. The verse read:

> Why is your face so white, Mother?
>   Why do you choke for breath?
> O I have dreamt in the night, my son,
>   That I doomed a man to death.
>
> Why do you hide your hand, Mother?
>   And crouch above it in dread?
> It beareth a dreadful brand, my son;
>   With the dead man's blood 'tis red.

I hear his widow cry in the night,
 I hear his children weep,
And always within my sight, O God!
 The Dead man's blood doth leap.

They put a dagger into my grasp,
 It seemed but a pencil then;
I did not know it was a fiend a-gasp
 For the priceless blood of men

They gave the ballot paper,
 The grim death-warrant of doom,
And I smugly sentenced the man to death
 In that dreadful little room

I put it inside the Box of Blood
 Nor thought of the man I'd slain,
Till at midnight came like a 'whelming flood
 God's word—and the Brand of Cain.

O Little son! O my little son!
 Pray God for your Mother's soul,
That the scarlet stain may be white again
 In God's great Judgment Roll.

AUSTRALIAN LABOR PARTY
Anti-Conscription Campaign Committee.

"VOTE NO MUM

they'll take DAD next"

VOTE ☒ NO

Authorised by
B. Mulvogue,
Trades Hall, Melb.

Another poster also appealed to the prospect that, despite Hughes's protestation that married men would be exempted from the call-up, fathers would be sent away to death on the Western Front. This was a cartoon of a small boy being embraced by his mother, her staring eyes reflecting both sadness and affection. The caption read, 'Vote NO, Mum. They'll take DAD next.'

The pamphlets included an extensive number directed to the woman voter, such as the song sung by Adela Pankhurst and her companion:

> I didn't raise my son to be a soldier,
> I brought him up to be my pride and joy.
> Who dares to put a musket to his shoulder,
> To kill some other mother's darling boy?

Hughes had stated that the only sons of families were to be spared if the referendum were carried. But were they? The *Worker* doubted it; it reported that at Cootamundra, Mrs Rocket, a prominent local labourite, had asked W. A. Holman if he considered it reasonable for single men to be exempt when married men were not. The Premier of New South Wales was reported to

THE VOICE OF THE TEMPTER

have answered that he did not think it a fair thing, but it was not proposed. Single men who were only sons would be exempted until the time came when it was necessary to call up married men. Thus, concluded the *Worker*, nobody would be exempt at all, and the promise made to only sons would be flagrantly broken; married men were simply being fooled by Hughes's statement.

The point was that there was a strong element of uncertainty in what the Commonwealth government might do, or be compelled to do, in the future; in order to pull its weight in the war effort, the federal authority might have to take virtually every man except those employed in vital industries. But how many men did Australia actually have at its disposal? Was it possible she might run out altogether? At least on this point the government could form some idea on what was practicable and what was not on the basis of the war census.

That calculation had led to the belief that there were 600,000 'fit' men in Australia between the ages of eighteen and forty-five. The number between eighteen and sixty was reckoned in the census to be approximately 811,000, of whom 339,000 were single and 455,000 married. On the basis of the census of 1911, and disregarding immigration and mortality among teen-agers, more than 40,000 males would turn eighteen in 1916 and similar numbers turn nineteen, twenty and twenty-one. The anti-conscriptionists did not take into account such a simple projection from 1911, but on the basis of the figures implied in Hughes's undertaking to send away 32,500 men and then 16,500 a month, they calculated away like mad. In a reprint from *Stead's Review*, entitled 'Conscription for and against', issued by the Australian Freedom League, much was made of the alleged fact that a nation could supply only 10 per cent of its entire population for soldiers. Thus only 450,000 men could go to the war; but within a year, ran the argument, Australia must find, at the rate of 16,500 men a month, 208,000 [*sic*] men, whereas conscription would give only 180,000 (450,000 minus 270,000).

In a special supplement the *Worker* lodged its protest against the 'conscription of human life for military service abroad', and proved to its own satisfaction that, if the referendum were carried, the turn of the married men for overseas service would arrive with alarming rapidity. It did this by drawing attention to the figures for rejection derived from the call-up of single men for home service on the eve of the referendum. Citing the cases of the three chief States, the *Worker* pointed out that of 63,000 men examined, only 29,000 were classed as fit, which meant there was a rate of rejection of 60 per cent! (In New South Wales and Victoria, however, 25,000 men had applied for exemption out of a total of 76,000 men who had reported.) The *Worker* then quoted Hughes as saying that at 6 June there were available 153,000 fit single men (other than those in camp) without dependents, whose ages ranged from eighteen to forty-four; by subjecting the figures to analysis, the publication victoriously concluded that only about 50,000 single fit men would be mustered. It therefore followed, pursued the journal, that because the Prime Minister's plea demanded 82,000 men by the end of the year, at that date married men would be drawn upon. There was only one way of saving the situation as far as the married men, their wives and children were concerned, concluded the *Worker*, and that was to vote 'No'.

Others argued that Australia was already doing enough, indeed more than enough, and drew attention to the offer of an extra 50,000 men made, it was alleged, in a silly desire to do more than any other Dominion. Comparisons were made with Canada: with its population of 7.2 million it had enlisted 308,000 men, on which basis Australia would have done equally well if it had enlisted 232,000 men. Instead, the Australian figure was 270,000.[44] With such superficiality worked the anti-conscriptionists. But they had a point.

H

6

Conscription Rejected

To the conscriptionists, it appeared foolish to be doing sums and making miserable calculations about precisely how many soldiers Australia could send away: the simple fact of the matter was that this was a just war waged against an enemy of unparalleled evil and barbarity. The Victorian Anti-German League entitled some of their leaflets *Make the Huns Pay*[1] and the Dutch cartoonist Raemaekers produced some powerful enticements to righteous fury and to confirmation that Australia should not pause to count the cost of victory.

As the referendum campaign raged on, the Commonwealth fanned the flames by accepting 25,000 cartoons by Raemaekers. Canada took 75,000. They were distributed by the various State War Councils and depicted German cruelty in Belgium and France. As early as April 1916, the Victorian Agent-General's office had accepted 25,000 of these cartoons from Hodder and Stoughton as a gift. Sent out to Victoria, they were distributed by the State Parliamentary Recruiting Committee, the Y.M.C.A., the Ballarat Mechanics' Institute, the clerk of the Legislative Assembly, the Portland Free Library, the Museum and Literary Institute, the State Forests Department, the Public Health Department and the Education Department, which sent copies out to all the schools.

Regarded as masterpieces of the cartoonist's art, according to the Agent-General, Raemaekers' work overflowed with a frightening hatred. It depicted the German soldier as unspeakably animal-like and filthy. The cartoons were truly obscene: the Kaiser stood on a grisly pile of corpses trying to see Verdun; Germany as a slavering gorilla crouched over the naked female bodies of Belgium and

104

Luxemburg; Christ crucified was mocked and reviled by German soldiers.[2]

The conscriptionist forces also produced pamphlets and used the newspapers to forward their campaign. Donald Mackinnon, chairman of the Victorian Recruiting Committee, produced one entitled *This is Worth Careful Study*; it noted provisions for recruits' dependents, and described service in the A.I.F. as a great adventure in which the mind would be broadened and the memory enriched. The rural beauties of France were touched upon, together with the happy prospect of taking leave abroad. The advantages of travel were also glanced at and the nature of repatriation described.[3]

The conscriptionists really based their case on the seriousness of the German threat and the immediate danger to humane values which Germany represented. Sir William Irvine, an arch-conscriptionist who had been Commonwealth Attorney-General in 1913–14 and who was to become Chief Justice of Victoria, said bluntly that if civilization were to be saved, Germany must be beaten and crushed and the heel of the Allies planted on the head of the serpent. Turning to the necessity for conscription, Sir William spoke with emotion of gallant France, a nation which had ennobled herself and the name of democracy, and significantly was the home of conscription. France's example should be followed by Australia, he concluded: no platitudes or talk of democracy would solve the question.[4]

The Church of England favoured conscription, if a Pastoral Letter from the Primate of Australia reflected the official view of the church. In this letter, the Archbishop of Sydney said that the splendid lead given by the Prime Minister ought to be supported by every patriot. The Archbishop warned against dangerous forces which were being exploited to nullify the efforts of Hughes, and expressed astonishment at the spectacle of a clique expelling Hughes from the labour movement. 'I appeal to all our church people to take their part in the poll, and to so vote that the Government shall have all the powers for which it asks, remembering those who have fallen and also recollecting those who at this very time are jeopardising their lives unto death, for us, and who ought to be supported by our last men, if need be so.'[5]

To make victory for conscription quite certain, a National Referendum Council was organized in every State, with prominent politicians and citizens urged to throw their weight behind its efforts to put the case for compulsion. Indeed, in September 1916, Hughes cabled all mayors and shire presidents throughout the Commonwealth asking them to take immediate steps to develop vigorous local organizations.[6]

Those in favour of compulsory service overseas also appealed to the women's vote, and drew attention to the plight of men at the front. 'Will you let them die?', it asked. The Prime Minister urged the women of the Commonwealth to play their part in helping the soldiers in Europe. Issued by the National Referendum Council, 395 Collins Street, Melbourne, this appeal dwelt upon what it termed the unspeakable and foul outrages inflicted on the women of Belgium by the occupying power, and it further noticed the horrors of the sack of Louvain, the murder of Edith Cavell (a British nurse in Belgium who aided prisoners of war and was subsequently caught by the Germans, tried and executed), and the sinking of the *Lusitania*. The only way to save countless lives was to vote 'Yes', urged the National Council; women should bid their men go forth and do battle for their country.[7]

The importance of the women's vote was also recognized by Hughes in a manifesto in which he said that in their hands was the destiny of Australia. He gave a number of other reasons why women should support conscription: women were consulted in emancipated Australia on all questions, even conscription, whereas in Germany they were not only denied the franchise but regarded as mere household chattels, the intrinsic coarseness and brutality of the German nature showing in its treatment of the female sex; women and children had been murdered by the Germans in Europe but, thanks to the British navy and the valour of the A.I.F., that fate had not befallen the women of Australia; a man who did not love his country and risk his life for her was like a woman who would not give her life for her child—both were decadent and unworthy; by voting 'Yes' women would save countless lives because lack of reinforcements meant greatly increased hardship, suffering and death; 'now is the hour of your trial and opportunity. Will you be the proud mothers of a nation of heroes, or stand dishonoured as the mothers of a race of degenerates?'[8]

So the Prime Minister of Australia appealed to women. Madame Melba did so too. In what was described as an exceedingly brief address, she favoured a 'Yes' vote on the grounds that if Germany won the war, the first thing that nation would ask for would be Australia. The *Argus* smiled upon the prima donna; more than any other woman in Australia, it announced in a leading article, Melba had a knowledge of the world and knew Germany well.[9]

The importance of the women's vote may have dawned upon the government rather late in the day, but the *Argus* recognized its importance by thoughtfully printing an editorial which suggested that separate ballot-boxes for men and women be established in the polling booths.[10] They were not.

Hughes was said to be sanguine of success. Perhaps he was, but in mid-October, only thirteen days before the poll, he sought the aid of Keith Murdoch in securing a victory, cabling that there must be heard the voice from the trenches calling on Australia to vote 'Yes' and send fresh troops. Hughes added that he was quite certain it would be easy to get such a resolution carried by a large majority of soldiers, and that it would have a powerful effect if cabled to Australia. In reply, he heard from Murdoch that the Prime Minister should arrange to have the A.I.F. votes in Egypt counted there because the Australian Light Horse provided the best chance of a solid 'Yes' vote.[11] The votes from the Light Horse or the whole of the A.I.F. were not released till well after the referendum was over; how individual units of the force voted has never been known, though the commander of the 10th Light Horse, Lieutenant-Colonel T. J. Dodd, sent the following cable to F. Wilson, Premier of Western Australia, on 13 December 1916: 'Just heard results referendum 10th Light Horse disappointed general result but proud of West Australia's effort.'[12]

If the government were successful in carrying the referendum, then certain arrangements would have to be made beforehand if it was to be capitalized on. One of these involved getting a flying start by having men already in camp, and although on the last day of August the Prime Minister made an eleventh-hour concession by postponing for a month a proclamation calling up the citizen forces,[13] at the beginning of October the government finally decided to call up unmarried men between twenty-one and thirty-five for military service inside Australia.[14]

This was not the cleverest of moves and suggests either that Hughes was airily confident that the referendum would be passed, or that he acted without much thought about the implications of what he was doing. Holman, the Premier of New South Wales, in a memorandum on the shortcomings of the federal government, concluded that this step was one of Hughes's greatest blunders.[15]

It was. The decision aroused yet more suspicion of his motives and once again reinforced the opinion of those Australians who feared militarism. These overnight orders made the people uneasy and they were further made doubtful when it was learnt that those called up were to be fingerprinted so that the men exempted would not be able to dispose of their certificates to others.[16] But over and above this, there was the simple inconvenience of being suddenly told to go into camp. Throughout the whole campaign, and indeed throughout the war, people could not be convinced that the threat to them and their families was immediate enough to justify all that the government of Australia demanded of its citizens. Hughes's action appeared yet another example of the incipient authoritarianism of the government. And there was no doubt that the men who were being compelled to go into camp would soon find themselves on the Western Front whether they liked it or not. The *Argus* glowed: 'It is certain that the new army that is being organized this week will not be distinguishable in conduct and bearing from those other glorious armies that have been raised in Australia', and the Prime Minister stated that there must be 32,500 men in camp in Australia that week who were not there when he had disclosed the government's war policy a month previously.[17]

It was typical of Hughes that he then sent to all Premiers a statement that when offences were committed by civilians against the Defence Act, it was most undesirable that the military police be used to make arrests. The Prime Minister informed the Premiers that he wanted the State police to do whatever arresting was necessary. At least one Premier, T. J. Ryan in Queensland, refused to have his police so employed and preferred that the military police perform such duties.[18]

In association with this call-up it was necessary to establish exemption courts all over the nation, and on 4 September the Minister for Defence sent to the commandants of the six Military Districts a letter which noted that the government had decided, if necessary, to bring into operation the provisions of Part IV of the Defence Act. (Part IV set out a list of persons exempted from service in time of war; they included the medically unfit, members of Parliament, judges, clergymen and prison officers, lighthouse keepers, aliens, conscientious objectors and persons employed in special occupations.) Also sent for guidance was a government pamphlet of fifty-nine sample cases for exemption by a central tribunal.[19]

The importance of the exemption courts lay in the fact that they brought before everyone a close-to-home example of what would happen if conscription were enforced. What did 'medically unfit' mean? Who was a 'conscientious objector'? What special occupations would be exempt from service? On what grounds would or could the government single them out?

Enormous confusion prevailed. Sections of the public service hastened to send in great lists of men reckoned to be indispensable to the administration of the country; the owners of the gold mines of Western Australia argued that men employed in the mines could be ill spared, and the various courts had to decide, in terms of regulations, who was an 'only son' and 'sole support', what was 'national importance' and what were 'exceptional domestic financial obligations'. Practical difficulties suddenly emerged: in Queensland there were problems of distance and lack of magistrates, those available having quite diverse opinions concerning the reading and interpretation of the regulations. A large number of magistrates in Queensland permitted applicants for exemption to make their claims on any grounds they could conjure up, and this led to the military representatives in the court being taken unawares because enquiries made to prepare their cases against a man seeking exemption were directed solely to the points alleged in the formal application.

The work was nevertheless expedited because applicants for exemption were forbidden legal representation. Some stirring exchanges were heard: in Queensland one applicant for exemption considered that his services would be of more use to his country in his position at home than in camp, which he likened to a convict settlement. This was R. J. Barrett, the Queensland Crown Solicitor, who afterwards apologized to the Prime Minister for his statement.[20]

The exemption procedures were far from satisfactory. Statutory declarations were made out in certain cases but there was only too much reason to suppose that many of their authors would not have lasted five minutes under cross-examination. In fact, the public mind was not only confronted with the conscripting state and its triumph (in Queensland only five cases opposed by the military representatives were successful in securing exemption) but was confused as well: in Western Australia the idea prevailed that the proceedings were a preliminary step to overseas service. Religion came under judicial examination in cases of conscientious objection and the military representatives sometimes found themselves in very strange and deep theological waters concerning the exemption of 'ministers of religion'. Magistrates in Western Australia took a stern view in such cases, and compared such people unfavourably with the economy and thrift of the man in a small private business.

One of the most interesting cases occurred in Victoria and concerned the headmaster of the Melbourne Church of England Grammar School. Archdeacon W. G. Hindley, acting on behalf of the council of the school and speaking in support of an application for exemption by Richard P. Franklin, the headmaster, appeared before the exemption court at Prahran on 17 October 1916. He applied for Franklin's exemption on the ground that his services to the school were indispensable.

In reply, Lieutenant Vines, representing the Defence Department, quoted the case of the headmaster of a Sydney public school who, unable to gain admittance into the Australian army because his eyesight was bad, went to England to join up there. Speaking as an old public school boy and as one who had enlisted as a private, Lieutenant Vines claimed to have knowledge of the ideals of a school such as Melbourne Grammar. The basis of those ideals was the principle of honour and self-sacrifice, he observed, and if the headmaster of an institution of that kind sought to despise the honour of the women of France and Belgium, and chose to stay home on £1,000 a year while those females were suffering, then, Lieutenant Vines declared, instead of the headmaster's work being of national importance, it was demoralizing to the boys he looked after.

The Archdeacon retorted with warmth: the headmaster in no way despised the honour of French and Belgian women, and if it were left to him he would vindicate his feelings as a patriot. But the fact of the matter was that Melbourne Grammar School's council considered that Franklin would be rendering better service to the state by staying at the school instead of going off in the army. What a school at Sydney might do in a special set of circumstances would not govern the action of another such school; it was disorganization for a public school to be bereft of its headmaster. The application for exemption was refused, but the decision was later reversed on appeal to the Supreme Court. Franklin enlisted in 1917.[21]

If Australia were to be put on a proper war footing involving conscription, it was clear that industries would have to be examined as well as men, in order to work out how important they were to the nation and how many men they could afford to release for the front line. On 11 September the Adjutant-General, Colonel T. H. Dodds, recommended that a committee be established to look into industries, occupations and services necessary to be maintained in the national interest, and guard against such employers who, to prevent financial loss, might claim exemption for employees or act in collusion with workers. Suggested as members were Professor Thomas Lyle (professor of Natural Philosophy at the University of Melbourne), Walter Leitch from the Department of Munitions and representatives of the Victorian railways, the Trades Hall Council, the Victorian Mines Department and the Associated Chambers of Commerce. This proposal was approved by the Minister for Defence.

Which industries should be concerned? It was perhaps significant, in view of the referendum's result, that instantly there was an outcry from the dairying industry for preferential treatment on the ground that men should not be taken from dairying and farming because the hands who dealt with cows received a special training for their work and could not be replaced. A deputation from dairymen expressed grave apprehension about what might happen to Australia if these trained men were called away suddenly from their cows; the deputation emphasized its unique position by pointing out that cows, unlike machinery, could not be stopped and started at will.

That was one trouble the committee struck; another also showed how the government's actions were dividing the nation rather than

uniting it for recruitment, because when the committee was formed
the Trades Hall Council took no action in reply to Pearce's request
that they send a member. The Minister then invited the Amalgamated Society of Engineers to nominate a man but their representative was subsequently withdrawn because the majority of
engineers were against being represented on such a committee. This
body shortly suspended its hearings.[22]

There was even conflict and confusion at the federal-State
government level; a fortnight before the date for the poll was
announced, the Defence Department asked the States to find out
dates of birth of the men coming forward, because obviously this
had to be known for the call-up; New South Wales and Tasmania
agreed to waive the customary fees for search but South Australia
would not.

The Commonwealth also asked the States to make referendum
day a holiday. To this New South Wales and Western Australia
agreed but Tasmania would not because it had a lot of holidays
already at that time of year. Then New South Wales thought again
and recorded that a holiday might be a mistake. The current state
of feeling about conscription being what it was, Victoria also
would not have a holiday because of the monetary loss to the
working classes. The federal system of government was in full
centrifugality.

More confusion ensued on whether there was to be closure of
hotels on polling day. The case of Western Australia was typical:
on 11 October Hughes wired the Premier, Frank Wilson, that the
Commonwealth desired a holiday for polling day and would
appreciate the issue of the necessary proclamation. Wilson agreed.
A few days later both the Women's National Movement and the
Women's Christian Temperance Union realized what an opportunity presented itself and urged the government to close the hotels
for the serving of liquor at six o'clock on polling day in order that
there might be a sober vote. Cabinet disagreed and would not
close them. Then the Chamber of Commerce weighed in, its president arguing that there should not be a holiday on referendum day
because it would take people out of town and therefore lose votes;
what was needed was a holiday in the country areas but a working
day in the cities and towns. This Cabinet approved, and so cancelled the holiday it had previously announced.

The next day the National Referendum Council of Western Australia decided that it, too, did not favour a holiday on the Saturday. In a dilemma, Wilson cabled Hughes asking what he should do. Hughes replied that it was Wilson's decision. The point was, of course, that no one was quite sure what effect a holiday would have and whether it would favour a 'Yes' vote or not.

The temperance people kept up the pressure, the Western Australian Alliance urging that the hotels be closed completely on the day of the referendum because, as they put it, the gravity of the occasion demanded the best and most unprejudiced thought and the calmest judgment; every precaution should be taken to safeguard those whose mental balance might be disturbed and whose passions might be inflamed by the consumption of intoxicants. There was also, considered the Alliance shrewdly, the danger of serious disturbances when feelings were now running so high.

There was no holiday. As Wilson finally cabled to Hughes, there was a day off on the following Monday and, anyway, business premises in Perth would be closed for two hours on the Wednesday before the referendum for a big military parade. Not only would a holiday militate against the success of the referendum, asserted the Premier of Western Australia, but it would not be in the best interests of traders and workers alike.

The campaign heated up: W. H. Lee, the Premier of Tasmania, asked that the Military Commandant of the 6th Military District hold the military in reserve in the event of the State police needing their help on the 28th; Hughes told all Premiers on 26 October that a regulation under the War Precautions Act had made illegal the opening of licensed premises on voting day, and the next day sent out another telegram telling them to arrange police protection for the polling booths and not to permit anyone to exhibit voting figures on hoardings. This followed telegrams from Wilson in Western Australia asking that the posting of any figures at all be put off till midnight on the Sunday because of possible disturbances when the figures went up, and from Vaughan in South Australia who said that if the returns were made known on Saturday, unruly sections of the public would wait up for their appearance. Vaughan, too, asked the military authorities to co-operate with the civil agencies on polling day.

It was a measure of the feelings of the people that in Western

Australia a body known as the All British Association was given permission to inspect the Crown Law Department's files on naturalized persons. This association had offered to scrutinize voters in order to pick out people who were debarred from voting because they were of enemy origin.[23]

Another indication of the people's temper may have lost the referendum for the government, because rumours swept the country concerning the alleged presence just out of sight over the horizon of hundreds of Maltese labourers waiting to take the jobs of men conscripted: in both Tasmania and Western Australia this rumour was strong enough and feared enough for the government to deny it yet be compelled to admit the damning fact that some Maltese of military age had landed at Sydney.

On Friday 27 October the Prime Minister wound up his campaign in Sydney with a spirited but rather tired appeal from the back of a truck in Martin Place. This was arranged to coincide with a march of newly-conscripted men, an event which the Premier of New South Wales regarded as Hughes's crowning act of folly because, concluded Holman, it was interpreted as a dictatorial threat to Australians of 'I'll make you give me the men!'[24]

After the partisan fervour and violently emotional atmosphere of the preceding campaign, the conscription referendum was expected to produce scenes of wild excitement and dangerous crowds. There were many who avoided the cities and even set out to vote at local booths in fearful anticipation.

But throughout Australia the polling was uninterrupted by any serious incidents. In Melbourne no election day within memory passed off more quietly. The heat which had been displayed at referendum meetings had burnt itself out.

Only where the compulsorily registered recruits from the military camps came into contact with conscriptionist groups was there any real threat of violence and even these clashes were quickly subdued. In Castlemaine a dozen or so of these recruits were engaged in singing something about 'Billy Hughes's Army' when a motor car passed bearing a calico placard with 'Yes' on it. One of the recruits snatched the placard from the car and tore it to pieces. A large crowd assembled but neither the military nor the civilian police took any action and the jostling soon died down.

A little excitement was caused at Fawkner, Victoria, by some persons, more or less angry, who indulged in the pastime of grab-bing at one another's 'Yes' or 'No' badges. At times threats were made and fists beat the air, accompanied by groans and hoots, but beyond this nothing happened.

Buttons, banners and signs abounded, so much so that one lady voter at Brunswick, after passing the lavishly decorated head-quarters of the 'Yes' supporters, asked a policeman to direct her to the place where one voted 'No'. In another instance a prospective voter asked which was the Labor side of the hall.

A diversion was caused at Prahran by an enthusiast bedecking himself with a large Union Jack and exhorting passers-by to 'Keep the Old Flag Flying.' After a boy snatched the 'vote Yes' cards he was distributing, he was mobbed by hoodlums but escaped unhurt.

A less happy fate befell a terrier who appeared at another polling depot branded on the back with a vermilion 'No'. Booted and mocked by an indignant crowd, the dog managed eventually to escape only to meet a drover's dog which swiftly added injury to insult.

For the first time in Australian history, the hotels were closed on a polling day and the federal authorities had forbidden the posting of progress returns. The issue to be decided was fraught with momentous consequences for the people, not only as a nation but as individuals. And there were no precedents. The quiet and serious atmosphere of the poll was perhaps not so surprising: there was nothing left to do but record votes and await the result.[25]

About midnight the day before polling, the Governor-General, who was in Sydney, received a phone call from Hughes. The Prime Minister announced that three Cabinet ministers had re-signed: the Treasurer, W. G. Higgs, the vice-president of the Executive Council, Albert Gardiner, and an honorary Cabinet Minister, Senator E. J. Russell. They had left the government because the Prime Minister had interfered unduly in the conduct of the referendum by issuing regulations under the War Precau-tions Act providing that military questions be put to voters at the polling booths. This regulation authorized polling officers to ask men who appeared to be aged twenty-one to thirty-five whether they were single and if so whether they had obeyed the Defence Act proclamation and entered camp. If the intending voter fell into that category, his vote was to be marked and placed aside, whether it was to be counted or not to be decided later. This regulation was scandalous, and, though passed by Hughes at a Sydney Executive Council meeting, it was quickly withdrawn when the resignations followed. The polling booths were not to be used to overawe or embarrass voters.

When the Governor-General went across the Harbour to meet Hughes, who was sitting hunched in a car, the Prime Minister announced mournfully that he had not a brain-wave left now, and that the resignations would undoubtedly influence the voting. Munro Ferguson thereupon suggested that the Prime Minister censor the announcements of resignation. Off went Hughes only to find that one of the three had beaten him to it and passed the news through the censorship. The Governor-General left Hughes forlorn on the North Shore, the Prime Minister saying that he would now 'pinch' ministers from the States and create a strong independent Labor Party.

By ten o'clock on polling night it was clear that the referendum would be rejected (see Table 2). For his part, the Governor-General regarded this as a serious blow to his confidence in the future of the country; and next day he suffered another blow when he discovered that his Prime Minister had misled him the night before: Hughes had not told Munro Ferguson that the order directing polling agents to 'spot' recalcitrants at the booths had

TABLE 2

Voting in Conscription Referendum 1916
(inclusive of soldiers' votes)

State	Yes	No	Soldiers' votes	
			Yes	No
N.S.W.	356,805	474,544	28,104	22,928
Vic.	353,930	328,216	20,683	16,612
Qld	144,200	158,051	8,608	7,052
S.A.	87,924	119,236	7,054	5,866
W.A.	94,069	40,884	5,820	4,680
Tas.	48,493	37,833	2,130	1,756
Federal	2,136	1,269	—	—
Total	1,087,557	1,160,033	72,399	58,894

SOURCES: *P.P.* (Cwlth), 1917-19, vol. 4, p. 1469; *Official History*, vol. 11, p. 352.

been rejected earlier in Melbourne. The Governor-General observed grimly that next time he would inform Hughes he should put all his cards on the table. Though the order had not been finally issued, recorded the Governor-General, its enactment by the executive meeting gave the three dissident ministers a better case than he had been led to believe.[26]

The Governor-General said that the referendum had been defeated by Irish Catholics, the women's vote and a large section of the agricultural vote, the latter opposing the government's proposal as a protest against the land being denuded of labour,[27] but the voting was so close that attention might just as readily have been focused on why the referendum came so near to success.

Though the plebiscite was defeated, there was a substantial increase in recruiting, nearly double the August figure, in fact. Perhaps this was due to a conviction that conscription was coming and that it might be advisable to join up before being drafted, or to the decision of certain of the men who had been called up for home service to stay in camp and join the A.I.F., although they were told by proclamation on 22 November 1916 that they might go home again. But the monthly totals in November and December sank to all-time lows. Perhaps some men were more or less forced into the A.I.F.; there were a number of objections about loss of jobs by some of those who had been compelled to go into camp but who then found themselves out of work because their employers had made other arrangements. The Federated Clerks' Union of Victoria asked the Prime Minister to receive a deputation on the subject of loss of occupation as a result of answering the proclamation.[28] They had some reason to complain: W. F. Finlayson, M.H.R., told Parliament at the end of November that employers were refusing to reinstate men released from camp and indeed refusing to take on discharged A.I.F. soldiers; in answer to a question from J. E. Fenton, M.H.R., the Prime Minister asked for details of particular cases, asserting that there could be no general statement made by the government.[29]

The final significance of the plebiscite was political. Munro Ferguson's comment was typical of the Governor-General on this point. Summing up the result, he said that Hughes had yielded to his better judgment, partly because none of his colleagues would follow him in taking the decision within Parliament, and partly because he was reluctant to smash the party which he had done so much to make without giving it a chance.[30]

W. M. Hughes practically single-handed destroyed the Labor Party. It was an indication of just how far apart he and certain of his sometime followers had drifted that the Labor rump could acclaim the final result of the referendum as the grandest victory of democracy over militarism in the annals of history.[31]

From the inception of the campaign, the New South Wales Labor Premier and the last two presidents of the labour movement in the State, R. D. Meagher, Speaker of the Legislative Assembly, and J. D. Fitzgerald, M.L.C., together with the majority of State Labor members and the whole of the State Liberal Party, had stood behind the Prime Minister in support of conscription. The metropolitan daily press had supported compulsory military service and so had nearly all the country newspapers, the Employers' Federation, the Chambers of Commerce, and the official classes generally. Hughes, it was said by the labourites in New South Wales after the campaign was over, had reacted to the challenge to his leadership and views by hurling reckless and hysterical charges of disloyalty against the anti-conscriptionists, and using press censorship to suppress whatever might have told against his personal and party objects. The Prime Minister was further accused of deliberately withholding the A.I.F. vote;[32] certainly it appeared with curious slowness and was the subject of speculation which led to a belief that the government had tampered with the figures.[33]

The government's proposal, then, failed narrowly, but it was a defeat nevertheless. The only question remaining was in what form the chief electoral officer should publish the final figures. He could see no objection to their publication in the press except that this might facilitate deductions by interested persons as to the voting by members of the forces.[34] He did not disclose why such deductions were undesirable, but perhaps it was because of the close vote and because an overwhelming 'Yes' vote in the A.I.F. had been predicted. (It is interesting to note that the rumour has persisted that the Australian army voted against conscription.) This was not so, as the totals in Table 2 show, but there were reasons for the rumour and the attitude of the chief electoral officer. The Australian newspaperman Keith Murdoch was a

Archbishop Mannix

Left, W. M. Hughes; right, General John Monash

close observer of the conscription campaign as it concerned the A.I.F. abroad, and it was his opinion that the soldiers in the front line voted against the government's proposals. He reported confidentially in October 1916 that the first 10,000 soldiers' votes counted were definitely against conscription, and feared that the votes from France would be even more decided.

In this situation, General Headquarters concluded that publication of the results would only prolong the war and cost lives, and consequently suggested that the Army Council ask Australia to merge all totals, so that the soldiers' vote could not be singled out. This was done, and Hughes did not allow the army vote to become known till long after, when perhaps his hand was forced by the publication of spurious totals.

In November 1916 Murdoch stated that voting in the field had been three to one against compulsion, but that a splendid majority in Egypt, where he said the Light Horse enjoyed the fighting, and a fifteen to four vote from the new Division and drafts at Salisbury Plain had led to an overall soldiers' majority of about 10,000.

Why did the men of the A.I.F. vote as they did? In Murdoch's opinion they were discontented, and he suggested that they be given a brief spell because of their distance from home and the strangeness of the climate and surroundings. He pointed out that the Australians were not, like the English, fighting at their own back door, observed that the real necessity was to increase the men's respect for Great Britain, said the men in the field cared little about the ballot-box, and stated that they could not be addressed without danger to discipline. In Murdoch's opinion, the tendency was for the A.I.F. to kick against discipline and register a protest against the powers who had put them where they were.

The man in a better position than anyone to gauge the temper of the A.I.F. and to assess the way they voted was probably the sensitive observer General Birdwood. Noting that there had been a considerable majority of over five figures who voted 'Yes', he concluded that there were nine reasons for the 'No' vote in the A.I.F. These were: (1) there was a strong objection to the Australian 3rd Division remaining in Britain, the men saying that while that unit was in England, they would not vote for more

I

soldiers to be sent from Australia; (2) the A.I.F. did not feel it proper for them to vote and bring men perhaps to lose their lives; (3) they would not have conscripts in the same units as the volunteers; conscripts should be in separate battalions; (4) they had not had enough leave; (5) Ireland did not have conscription, so why should Australia?; (6) Australia had nothing to do with declaring war; (7) the A.I.F. was not satisfied that conscription would be for the term of the war only, and did not want it permanently in a free country like Australia; (8) when asked by Sir John Cockburn, one of the delegates who came over to France at the Prime Minister's wish to interview the men, if they did not want to see the Australian army at full strength, some soldiers ejaculated that there was no Australian 'army'; (9) a very few men complained of insufficient rations.

Birdwood observed that the 'No' vote would be quite heartbreaking for Hughes who had told the General that he was completely confident of success. Birdwood, however, failed to see why Hughes had been so confident when, in Birdwood's view, any country at all would vote 'No' if asked about conscription. Yet, he concluded, if there should be a second referendum in Australia, it was quite likely that the 1916 decision would be reversed.[35]

In August 1917, well after the referendum, Senator Ferricks quoted the Dublin *Freeman's Journal*, cited in the Melbourne *Socialist* of 6 April 1917, as reporting that the 'Anzac' vote had been 106,000 for 'No' and only 40,000 for 'Yes'.[36] The next month a summons against the *Socialist* for publishing an article from the *Glasgow Herald* purporting to give the result of the soldiers' vote was withdrawn by the government because permission had been granted on the understanding that the authority be cited. There was also an apparently innocent cable concerning 'ewes' and 'wethers' which was said to represent the A.I.F. vote.[37]

The effect of the conscription campaign was the disruption, if not the effective destruction, of the Labor Party at the federal and State levels, and the union of conscriptionists from both parties. In New South Wales there were negotiations between Holman and the State Liberals to form a 'National' coalition, held to be justified because prosecution of the war should lead to all party political differences being buried until peace was secured. The

Labor rump or 'Caucus party' attributed this to less noble motives, asserting that the Parliament of New South Wales had no responsibility for the conduct of the war, and that this pretext was intended only to blind people to a process of sordid bargaining for keeping place and pay. Thus was W. A. Holman accused of a great betrayal, compounding his offence by extending the life of Parliament a year beyond its statutory limit.

Five of the six State labour organizations expelled the members of the federal Labor Party who had followed the Prime Minister; opinion was divided in Western Australia and the matter left open. Before federal Parliament met, a caucus of the Labor Party was held and a resolution moved expressing no confidence in the Prime Minister. After confused argument, Hughes dramatically called on those who agreed with him to follow him, and left the room at the head of thirteen followers in the Lower House and twelve in the Senate. These twenty-six numbered less than one-quarter of the number of Parliament's 111 members. The other Labor men chose Frank Tudor as their leader and Senator Gardiner as deputy leader.[38]

As the Governor-General reported it, Hughes then appeared at Government House after his caucus defeat and concealed his cronies in another part of the building after the manner of Ali Baba; here they were discovered with Bibles at the ready, and were duly sworn in.[39] Thus did a fresh Australian government emerge.

Following this transaction, a special conference of the Labor Party met at Melbourne on 4 December 1916, and by twenty-four votes to four adopted a resolution that federal members who supported compulsory overseas service, or who had left the parliamentary Labor Party and formed another party, should be expelled from the movement. The minority of four included three from Western Australia and Senator Gardiner from New South Wales.

Hughes then did a deal with the Liberals and formed his first coalition of National Labor and Liberals, controlling the House of Representatives by a majority of twenty-three. A minority of four in the Senate was reduced by underhand means and when two affronted Liberal senators voted against Hughes, Parliament was dissolved and a landslide victory won by the coalition at the polls, Hughes promising there would be no conscription for over-seas service without another referendum.[40] This whole unsavoury business was succinctly described by Munro Ferguson: the minority in Parliament had been turned into a majority all right, but whether by bribery, threat or hemlock, he was unable to say.[41]

7

The Recruiting Campaigns of 1917

The disastrous referendum of 1916 was over but the war in Europe and the Middle East was not. For two and a half years now the Central powers and the Allies had gripped each other by the throat: at the end of December 1916 18,652 men of the A.I.F. were dead and 27,290 wounded; 3,354 were missing, 18,074 were sick and 908 were prisoners of war. The number of men who had joined the Australian army was 342,825.[1]

Against this background, the Official Historian, C. E. W. Bean, describing the very severe European winter of 1916–17, spoke sorrowfully of the referendum campaign at home:

In the long line, through the long long nights, the troops look out over the wide moonlit snows in the teeth of a bitter wind. But more bitter still is the thought which I hear expressed on every side that, after all these men had done, the Australian party politicians cannot sufficiently sink party gain and loss whole-heartedly to represent in the Imperial Conference the Australian ideas of justice and right for which they are fighting.[2]

What was to be done? Would there be another Somme? If there were, would it not lead to the breaking up of the A.I.F.? The A.I.F. and Captain Bean might consider they were fighting for justice and right, but party politicians in Australia were asking questions about justice for whom and the right to do what? The war might go on for ever, and the government, defeated in its proposal to reinforce the army compulsorily, could only try now to keep up recruitment at a level it hoped would prevent the diminution of the A.I.F. This was 5,500 men a month, but to ensure that that number arrived in the theatres of war, it was necessary to try to get slightly more to enlist in Australia.[3]

Having arrived at this figure, the government looked out for a man of action, determination and enterprise who might persuade Australian men to enlist at the decided rate. He was found in Donald Mackinnon, the member of the Victorian Cabinet who had so successfully organized that State's recruiting drives, and he was made federal Director-General of Recruiting.[4]

Out of the ruins of the conscription campaign Mackinnon was asked to organize recruiting on a Commonwealth basis, and at the beginning of December he issued his plan for nation-wide action to reinforce the A.I.F. That plan was business-like: a Recruiting Committee in each State was nominated by Mackinnon who corresponded with it directly on general matters affecting the civil organization of recruiting. State organizing secretaries were appointed to the State Committees and generally given a free hand under the Committees and the Director-General. Arrangements were also made for federal Electorate Committees and local Recruiting Committees, the latter formed in each local government area or centre of population from existing War Service Committees and local recruiting bodies. Recruiting officers, not necessarily holding military rank, and controlled by the State secretaries, were stationed in central towns in each federal electorate, a civilian to receive a yearly salary of £250 with travelling expenses.[5]

The organization of Mackinnon's recruiting scheme may be gathered from the example of Western Australia. Here headquarters in the various recruiting areas were established at Fremantle, Perth, Bunbury, Northam, Katanning, Geraldton, Kalgoorlie and Leonore. In each of these centres a recruiting officer was stationed, assisted by paid recruiting organizers who received £4 a week, and committees were also formed in the various centres, their officers and members working on a voluntary basis.[6]

So was started the great recruiting drive of 1917, headed by a man who dedicated himself to making the voluntary system work. He tried everything, including the production from his office of a pocket volume called *The Speaker's Companion* to help in making the correctly-directed stirring appeal to the men of Australia. Its foreword stressed that the recruiting campaign for 1917 must not by a single word or deed be offensive to anyone; the tone of the book was that everybody had a united interest and that this was a people's movement. The note to be struck, stressed the Director-General, should always be consistently conciliatory and persuasive; as far as possible, all objections to recruiting were to be answered in a friendly way and complete information given to those who sought it.

Those who wanted information were not always friendly, thanks to the referendum campaign and the apparent stalemate on the Western Front, but Mackinnon's directions assumed an earnest interest. The manual was full of verse and prose such as Kitchener's message, statements on the war by Lloyd George, comments about Gallipoli, a famous speech by Mr Asquith, and something called 'Sister Susie's Creed'. This statement of principle was an interesting measure of recruiting efforts in Australia. It ran:

I believe in Australia inviolate, and in those who bear arms to keep it so. I promise to love, honour, and if necessary to obey any unmarried soldier who has seen active service, and has obtained an honourable discharge . . . I promise to be a sister to any reputable member of the Australian Military Forces, provided that he is debarred by youth or other good and sufficient cause from going to the front. I refuse to establish propinquity to or flirt with any male who cannot produce statutory evidence of ineligibility for active service. If there are not enough soldiers to go round I will cheerfully die an old maid . . .

Henry Lawson, billed as 'Australia's democratic poet', had some verse in the recruiting book:

> There are boys out there by the western creeks,
>   Who hurry away from school
> To climb the sides of the breezy peaks
>   Or dive in the shaded pool
>
> Who'll stick to their guns when the mountains quake
>   To the tread of a mighty war
> And fight for Right or a Grand Mistake
>   As men never fought before:
>
> When the peaks are scarred and the sea-walls crack
>   Till the furthest hills vibrate
> And the world for a while goes rolling back
>   In a storm of love and hate

And this you learn from the libelled past,
  Though its methods were somewhat rude—
A nation's born where the shells fall fast,
  Or its lease of life renewed

We in part atone for the ghoulish strife,
  For the crimes of the peace we boast,
And the better part of a people's life
  In a storm comes uppermost.

Also sketched out for the recruiting agent was the basis of an address to a sports club; this directed the speaker to recognize the splendid spirit which had always animated the followers of sport in Australia, tell his audience that many leading sportsmen were already at the front and had won high honours, and confidently expect that the call to sportsmen had only to be sounded to bring forth a hearty and unanimous response.

The poet Alexander Pope could be cited, 'The gallant man, though slain in fight he be/Yet leaves his nation safe, his children free.'

Humour was to be used too, and sample jokes were offered: 'We were on parade one day, and one chap had no chin-strap to his hat. The inspecting officer paused. "Haven't you a chin-strap?" "No", replied the private. Especially on parade, an officer must be addressed as "Sir". This one glared at the offender. "No what?" he sternly demanded. "No chin-strap", said the other quite cheerfully, and even the officer joined in the audible smile that resulted.'[7]

With and without the aid of this *Companion*, Mackinnon's recruiting organization swung into action with personal appeals. In one of his first statements the new Director-General declared that he would do his best to retrieve the 190,000 men who had gone into camp as a result of Hughes's proclamation earlier that year, and to those men who nevertheless went back to civilian life after the compulsory call-up, State Recruiting Committees made an urgent appeal (with the usual split infinitive) for them to come back into the army:

Can we depend on you? Perhaps you have a mate who will come along with you. You may be sure that as volunteers the Anzacs will welcome you in their battalions, and the pleasure, interest, and honour of your experiences abroad will be something to look back on in after years. Will you make a New Year resolution to carefully consider the claims your country has on your services in this time of national peril?[8]

Typical of another sort of appeal to the eligibles was that made by three returned soldiers in front of the Melbourne Town Hall in mid-January 1917. 'Must we go back?' ex-Sergeant Conbrough asked the crowd dramatically, adding that it was not the Turks but the failure of Australia to send reinforcements to Gallipoli that had made the Australians quit. Were not Australians moved with pride at the capture of Rabaul, and by indignation at the Germans calling them sons of convicts, murderers and thieves? concluded the sergeant, evoking an aspect of Australia's history which most people carefully disregarded in 1917. He netted seven recruits, of whom five were ex-soldiers.[9]

Not only men addressed the eligibles. No effort was spared to play upon every feeling which might induce a man to join the colours; but at a recruiting meeting in Bridge Road, Richmond, Victoria, only one man and nineteen boys were secured: 'How young, how young—didn't that thought strike you—won't one man come forward?', sobbed the young woman who had concluded a recitation of Kitchener's Call at that meeting, looking through brimming eyes out over a sea of faces.[10]

The numbers did not come forward, even though the National Council of Women resolved that women and girls should refuse to play tennis, golf or join in sport of any kind with eligible men.[11] A desperate situation required desperate measures; in early 1917 it had not yet been suggested that men in gaol be sent off to fight for their country, but it was urged that energetic and well-considered action be taken to round up deserters from the A.I.F., of whom there were thought to be about 2,000 in Victoria alone.[12]

A different note was struck when men were advertised for:

200 Daily

VICTORIA'S SHARE

In the coming spring, the Allies, it is expected,
will begin a great offensive.
It will, it seems, be a great advance.
Will YOU be there?

> This may be your last opportunity of helping to
> win the final victory.
> Delay may rob you of a splendid distinction.[13]

In February Mackinnon urged all his recruiting agencies to push their efforts yet further, noting that the American situation had undoubtedly improved the atmosphere, and that the opportunity should not be missed to use this fact to secure more men.[14] Posters urged men to join a 'Sportsmen's Thousand', a battalion which was to enlist in the ordinary way and then be formed in groups of 150 by those who wanted to join it till seven such groups were completed. The slogan was 'Camp together, train together, embark together, fight together.'[15] Again, when Hughes and the Nationalists went to the country in the general election of May 1917, all candidates were asked to appeal for recruits, and the leader of the Labor Party, F. G. Tudor, also stated that his candidates would be asked to appeal at meetings for men to join the A.I.F.[16] All sorts of clever ideas were tried out. In Sydney, for instance, at an open-air meeting addressed by Hughes, fifty mounted horsemen paraded leading fifty horses with empty saddles. Immediately the horses had been led past the speaker's rostrum, the fifty saddles were filled with recruits. At once the experiment was repeated and in this way more than one hundred recruits were secured, with forty more the next day.[17] But ingenious ideas could be taken too far, and a line had to be drawn to prevent a member of a recruiting committee trying to get recruits at a Government House ball.[18]

Recruiting films were also used. Those sent to Tasmania were well received, Mackinnon's recruiting agents reported encouragingly, and in Brisbane the film 'Why Britain went to War' led to fifteen men joining the A.I.F. when it was screened in the open air.[19] The same film was also successful in Lithgow, where forty-eight recruits were traced to the effect of its screening,[20] and in Victoria it was said that 40 per cent of recruits were being obtained by movies advertising the plight of the Empire and the duty of its sons.[21] But not all films showing highlights of the war effort were suitable, the authorities considered: when rodents and then weevils attacked Australia's huge wheat stockpiles in 1917, the film 'Fighting the Mice Plague' was prohibited by the censor from exhibition, though no reason was offered.[22]

Some of the films used for recruiting purposes were, 'Battle of Ancre', 'Advance of the Tanks', 'Australians in Egypt', 'A Hero of the Dardanelles', 'Will They Never Come?', 'La Revanche', 'A.I.F. in France', 'Why Britain Went to War', 'A Soldier's Life in the A.I.F.', 'Australia Prepared', 'Australian Soldiers in the Making', 'Australia at War', 'Sons of the Empire', 'Australia's Peril' and 'A Man, that's all'. The great majority seem to have been Australian productions. A series of lantern slides was also produced, showing scenes of munition workers, physical training and building soldiers' cottages at Oakleigh.[23]

In July 1915 there was produced by Australasian Films under the authority of Senator Pearce the feature called 'Will They Never Come?'. Written by Phil Gell and Louis Brown, 'A Hero of the Dardanelles' was the sequel given a private showing at the Majestic Theatre in Melbourne in the presence of the Governor.[24]

The scenario of 'A Hero of the Dardanelles'[25] exemplifies the propaganda film of the war.

CAST

Father
Mother
Gordon Brown (the Man who did his Duty)
William Brown (the Man who followed his Example)
Lily Brunton (William's Sweetheart)

(Subtitle) 'HE HAS COME'

SCENE 1   After having been inspired by his brother's noble self-sacrifice, William is shown in bedroom (in private's uniform) gazing aimlessly at the sporting requisites which he had cast aside. With a significant shrug he turns and examines his rifle. Glancing through the window he sees the 'Will They Never Come?' tableau as a vision against the starlit sky.

SCENE 2   Leaving home for encampment. Mother and father escort William to gate while the convalescing brother waves farewell from the verandah.

(Subtitle) 'A SOLDIER IN THE MAKING'

SCENE 3   William at Liverpool undergoing course of training. This section of film to illustrate the full course of instruction for recruits. (All the various forms of drill, rifle practice, trench digging etc.)

(Subtitle) 'NOW HIS SWEETHEART'S PRIDE'

SCENE 4   Sunday in Camp. William effusively welcomes his sweetheart who gazes at him with unaffected pride. The great love that has been kindled in her since his enlistment is plainly indicated as the young soldier shows her over the camp.

(Subtitle) 'HE DID HIS DUTY—WILL YOU DO YOURS?'

SCENE 5   On a visit to the City, William meets a number of his old Sporting associates who adopt an air of ridicule in regard to his rallying to the colours. He joins them in a drink at the Club. The crowd jolly him over wearing the uniform and one of their number suggests another round but the soldier indicates that he has had sufficient and proceeds to explain the reason for his enlistment. During the telling of the story there appears a vision of brother lying wounded. He takes from his pocket a small recruiting poster (Lord Roberts) and pins it to the wall. One of the party moves to tear it down but the temper of the crowd has changed as a result of the soldier's appeal and the others pull him back. (Business will create the desired impression.)

(Subtitle) 'ON FINAL LEAVE'

SCENE 6   At Manly, William is shown on the rocks with his sweetheart. (After love business) William takes ring from pocket and places it on her engagement finger. They embrace and scene fades out showing figures silhouetted against setting sun.

(Subtitle) 'GOODBYE AND GOD SPEED'

SCENE 7   Last night at home. Banquet to the departing soldier. Around the table with parents and invalided brother are his fiancée and family friends. Father calls on company to drink to their son's safe return. In responding William by business suggests that he will follow his brother's noble example. Scene concludes with soldier leaving home (night effect). Mother seems to give way but father and the boy's sweetheart cheer her up.

(Subtitle) 'FOR KING, FOR COUNTRY'

SCENE 8   Scene in camp, packing up kit etc., embarking on train. On the transport at Sea. Night time; William peering over rail (flash back short scene) Mother and Sweetheart at prayer.

(Subtitle) 'FOR THE DARDANELLES'

SCENE 9   Scene showing William in camp in Egypt (show only few bell tents and then a panorama of camp—this can be obtained from negative taken for us by Pathé Frères). There is a stir in camp when a soldier rushes up to William's tent with the news that the Australians have been ordered in to the Dardanelles.

(Note)—All scenes at Dardanelles to be produced according to Ashmead-Bartlett's report.

(Subtitle) 'THE LANDING AT GALLIPOLI'

SCENE 10   On the transport. Men waiting on deck prior to embarking in boats. Officers examining kit etc. (according to military custom). Men shown coming down gangway to naval cutters manned by bluejackets. Boats being towed ashore by pinnaces. (Flash back close view of gunners loading and firing. This can be made from stock negatives and will suggest navy covering landing.) On the way to the shore the men discover magazines empty and with a grim determination fix bayonets. Nearing the beach bullets from the enemy splash all around boats and several fall.

(Subtitle) 'AUSTRALIA FOREVER'

SCENE 11   Men jump from boats into water up to their necks and storm the heights. Driven back they charge and charge again until finally the position is won. (Charges to be made in face of heavy fire, the enemy always being suggested.) During the fighting William is brought well into the limelight. Red Cross and A.S.C. shown at work. Then follow scenes illustrating the taking of the enemy's trenches. (Flash back: Scene of Australians indulging in swim under shrapnel fire.)

(Subtitle) 'WHEN AUSTRALIAN MEETS TURK'

SCENE 12   During the battle William meets a Turk on edge of cliff and in the scramble both lose their rifle. There follows a life and death struggle (as described in cable). Men fall over into water and William drowns his adversary and struggles to shore badly wounded.

(Subtitle) 'HE DID HIS DUTY!'

SCENE 13   In hospital writing letter home. Flashback scene showing parents reading letter as follows:—

Military Hospital, Cairo
28/6/15

Dear Mother & Father,
    The Turks winged me early in the piece but I more than got my own back for Australia. My leg is completely useless and much as I would like to be back with the boys it's now

up to the others to carry on the game. Don't worry, I'll be back with you all in a very few weeks.

Your loving son,
William.

Another scene showing fiancée reading letter.

SCENE 14   Enthusiastic welcome to wounded hero on crutches. Father, mother, brother (well but still limping) fiancée. (Business ad lib.)

(Subtitle) 'A SOLDIER'S REWARD'

SCENE 15   Quiet wedding at little rustic church. After ceremony bridal party walk down path, the scene fading into the 'Will They Never Come?'

Tableau.

So was recruiting encouraged by modern techniques. Some people adopted other methods or wanted other ideas tried out: certain women still urged that conscription be introduced but were discouraged because the government's policy was voluntaryism;[26] the secretary of the Recruiting Committee in Adelaide noted a point observed by others throughout the war when he asked the Director-General of Recruiting to use his influence to persuade newspapers to adopt a more pessimistic attitude towards war news: good news had the effect of discouraging recruiting;[27] it was urged that articles in newspapers be censored if they referred to conditions at the front likely to prejudice recruiting; others yet again thought that the use of 'returned soldier' to describe people brought before the courts should be stopped because it militated against recruiting.[28]

The Governor-General observed some of the same factors, pointing out to the King that if Australia had fallen below the high standards of her promises at the beginning of the war, this was due to the repeated English news that victory was assured, and to press accounts which over-emphasized Australia's role at the front.[29] The Rockhampton Recruiting Committee felt rather the same way: it wanted the release of war news that would enable the public to realize fully the gravity of events.[30]

In mid-May 1917 the number of casualties suffered by the A.I.F. was calculated from 1 July of the preceding year, and turned out to be 9,354 killed, 3,168 missing and 30,351 wounded.

advertising gave all its space for recruiting purposes. Members of nearly all specific institutions were circularized to help recruiting, and local women's recruiting organizations had considerable influence, especially during an appeal made on the King's birthday.

Novel ideas were tried: huge footprints were placed on city footpaths directing men to recruiting depots; recruiting slides were shown at the pictures; cards were hung up in public transport, and handbills to wrap up in parcels sent out to commercial firms; box kites bearing messages about joining the A.I.F. were flown over the racecourse; voluntary women helpers stationed at different stopping-places put recruiting literature into all race trams and trains; women in local towns were encouraged to plant a tree in honour of every soldier killed at the front; children were lectured at; there were recruiting trains, route marches and military displays of all kinds. And to crown it all, scones and cakes were thrown out to crowds from travelling kitchens, the food containing slips of cooked paper inside telling the eligible he ought to enlist.

In the six months after the Director-General of Recruiting had been appointed, Queensland raised nearly 4,000 soldiers by these means, but it was less than one-third of the total stated to be the minimum needed, although in that State there were calculated to be 7,500 fit single men between the ages of eighteen and twenty-one, 15,500 between twenty-one and thirty-five, 7,000 between thirty-five and forty-five, and about 40,000 married men between eighteen and forty-five. Why was it impossible to get many more men? Because about half the twenty-one to thirty-five age-group had come under exemption during the 1916 call-up for home duty, whereas the other half of the number of fit single men in that group had emerged from the compulsory service more case-hardened than ever. The fringe of this group was driven into the A.I.F. camps in dribbles as a result of economic and other conditions, but it was the married men between eighteen and twenty-one who made up the bulk of Queensland's enlistments in mid-1917, despite the fact that the recruiting committees had never told married men that things were so bad at the front that it was time they, too, went to the war.

The voluntary system, then, had been given a very good trial in Queensland; only in rare cases did the anti-conscriptionists actively work against recruiting under the Mackinnon scheme,

K

and the most rabid newspaper opponents of compulsory service for overseas gave the committees a very fair run and kept quiet about their opinions. Hence, to a large extent it appeared that the bitterness of the referendum campaign had been removed, yet still not nearly enough men had come forward.[34]

The experiences of recruiting in South Australia were somewhat the same as those of Queensland, the State Recruiting Committee reporting that, although satisfactory work had been done, there had not been enough recruits. The State was split up into the seven districts of the federal electorates (Adelaide, Angas, Barker, Boothby, Grey, Hindmarsh and Wakefield) and subdivided into a total of fifteen recruiting centres. The recruiting figures are shown in Table 3.

Boothby and Hindmarsh produced few recruits because they were in the suburbs or on the outskirts of Adelaide and men were sent to the enrolling officer in the city to be medically examined and attested.

The best recruiting results were obtained from stirring open-air appeals made by recruiting officers and organizers assisted by returned soldiers and representative citizens. Unlike the Queensland recruiters, the South Australians found that the public appeal from a street platform was better than getting into direct touch with an eligible man because, as a report put it, the message or appeal eloquently delivered in the open air touched the hearts not only of the audience but also of those who listened to the addresses, who became unconscious organizers, spread abroad among their relations, friends and acquaintances, and ultimately reached the eligible man who would never listen to arguments and facts regarding the absolute necessity for reinforcements and the duty Australians owed to the Empire and the Commonwealth coming from any other source.

Boy Scouts were used for recruiting purposes by the Scoutmaster, Gordon Spry, a returned soldier, and every evening for a week in November special street meetings were held in a number of centres in the city and suburbs. Round each recruiting stand, a strong guard of Scouts was mounted after the boys had marched through the principal streets of the particular suburbs to which they had been allotted. Special appeals were made from all platforms by returned soldiers and others. The usual programme was

TABLE 3

Recruiting in 1916-1917*
Australia

State	Population	Recruits	Percentage
N.S.W.	1,858,544	17,527	0.94
Vic.	1,398,884	11,471	0.81
Qld	669,467	5,798	0.86
S.A.	432,709	4,258	0.98
W.A.	308,806	4,896	1.6
Tas.	199,925	1,944	0.97
Total	4,868,335	45,894	0.94

South Australia

District	Enlisted	Volunteered
Adelaide	2,393	3,986
Angas	158	357
Barker	376	709
Boothby	15	31
Grey	1,044	1,732
Hindmarsh	111	275
Wakefield	161	387
Total	4,258	7,477

*It is not clear what part of 1916-1917 is referred to here; the population mentioned appears to be that for 1914, but the *Official History*, vol. 11, pp. 882-7, gives slightly higher totals for 1914; e.g. New South Wales 1,861,522, Victoria 1,430,667.

SOURCE: Defence Dept, MP 367 582/1/252, 22 January 1918, C.A.O., Melbourne.

changed and many Scouts and other children sang songs and recited verses. A special final rally was made at the end of this particular week when all the Boy Scouts in the metropolis, accompanied by several bands, marched through the city to the Returned Soldiers' Memorial, North Terrace, where an address was delivered by the Governor, Sir Henry Galway.

The Women's State Recruiting Committee was also resolute in the recruiting drive of 1917 and concentrated every effort and used every method to counter the effect of women who opposed recruiting. On 27 April there was a great procession of women relatives and workers, a silent march which it was thought would never be forgotten.

The 'Win the War League' in 1917 contributed more than £4,000 to war funds to help keep up the spirit of the Empire. Every factory in the capital which employed women was visited and employees addressed during the lunch hour with the object of breaking down apathy; when various reasons were offered why men were not enlisting, an army representative met the committee and explained what had been represented as stumbling blocks.

One week was designated 'reinforcement week' and was the result of concentration by the Women's State Recruiting Committee on a special effort when all-day appeals were made by relays of speakers in the city and at every picture show and place of amusement. Pertinent cards of appeal were delivered to eligible males by women and girls, and every hotel, café and restaurant had special cards in the form of menus placed on each table so that when the diner picked up the menu he was confronted with an appeal to enlist in the army. This effort led to an increase of from 79 to 111 enlistments, a result sustained for several weeks.

In South Australia there was also established an advisory body on soldiers' dependents, a group which realized that complaints about treatment of dependents had the closest connection with recruiting. Publicity for the recruiting scheme initiated by Mackinnon was also kept up by street posters, advertising at the pictures and other places of amusement, the placing of dodgers on trams and trains, and by the use of painted signs, streamers and notices anywhere they might catch the eye and reach the heart of an eligible man and lead him along that path which terminated in the training camp.

All through the year also the business men of Adelaide were kind to the recruiters, donating flags, chairs, tables and a lock and key for the 'dug-out' (recruiting office) door. Merchants on several occasions placed at the disposal of the committee a part of the space contracted for by them in daily papers free of charge, so that it might make special appeals by medium of display advertisements.[35]

These were some of the devices used to get South Australia's quota of 1,000 men a month. The general organizer of the South Australian committee was Walter Stutley, the chairman Senator

J. Newland who in his first instructions to local committees sought to arouse what he termed 'local emultation' [*sic*]. There were a thousand and one details involved in the recruiting drive directed by Mackinnon in 1917. In South Australia, for instance, nothing was left to chance so that people would not be offended: recruiting officers and committees were charged to remember that the people were not going to be conscripted, they were going to volunteer; organizers were urged to avoid all references to cowards and shirkers, not to lose their temper, not to be aggressive and to remain tactful and calm.

Such tact and patience were beautifully exemplified in the sort of letter sent out to eligibles who would not enlist when interviewed by recruiting officers. This refusal was termed 'your disinclination to undertake in the common cause a share proportionate with your power and opportunity. Health, youth and vigour are yours. To no better service will you ever be able to consecrate these gifts.' Such men were asked to reconsider their decision because they would be remorseful later when it would be too late, no matter what good works they subsequently did.

The bitterness aroused by the late conscription campaign was one difficulty which the recruiters, who were nearly all returned soldiers, had to face; another was associated with the record harvest of early 1917, the high wages offered in South Australia and the associated shortage of labour; another was the adverse comment caused by the number of eligibles who were said to be employed in government service, and particularly the Department of Defence.

Stutley took his work seriously, determined to leave far behind the memory of the preceding months. On a trip into the country he dismissed an organizer at Burra because the man drank too much. At Peterborough he found that the recruiting office was too remote from the town (so far indeed that the general organizer got bogged) and at once secured other premises for his man on the spot. At Gladstone he discovered that the organizer drank because he had been a victim of shell-shock, and he dismissed the man at Port Pirie because he, too, was a sufferer from shell-shock. Stutley recorded his pity for such men; their nerves shattered by the ferocity of combat, they were either disregarded by the public or sneered at, whereupon they sank into excessive drinking.

But the memory of the conscription upheaval was all too evident. At Peterborough some labour bodies would not be represented on the local committee; at Gladstone there was also great bitterness because of the impact of the conscription campaign of 1916, and throughout the country areas there was great opposition to conscription. In Strathalbyn, for instance, where there were several hundred eligibles, only two recruits were got in nine weeks. It was in 1917 often a question of harrying men into the army; as one recruit said, 'I could stand it no longer, I had to enlist.' But others would not go, excusing themselves with 'There is a shortage of labour', 'There should be Home Rule for Ireland' and 'I have a brother at the front.' The mining districts of Kadina and Moonta were most irresponsive, reported the general organizer, and he sought to arouse interest in recruiting by organizing a 'Win the War' day for 6 June 1917 at the Exhibition Building, Adelaide. Addressing the clergy, Stutley asked them to arrange for appropriate music in church the week before this meeting, and suggested Kipling's 'Recessional', 'Lead Kindly Light', 'Onward Christian Soldiers', 'O God Our Help in Ages Past', 'The Marseillaise', 'John Brown's Body', 'God Bless our Splendid Men' and the Russian National Anthem ('perhaps').

By mid-year the recruiting committees, especially in the country, were losing heart, especially at the rebuffs from men at Port Pirie and Broken Hill who said they would not enlist while men from Allied foreign countries stayed back and threatened to take their jobs. Other sorts of trouble also emerged; an organizer made a trip out along the east-west railway line but when he asked men for their names he was told he had better not if he wanted a safe passage; here men would not join up because they had good wages and because they said Greeks and Maltese would take their jobs. The latter would not join the A.I.F. because they said Australia was not their country and replied to counter-arguments with 'No savvy Australian.' It was quite a trip for the organizer: on the way a railway guide told him, 'If you don't want to be hit on the head with a fish plate, you won't talk recruiting here'; but generally the recruiting man reported he was not ill-treated.

Senator Newland put pen to paper and told Mackinnon about all his troubles. For one thing, South Australia was too big for effective and economic canvassing: the expense involved in covering the West Coast (the Eyre Peninsula) led to the buying of a Ford motor car; there was a lack of interest by the anti-conscriptionists; the aliens such as Greeks and Italians were a problem because they would not enlist; deferred pay due to dependents was delayed; newspaper proprietors would not reduce their charges for advertisements or allot a certain fixed amount of advertising space for recruiting appeals and notices; editors sometimes reduced recruiting copy by upwards of one-half or else left it out altogether, with the exception of the labour daily.[36]

Throughout Australia, recruiting was going down and down, and the Director-General instructed local recruiting committees to stop passing resolutions that the voluntary system was exhausted.[37] But it was, if people expected the A.I.F. to be reinforced by the tens of thousands; in the countryside of South Australia the little towns were completely canvassed; only a very few men had not been tackled by the recruiting officers, and those lived a long way out in the backblocks and rarely appeared in towns except for a social or a dance, when they came late in the evening and left early in the morning.

In these places the casualties on the Western Front did not arouse the eligibles but discouraged them. In one such little town four brothers enlisted in the army and by 1917 two of them were dead and one badly wounded. Everyone knew this and people were not encouraged to join enthusiastically in recruiting drives.

Stutley visited Wakefield and Grey and could only sadly report indifference and even hostility to recruiting there: store-keepers who showed any interest in recruiting were boycotted. A fresh idea was tried, cards were distributed which read: 'A man has left this house to fight for liberty.' One recruiting officer, leaving such a card, heard that a son of the family had been reported 'missing', and was told by a disappointed mother that she had hoped, seeing his uniform, he brought good news of her son. As the officer reported, 'We cheered her up with possibilities.'[38] There was a lot of cheering up needed in Australia if the Commonwealth government expected to recruit 5,000 men a month, because that figure was down to about only 2,500 by the end of 1917.

8

Patriotism and Paranoia

The year 1917 was one of growing conflict in Australia. Though enthusiastic recruiting agents tried all manner of means to induce enlistment, this led only to more and more conflict; sectarianism, anti-German feeling and political fights remorselessly destroyed any spirit of unanimity and created an atmosphere of nervous tension.

There was no possibility of Australia supplying the monthly reinforcements said to be necessary to maintain the A.I.F. at full strength unless men were compelled to enlist, because every device that human ingenuity could think up was tried out in the first six months of 1917 to secure the 5,000 men a month. The letterhead of the Queensland State Recruiting Committee drew constant attention to the size of the task. A red map of Australia had on it the number of men available from the various States in order of population: 48,000, 41,200, 26,700, 14,100, 10,000 and 5,000. Towards the end of 1917 the Committee informed everyone who received a letter from it that there were still more than 140,000 eligible single medically-fit men of military age in the Commonwealth, distributed as shown among the States. Asserting that these figures were the federal statistician's calculations, the Queensland body said that this estimate was extremely conservative.[1]

The Director-General had been given a task which he came to suspect was based on information of dubious accuracy, but it was a measure of Mackinnon's qualities of determination to do his best for Australia that he continued his work. Was the number of necessary reinforcements for the A.I.F. arrived at by the British Army Council and accepted by Hughes's government a realistic and cool estimate? Mackinnon suspected that it was a hair-raising overestimate and a hindrance and a discouragement to earnest and loyal recruiters everywhere. That estimate gave encouragement to the feeling of hopelessness voiced in South Australia and to the same reaction in Victoria. The campaign of 1917 never had the full support of the Victorian public. The presence of eligible men in the Defence Department and especially at the Victoria Barracks in Melbourne was a heavy handicap to getting the quota of men, and a very convenient excuse for people refusing to rally to the colours. Furthermore, there were influences at work which fomented political strife and damaged the voluntary effort. For instance, opposition to the leader of the Labor Party, F. G. Tudor, at a Melbourne Town Hall meeting was almost certainly premeditated. At this meeting, Tudor appeared with Mackinnon. The crowd was very unfriendly to Tudor, and especially hostile were female members of the audience who persistently interrupted him. Tudor denied an interjection that he had advised that no one else should go to the war, and likened those who shouted out from the audience to a pack of dingoes.

Mackinnon continued to make various suggestions about ways and means of increasing the number of recruits; he said that the attitude of the government towards reinforcements should be made public and the people told how many men were needed, members of Parliament should start a recruiting appeal and more men and money be put into a short and enthusiastic campaign instantly, there should be increased allowances for wives and children of soldiers, a repatriation scheme should be announced, fit men over forty-five should be enlisted, more military bands used to encourage recruiting, members of Parliament speaking at the declaration of polls should appeal for recruits, race meetings should be curtailed, the religious composition of the A.I.F. made public, and men with German names removed from the public service and especially from the Defence Department.[2]

But inducements to enlist could be taken too far, added Mackinnon, and he disapproved of the practice of well-meaning citizens giving premiums to encourage men to enlist: many of the high-spirited men objected. For instance, in June 1917 Sol Green, a bookmaker in Melbourne, offered a £5 note to the first five volunteers to come forward at a recruiting appeal at the Majestic Theatre.[3]

Women of the Commonwealth continued to strike their blows to assist recruiting, and were urged to say to eligible men, 'You must go! While you fail to do your duty, you shall no longer be a friend or associate of mine.' Women were told to work and consult together, discriminate in shopping between the apathetic and enthusiastic and protest about anyone who was not encouraging recruiting, and hold aloof from any social functions not designed for recruiting and patriotic purposes.[4]

There were more positive ways of getting Australian men into the front line. For instance, a Miss Temperley, speaking at one of her 'one woman, one recruit' meetings, urged the female sex to fix upon one man, even if he were the poor, unfortunate but eligible tradesman who knocked at the back door each day. She implored ladies not to be discouraged if the object of their attention was adamant at first, and certainly not to lose their temper and tell him not to call again. She cited the heartening tale of one woman who had recently converted her baker after two years of unremitting effort. The baker had finally enlisted and rushed back from his rounds to tell her.[5]

This 'one woman, one recruit' league was formed by Miss Temperley in mid-1917, and by early 1918 had grown to a membership of two hundred and raised more than two hundred recruits without any cost to the government. The pledge of the league was 'To do my utmost to enlist one man by appealing through my Womanhood to his Manhood', and was established in connection with the State Recruiting Committee of Victoria with the object of gathering to its banner all women who were prepared to help win the war for the Allies. It appealed to members on the grounds that somewhere in the firing line a man was fighting that a woman might live. Such a man, tired and weary, should have a rest by having his place taken, stated the league, and called upon women to set out one soldier on his march and to justify themselves as women in their country's hour of need. As one of their circulars proclaimed, 'Anzac! Anzac! That little name will ring down through the ages! Women of Australia, set your seal upon it!' Members of the league wore a medallion bearing the figure of a soldier and the words, 'Qui s'excuse, s'accuse.' They tried to make men wear such a medallion as a pledge that they had promised to enlist.[6]

There were other ways that women might be the cause of enlistment during the recruiting campaign of 1917. Mrs McPherson, president in chief of the Australian Women's Association, spoke at a meeting to organize a woman's recruiting committee in Kooyong, Melbourne, and said that when a chaplain had asked one man why he enlisted, the soldier answered, 'Because my girl asked me to.' The next reply was, 'Because the old woman roused me', and a third had told the chaplain to look at Proverbs xxv. 19 ('It is better to dwell in the corner of the housetop, than with a brawling woman and in a wide house'). There were thousands of eligible men, she said, and the women she was sorry for were those who had married since the war, because the children of those would come into the world as cowards.[7]

Patriotism reached great heights in Melbourne: in Preston a lady sought permission from the Defence Department, whether she needed it or not, to name her baby daughter 'Queen of the Allies'.[8] Others were not so pleased when so blessed because they were unmarried and the father was a soldier gone away to the war. Attempts were made to pass an Act of Parliament enabling proxy marriages but this was defeated.[9]

The urgency of the recruiting situation during the summer and autumn of 1917 was never to be lost to mind or sight. In July arrangements were made for tables to be placed at forty-eight street corners in Melbourne, with Boy Scouts in attendance, and enrolment forms provided for men who could be persuaded to join the A.I.F. The forms bore the undertaking, 'I promise to be examined at a recruiting depot, and if fit, sworn into the King's service, and will enter camp within one month.'[10]

The pay of the private soldier was not increased during the war but in July the Director-General announced that dependents of married soldiers would in future have their allowance augmented from the patriotic funds; he noted that in Queensland a larger proportion of married men had enlisted than in any other State, the reason being that they were able to leave their wives and children in better circumstances; in Victoria the scale of allowances was the lowest in Australia.[11]

This increase was partly responsible for the greater numbers of men aged between forty-five and fifty who volunteered in mid-1917. When the British War Office was asked whether such soldiers were wanted, it replied that they certainly were, but a month later the Commonwealth declined to raise the age limit above forty-five on the grounds that older men and those less than 100 per cent fit who were available abroad were evidently not being efficiently and economically utilized. The War Office withdrew its request.[12]

In 1917 voluntary recruiting became a dead horse which could neither be flogged into fresh life nor killed a second time, if large numbers of men were expected from it.[13] The conscription referendum had destroyed the hearty unanimity of purpose which might have led to the voluntary system securing the number of men the government wanted, though thousands of reasons were offered privately and publicly why men did not join up in the numbers hoped for; now it was that larrikins wrote obscene language on recruiting posters put up on railway train windows,[14] next it was that eligible men were in cosy billets in the public service, then it was inadequate pay.[15] And there was sport. Some thought it ludicrous to expect men to enlist while sports such as horse-racing and boxing were conducted full blast as though there was no war on at all. Action was taken, and racing and boxing were limited in September 1917.[16] The participants and spectators did not join the A.I.F. in numbers sufficient to be noticed.

Not only was sport curtailed, but so were the hours for sale of intoxicating liquor. His Majesty the King undertook to refrain from drinking during the duration of the war, and so did members of the staff of the University of Melbourne.[17] The war was serious. Impressed by King George V's action, and the mutiny at Casula Camp, New South Wales, in early 1916, temperance people and others succeeded in reducing the hours of hotels very drastically from the pre-war 6 a.m. to 11 p.m. hours. By the end of the war, Australian hotels were closing at 6 p.m., a 'temporary' measure which remained in Victoria and South Australia for fifty years. Whether or not early closing led to thrift and more sober attention to employment cannot be known, but it did not lead to the required increase in recruiting.

The general election of 5 May 1917 was another factor which destroyed that harmony which people perceived in the months immediately following the declaration of war. The recriminations which followed the split in the Labor Party in 1916 were raised to boiling point again during that campaign: in the Victorian House of Assembly it was said that workers and labour men who had been called pro-German could not be expected to enlist. The *Geelong Advertiser* carried an advertisement which, giving reasons why not to vote Labor, said 'You also will be a traitor if you vote for the candidate who represents the extreme Labor section.'[18] Sectarianism once again figured as Protestant conscriptionists left a Labor Party associated in the public mind with Catholic anti-conscriptionists.[19]

In the irritated condition of the Commonwealth, it needed little in 1917 to upset people. Recruiting agents could do this, and in Victoria Sergeant Galli, a French-Italian who had enlisted in Australia and been wounded at Gallipoli, provided an example of how recruiting efforts could lead to jarring repercussions, because he was a Catholic who offended some Protestants by the way in which he appealed for recruits. He particularly angered the secretary of the Ballarat branch of the Victorian Protestant Federation, C. D. Ross, who asserted that Galli had lauded Catholics and belittled Protestants, thus disgusting Protestants and hampering recruiting.[20]

The sectarianism aroused by Galli's exertions was not smoothed over by the conduct of Archbishop Mannix who went so far as to say that in his view the struggle in Europe was a trade war. His Grace not only offended Protestants but some of his fellow Catholics as well, because in March 1917 a deputation of leading Catholics waited on Archbishop Carr to protest that Dr Mannix's statements were disloyal and inimical to the interests of the church. Carr received the deputation but declined to take any obvious action.[21]

Mannix was angrily attacked for casting doubt on the nobility of the cause for which Australians were fighting; the Rev. J. Snell at Ballarat said that it made his blood boil when he read that a church dignitary had had the callous and unfeeling brutality to characterize the conflict as a trade war: if the Australian boys fighting in the A.I.F. lived to be a hundred years old, they could never be identified with a more sacred cause.[22]

Perhaps not, but there were those who had their doubts about men who sought to compel others to fight in that cause. In Sydney there was a demonstration against Holman and the Lord Mayor, R. D. Meagher, at the St Patrick's Day sports, of all places, and an apology for the hooting and shouting that had gone on asserted that the culprits could not have been Irish because the Irish would have respected the presence of the Apostolic Delegate and the Archbishop. This concluded by applauding the stand of Holman and Meagher in favour of Home Rule.[23]

A lot of people had no time for Dr Mannix, and one of them was the Governor-General. He told the Secretary of State that Melbourne's turbulent priest had made yet another violent speech in which he had said that the conflict in Europe was 'a sordid trade war', and spoken of men being hustled to their death by the recruiting campaign.

It was therefore not to be expected that the Governor-General would cheerfully agree to the calling of Mannix to high public office. He certainly did not, because when the Archbishop was gazetted Chaplain-General, Munro Ferguson remembered Mannix's statement that people should not worry about the disgrace and obloquy attached to him in 'putting on the King's uniform' because in fact he had not any of the King's uniform to put on. For this and earlier comments on the war, the Governor-General refused to sign Mannix's commission.[24]

There was an Irish question in Australia, as Mannix and the 1916 referendum had made perfectly clear. Hughes did not like the Irish question, and begged the British government to come to some sort of agreement with the Irish so that the work of reinforcing the A.I.F. could proceed. In reply, Lloyd George curtly informed Hughes that it was not possible for the Irish question to be settled as he pleased, and explained to the Australian Prime Minister, obsessed with the defeat of Germany at all costs, the main troubles—or some of the main troubles. The point was that the Nationalist majority wanted a united Ireland and the Ulster men refused to accept the existing Home Rule Act. Hughes was informed that the best help he could render therefore was to induce Irish-Australians to put pressure on the Irish leaders to accept any settlement which would not involve compelling Ulster by force of arms to accept Home Rule.[25] But Hughes's conduct in the referendum campaign had not put him in a powerful position to bargain with the Australian-Irish; and no matter what anyone claimed, the constant sectarian strife had not led to a decrease in the number of Catholics who volunteered.[26]

The heat of the war kept sectarian animosity on the boil. In June 1917 strong exception was taken to a letter published by one J. Fegan in the Brisbane *Daily Mail* of 22 June, and the Loyal Orange Institute asked for governmental action against the man Fegan for his views. The United Irish League had other ideas on the rights and wrongs of the Irish question and, in connection with the conduct of Sir Edward Carson, asked the Commonwealth government to express disgust. Dr A. Leeper did not want anything of the kind done, and the government replied that it certainly had no intention of forwarding a request from the United Irish Lodge for the removal of Carson. Amid a welter of angry communications to the central government, the United Irish Lodge protested against the Protestant protest about the anti-Carson cable it wanted transmitted, pointing out the different attitudes the government appeared to have towards the League on the one hand and Dr Leeper on the other.[27] (Speeches in the *Argus* reported on 25 October 1917 are fine examples of the respective positions of Dr Mannix and Dr Leeper.)

Sometimes it seemed that the war was a skirmish connected with the Irish troubles: the Prime Minister's Department had its attention drawn to the landing on Australian soil of Father J. A. Roche, fined in New Zealand for disloyal utterances; a man named McInerney in Gormanston, Tasmania, was the subject of statutory declarations concerning his alleged disloyal comments; people named Daley and Sheehan at Oakleigh, Victoria, were informed on by someone named Galloway;[28] and the Temora branch of the Catholic Federation lodged a protest against the circulation of Critchley Parker's works, which had appeared during the referendum campaign and were still going the rounds. Such sectarian literature was described by Senator E. Needham of Western Australia as scurrilous, the cause of disaffection and the source of outrageous insults hurled at the parents of Catholic soldiers at that very moment fighting and dying on the battlefields of France.[29]

Everywhere there was conflict connected with the recruiting drive of 1917. Another storm blew up concerning Captain (later Sir) Gilbert Dyett. He was to become federal president of the precursor of the Returned Services League in 1919 but at this time was organizing secretary of the State Recruiting Committee in Victoria, and tried to talk theatrical managers into permitting recruiting speeches during performances. The managers were far from keen, pointing out that it was unpopular, that speeches spoilt their attendances, and so on. To this Dyett replied that if conscription came in, they would have no young men in their audiences at all for theatrical entertainments, and in answer to a question he pointed out that conscription was possible under the War Precautions Act.

As a result of these alleged remarks, the governing director of Tivoli Theatres wrote to W. A. Watt, Treasurer and Deputy Prime Minister, and the Minister for Defence complaining that Dyett had practically blackmailed him with the War Precautions Act; both J. C. Williamson Ltd and the Tivoli, he said, felt it was most unfair that such a request had been made to have recruiting speeches from the stage. He asked whether Captain Dyett had official authority for stating that the Act might be used to compel theatrical managers to permit speeches to be made on the stage, and also whether it was intended to use that Act to prevent eligible men from attending the theatres.

Captain Dyett, asked for a report, wrote that he had told two people at Her Majesty's Theatre, one the manager, that the Recruiting Committee would like to have recruiting speakers at the theatres. They had not been eager and said they had done all that might be expected of them. To this Dyett had replied that if the request were granted, the speakers would be instructed to make no discourteous or insulting remarks and, so that the time allotted would not be exceeded, that one of the theatre's employees should ring a bell for the speaker to come on and ring again when it was time for him to stop speaking.

To this, one of the managers had replied that Dyett was fighting for the best cause in the world, but thought that if such interpolations were permitted in the show, eligible men would not come. Dyett retorted that most men had girl-friends, that these girls would insist on being taken to the theatres and that the young men would rather come than lose their girls. He went on, Captain Dyett reported, to stress that the war situation was very serious, that only about half of Australia's quota of reinforcements was being obtained, that the projected scheme would have a very beneficial effect on recruiting and that if, after a month's trial, it could clearly be shown that takings were seriously down because of the recruiting appeals, Dyett would recommend to his Committee that the practice be stopped. He had gone on to say, 'Now, look here gentlemen—between ourselves—supposing that conscription were to be introduced tomorrow, would you not lose the patronage of the eligible men?' They had agreed on this point, and asked could the government do it if it wanted to? Dyett had replied that the government could do anything under the War Precautions Act. Captain Dyett then said he would see Hugh D. McIntosh, the general director of Tivoli Theatres. He found out where the director was, thanked the managers and left for the Tivoli, suspecting however that McIntosh would receive a phone call before he could get to him. He failed to get an interview with the director.

The Minister for Defence, Senator Pearce, looked into this incident and minuted that he could see nothing to object to in the report, but five days later the secretary to the Director-General of Recruiting sent a memorandum to Captain Dyett in which he pointed out that perhaps it would be as well not to refer to the power under the War Precautions Act when seeking the co-operation of public men who were in a position to help the voluntary recruiting movement.[30]

The prospect of dragooning was not necessary for other people to reinforce the discord in Australia. The honorary secretary of a public schools athletic association, Brother Edwin of St Joseph's College, Hunter's Hill, wrote to H. J. Braddon, chairman of the Sportsmen's Recruiting Committee, that a sports master at one of the colleges would not permit his team to play matches with teams of young men who had left school, sternly deeming that they should be at the front. And at a meeting of the Committee, Lieutenant R. MacLean, appointed to the sportsmen's unit, was mentioned with pride: for several years he had held the position of sports master at Cook's Hill school at Newcastle and now wished to see some of the old boys with him in the greatest sport of all, Hun-hunting.[31]

Not all schools had such teachers. In South Australia it was stated that in a German school in the Barossa District, the teacher used to haul down the British flag, wipe his feet on it, spit on it and then hoist up the German colours. Whether there was any truth in this or not, early in November 1917 the Lower House in South Australia passed a Bill prohibiting the teaching of the

L

German language in primary schools, and a clause was inserted closing forty-nine Lutheran primary schools.[32]

There was always suspicion of German-Australians to fall back on in explaining why the enlistments were not up to scratch. It may be doubted whether actual fear of Germans at home prevented many men from volunteering for the A.I.F., but some people certainly thought that the enemy within the gates was in some mysterious and sinister way sowing discord; Pearce himself considered there was a German spy system in Australia. In March 1917 he wrote unofficially to the Chief of the General Staff that it had been suggested by the editor of the *Argus* that an article on the subject would be beneficial. Pearce asked Brigadier-General H. J. Foster, Chief of the General Staff, for his views, concluding that he should have some interesting data in his archives. The next day, however, Foster replied that the Director of Military Intelligence, Major E. L. Piesse (later to become Director of the Pacific Branch of the Prime Minister's Department) had stated that there had been no case of hostile spying in Australia since he took office in November 1914.[33]

No German spies were identified in Australia during the war,[34] but this did not prevent spy hysteria from creating dissension and suspicion, thus leading to the development of more disharmony in the community. There were thousands and thousands of letters to the authorities in which people sought to have strange events investigated and apparently suspicious people brought under surveillance and interned because they might hamper recruiting by dropping the occasional cunning word here and there. Strength was lent to this witch-hunting when less than two months after the landing at the Dardanelles there was a rumour, referred to in Parliament, that an Australian-born soldier (the censors changed the word 'officer' to 'soldier'), who enjoyed the reputation of being a first-class sniper, used to go out and snipe his own men.[35]

The reports from England in 1915 about concrete gun emplacements concealed in private houses increased the hysteria in Australia, and even suburban cricket clubs, particularly a club whose secretary had a foreign-sounding name, were unable to put down concrete cricket pitches without it being reported by 'Britisher' or 'Loyal Australian'.

Suspicious signalling was reported all over the place; 'aeroplanes' seen at night by some people turned out to be flights of migratory birds. Neighbourly curiosity, inflamed by press reports of the immense sums spent by Germans on secret service work, was responsible for such communications as: 'Mr A——, of —— Street, does not work, but he is plentifully supplied with money, which he spends freely. His wife pretends to go out washing, *but she has not been out for four weeks; this does not keep him!* (Signed) "All for Empire".' Another characteristic communication read: 'There is a man in this street who does not work, but has lots of money. His wife has no children, and I don't think ever will, but she goes about with a perambulator; in this have been packets, like packets of candles covered over with a rug; they are not candles, however, for they have gas laid on in their house; they are bombs, which he makes.'[36]

The Australian body politic was evidently hopelessly riddled with spies and with people who behaved as if they might be German agents. Public-spirited citizens in 1914 suggested that people overheard discussing military tactics be placed under observation, informed the authorities that a German family at Bannockburn wanted watching, said that there was a suspected German at Cheltenham, told the Defence Department that the Swiss consul-general was of German extraction and would bear watching, wrote that a suspicious airship had been sighted over Wonthaggi, intimated that Germans in detained ships were signalling to something or somebody by means of a box kite, and concluded that there was an unauthorized wireless station operated by a German at Inverloch in Gippsland.[37]

It was held by responsible people in Australia that there were indeed German spies in the Commonwealth. A month after the outbreak of the war, a circular from the Prime Minister to the States asked them to uncover the working of spying wireless telegraphy stations supposed to be operating in the nation. In helpful hints, the author of the circular noted that such wireless operators would of course use unfrequented places for their activities, and that the necessary masts would probably be put up during the night and taken down during the day lest they be seen. A mast or tree of medium height if near the coast would serve and a motor car could be used to supply the necessary power effectively to transmit information. Local authorities were to be warned to look out for suspicious characters, that is, people in a district with no good reason for being there. Such individuals were to be carefully watched and plans laid for their capture and search if they were found in possession of a wireless telegraphy station or apparatus. These temporary transmitters, it was stated, could be established with such ease and, when near the coast, be capable of such dangerous work that no vigilance was to be spared in order to apprehend their users and capture the infernal apparatus. In New South Wales the circular was extended: police were to guard against accepting views touching on the limitations of wireless telegraphy, the potentialities of which were not fully understood even by the best informed on the subject.[38]

Whether wireless signals were getting out of the country or not, unauthorized letters, it was thought, were getting in. The deputy chief censor in Brisbane sent one such to the Defence Department, noting that former communications had been sent in a sardine tin, now held by the police, to their suspect. There was danger everywhere if you looked carefully: in Brighton, 'True Englishman' found to his consternation that the electric cars on the Brighton tram line had been designed by a German, a fact which allegedly hindered recruiting. Pigeons were also considered dangerous, for might not the birds be used by the spies to send off messages to vessels, should wireless transmission be impracticable or foiled? They were grounded for the duration of the war, the Minister noting that permits were to be required to fly pigeons, though not merely to house them in lofts.

There was danger from below as well as above and at sea, and the terrifying possibility that Germans might place explosives in drains and sewers and thereby blow up an unsuspecting Melbourne was noted. In Queensland the town clerk of Townsville considered that the Cairns [*sic*] water supply had been tampered with, and he asked that the water catchment area be guarded lest the whole community be suddenly poisoned. Melbourne was also endangered in the same way: a correspondent stated categorically on 7 July 1915 that the water would be poisoned on the following Tuesday.[39]

The Minister for Defence might well take very seriously a number of such reports and warnings; as he reminisced years later, there was undoubtedly a secret German war organization in Australia, its task made easier by the unsuspicious and friendly

character of the Australian people who had regarded the German
settlers with affection before 1914.[40] Perhaps the most sinister of
these activities in the midst of a people not quite as amiable as the
Minister thought was the supposed existence of a German secret
society which flew a flag decorated with a picture of an ape; yet
no trace of it could be found upon official investigation.[41]

In Stanhope Street, Malvern, someone saw a revolving light on
a roof at night and thought the worst, another correspondent forwarded a threatening letter for transmission to the Emperor of
Germany, in Newcastle an impressively loyal citizen informed the
Defence Department that he was planning the destruction of all
Germans in Australia, but another citizen urged a less short way
with the enemy in the midst: all able-bodied Germans should be
sent to the front or else interned. At Phillip Island a lady wrote in
to say that two unnaturalized Germans at Western Port went out
fishing over the cable; she did not know their names. An anonymous writer more than usually enigmatic discovered that the
Germans in a country town not a hundred miles from Brisbane
were laying in stores of ammunition, another German was inventing a flying machine, others yet again were signalling to mail boats
at night from Torquay, and a building near the corner of Queen
Street and Flinders Lane, Melbourne, was under notice because
shooting lessons appeared to be given on the premises. Ten days
after the outbreak of war, three very distinct smokes were sighted
west of Dirk Hartog Island at sundown; they were travelling, as
do such mysterious objects, at high speed.

Not all the enemy were moving away; some were close to home
operating with a fiendish cunning in unexpected areas: information was lodged about the supposed existence of a secret wireless
near Bishopscourt, Melbourne, and an informant in the same city
told the Defence Department that information might be had on
application concerning the movements since 1916 of a man with a
German name.

Anonymous correspondents remained alert in seeking out the
enemy: one Feitz was observed to be up to no good, for was he
not riding about in a motor car at night? and at Roseneath Street,
Clifton Hill, a man of German descent was busily inventing an
aeroplane. The Minister still thought there was a German spy
system, and late in 1917 sent to the *Argus* a copy of notes on the

subject for that paper to use for articles. This had at least one result, because a few months later 'Vigilant' at Bendigo informed the Department that advertisements for London Stores in that same newspaper contained possibly secret writing.[42]

Germans in Australia were the subject of violent attacks throughout the European conflict. Only two months after the war started, 'Scotsman' from Gayndah on the Darling Downs hysterically wrote about the Germans at Binjour settlement which, he alleged, was distinguished by squalor and typhoid among aliens, one of whom boasted that if only he could get back to Germany he would 'blow the —— British up'. 'Scotsman' considered that the 'animalism' displayed by the Germans at Brussels and Louvain was not surprising: the government could not expect Australians to volunteer and leave their wives and children in such company, the scum of Essen and Dusseldorf, 'some lack fingers, others are almost blind'. A schoolteacher also wrote about the Germans who, he said in a panic, were slowly and slyly arming, the nearest one to him having bought a new Winchester rifle and a hundred rounds of ammunition.

The government was not going to be caught napping; the Commandant of the 1st (Queensland) Military District was instructed to search certain houses and, when he sought the help of the Queensland State police, the Premier agreed to co-operate, asked the Military Commandant to call in all arms held by the Germans, and to institute a secret service in German districts. Brisbane was full of rumours about the danger of Queensland Germans.[43] Two loyal citizens reported one such individual after the sinking of the *Lusitania*; he was supposed to have said, ' "She was carrying arms and trying to starve Germany". He stamped his foot and said, "I am proud of the German army and the country I come from".'[44]

Fear of the Germans in Australia continually led to complaints about them and suggestions of how they should be treated so that the nation could get on with recruiting men for the A.I.F. A writer to the Premier of Queensland spoke of the situation at Eidsvold, and wanted a war tax imposed because the Germans in the area gave little or nothing to war funds, 'A lot of Germans hold meetings and have a great day when the Kaiser has a victory. They breed horses and cattle and won't give even a dozen eggs.' This complaint was looked into by the police, as were all complaints during the war, who reported that the writer of the letter also bred horses; admittedly, very few German settlers had given anything towards the Patriotic Fund, went the report, but the enquiries had led to no evidence of meetings to celebrate victories by the Central powers.[45]

The problem of how to deal with Australians of enemy origin, or apparently enemy origin, was never solved because only a limited number were interned. They presented a dilemma; they could not be permitted to enlist because they might turn on their Australian comrades or desert to the enemy; on the other hand, if they did not enlist, they were the excuse for some Australians piously refusing to join up and risk their necks on the Western Front.

Not only German influences were thought to be alive and well in Australia. There were other, perhaps more insidious, means by which some people thought dissent was being nourished and the war effort slowed down. Another factor, which went part of the way to destroy the cohesiveness of the Australian people and to raise doubts about the intelligence of the federal government and its agents, concerned further censorship of material thought to be prejudicial to recruiting. Such works were not necessarily the newspapers and books imported from neutral countries which cast grave doubts on the purity of Britain's motives. There were other publications which were held to be prejudicial to recruiting. Senator Pearce himself defended the prohibition of such an item. This was *The Fiddlers: Drink in the witness box* by Arthur Mee, described by the Minister as a book ostensibly aimed at the drink traffic but one which took none of its horrible examples from the civilian population. Instead of that it selected all of them from men who enlisted in the forces. The book went even further than that, continued Senator Pearce, because it picked out frightful instances of what drink did in the home, citing the cases of soldiers' wives and soldiers' daughters, apparently with a view to demonstrating that if a father, son or husband enlisted as a soldier, he became a drunkard, that for him to fight for his country was to imperil not only his moral character but the moral character of his wife, his daughter and his home. Could anyone say, concluded the speaker, that the circulation of such a book among Australian women was not prejudicial to recruiting?[46]

They could, and did. There was a great outcry against this embargo on *The Fiddlers* and on a companion temperance paper called *Defeat*, from the Independent Order of Rechabites in Tasmania and in Adelaide, Presbyterians in Queensland, Baptists in Victoria, Methodists at Charters Towers, Seventh Day Adventists and the Adelaide Synod of the Methodist Church. The Defence Department did not promote healing and settling by mollifying its outraged critics; instead it chose to raid premises of the Rechabites in Tasmania and seize copies of the offending works. This was too much for the Congregational Union of Western Australia which raised the matter to a lofty height beyond the understanding of some when it said, harking back to another mighty struggle, that as the spiritual heirs of Oliver Cromwell, the Union resented the action of the Hughes government.[47]

Not everyone agreed that the A.I.F. should be a teetotal army and when the Women's Christian Temperance Union sent a letter to Lloyd George asking him to stop the issue of rum to the Australian Diggers in the trenches, a newspaper correspondent signing himself 'Christian' defended rum with some vigour, pointing out that he had recently returned from the Somme after experiencing the worst European winter for forty years:

I can say how indispensable is our little tot of rum. It is absolutely impossible to replace it with anything that would warm the half-frozen bodies of the men. On one occasion our rum issue went astray, and one man, on being told of the fact, remarked, 'My God, sir, I will never last the night out. My little tot of rum is better to me than a blanket.' It is not used as a drink, but as a medicine. The Germans have their issue of brandy, and that of the best quality available.[48]

No matter how carefully and wisely the government censors operated, they were, of course, bound to offend someone with their decisions, given the necessity for censorship. But it was capricious, that was the trouble, and tended not only to annoy quite loyal people and alienate their sympathy from the government's object in recruiting, but also to lead to the suspicion that the censors sometimes exceeded their authority in an excess of zeal. For in-

stance, the Governor of South Australia had occasion to complain
that a telegraphic message from the Secretary of State conferring
the chief justiceship upon His Honour Mr Justice Murray was
unnecessarily detained by the censor.[49]

In other cases the censors attributed to Australia mighty powers
of influencing world opinion: the Brisbane *Daily Standard* thought
fit to produce, on 31 January 1917, an article on Russia and
Constantinople. The opinion of the Crown Solicitor was sought
and he gravely found that under the circumstances of the cases
there was no likelihood of the statements referred to ever coming
to the notice of any foreign power interested, or of carrying any
weight, and that consequently there was no real likelihood of His
Majesty's relations with any foreign power being affected.[50]

Donald Mackinnon, the one man who ought to have known,
spoke vehemently on the subject of censorship at a recruiting
meeting outside the Melbourne Town Hall saying that the newspapers told the Australian people only what they wanted to hear;
that the people were kept in ignorance of what was really happening on the other side of the world; that they were not informed
that meat was two shillings a pound in Britain and that many
people there had not tasted potatoes for two months; that vessels
were being sunk, a point gradually dawning on the Australian
people because their letters to England were not reaching their
destination; that Germany was building 5,000-ton submarines to
challenge the British navy and sink the remaining vessels of the
British merchant marine. How could any decent Australian hang
back from recruiting, Mackinnon wanted to know, when 5,000
girls of tender years were being sent to Constantinople to appease
the lust of the brutal Turks? The Allies were not winning and
Russia was now practically useless.[51]

Even the conservative daily press, which stood four-square behind Hughes's government once he had merged with the Liberals,
spoke out strongly and with marked uneasiness about this aspect
of his government. The Melbourne *Age*, for instance, noted that
the sole justification for the spending of £30,000 a year on military
censorship was that the service prevented news of military importance from reaching the enemy. But what if the system were
used for political purposes? The paper proceeded to lay before its
readers an example of how the government was using its tre-

mendous powers: there was the text of the official invitation from
the imperial government to Hughes to attend the Imperial Conference. This information had reached Australia two days previously and had already been published in Great Britain and issued
to the world at large. Despite this, the Australian censors had
refused to permit local papers to publish the news! 'In as much as
the Australian censor acted deliberately, and in pursuance of
deliberate political instructions, it is now obvious that the censorship system has a dual character and pursues two separate
objectives. It is used in part to prevent news of military importance
reaching the enemy; and it is used in part to prevent news of
political importance from reaching the Australian people.' The
Argus published a similar though shorter and less direct complaint.[52]

Censorship of letters and other communications led to the
identification of those termed 'suspicious persons', and early in
1917 Hughes asked the Premiers to release their commissioners of
police to attend a Melbourne conference which would include the
director of the Commonwealth section of the counter-espionage
bureau. Business to be done would include counter-espionage
matters and the centralization of information; the chief duty of
this bureau would be to watch suspected persons. In Queensland
the Labor Premier, T. J. Ryan, agreed to permit his police commissioner to go down to Melbourne but wanted to know what was
going on in the bureau. A month later Hughes agreed to inform
Ryan of the bureau's proceedings and the Prime Minister took the
occasion to speak to Ryan of the necessity for hearty co-operation
with the State governments in the work of detecting and countering
hostile enemy agents.[53]

Not only the insidious work of shadowy foreign agents was
suspected of hampering recruiting. Clearer to some was the influence of economic inflation. J. H. Catts, formerly secretary of the
New South Wales Recruiting Committee, argued this, saying that
the minimum rate of six shillings a day paid to private soldiers
might have been all right in 1914 but that in 1917, largely due to
the neglect of the regulation of prices, the cost of living had
increased 33 per cent, which meant that soldiers should be getting
8s 6d a day. Thus it was impossible for men of the A.I.F. to maintain their dependents, Catts said, and he alleged that men were

being forced out of jobs to join up because of the government's inaction in the matter.[54] J. E. Fenton, M.P. for Maribyrnong, drew disgusted attention in the House of Representatives to a letter in the press which appealed for warm clothes for soldiers' children, stressed the damage being done to the recruiting movement, and said that men were being dismissed by government employers, notices being put up and censuses taken, to find out what men were eligible for the front line. This was all evidence that economic conscription was being applied.[55]

During the year an appeal to sportsmen met with very fair success and a Rifleman's Thousand was well filled, but an attempt to organize a battalion of railwaymen was a failure and had to be abandoned.[56] A sportsmen's committee organized in New South Wales was an addition to the official recruitment agencies but when it visited Lithgow in August 1917, the town was unsettled because of industrial trouble, and business people were totally opposed to identifying themselves with any meeting or taking part in any rally.[57]

This 'industrial trouble' was a very widespread strike which began in 1917 with railwaymen downing tools because they objected to a fresh system of time-cards which they asserted would lead to speeding up and other undesirable things.[58] It is impossible to say precisely what effect the great strike of 1917 had on recruiting; it might have been that men out on strike finally joined the army but it is certain that the bitterness of the strike further isolated the industrial wing of the Labor Party and further polarized Australians into 'industrialists' or Labor, and the 'Win-the-War' Party, as Hughes's followers were called, or Nationalists.

The political battles were deplorable in a situation where the government was trying to get every possible man to enlist. Special police had to be sworn in at Melbourne to preserve law and order in the streets when Adela Pankhurst was arrested (not for the first time) on charges of having encouraged damage to property on the occasion of a torchlight socialist demonstration at the Yarra Bank. The charge was quashed, but a day later on 24 September 1917 there was mob violence at Richmond in Melbourne when 2,000 persons singing socialist songs and led by women carrying red flags were on the march. Windows were smashed by the more lawless element. Police captured some flags which bore the words 'Arrest

the Profiteers' and 'Why Starve when Mice and Rats Grow Fat?'
(a reference to the mice plague among the wheat stockpiles in such
places as the Mallee where wheat bought by Britain was awaiting
shipment). This riot was said to have had its origin on the Yarra
Bank where a Mrs Wallace addressed the crowd and sought to
find out why the special constables had not enlisted in the A.I.F.
In the business section of Richmond, windows were broken in
premises conducted by W. H. Angliss, the Richmond Furnishing
Company, Maples and Tyes.

The same day Beatrice Keon and Doris Donnison were fined
£3 each for offensive behaviour during a riot in the city. Police
evidence showed that the defendants had headed a crowd of 2,000
people trying forcibly to enter Parliament House. Both ladies had
been hooting and shouting, said the police, and one was carrying a
red flag which measured six feet by three feet.[59]

Labour militants opposed the war for all kinds of reasons. One
Timothy McCristal, for instance, the president of the Sydney
branch of the Wharf Labourers' Union, was arrested at the end
of August 1917 on a charge of sedition which arose from remarks
he was said to have made in the Domain. These were that kings,
governors, parliamentarians and bosses were parasites fattening on
the workers, and must be destroyed. McCristal, said to be a returned soldier, was also alleged to have informed the public that
he had not gone to the other side of the world for love of the King,
but to get the necessary knowledge to be able to stand side by side
with his fellow unionists in the great fight against the parasites of
whom he had just spoken.[60]

Comments such as those made by McCristal were also to be
found in the *Worker*, edited in Sydney by the very able H. E. Boote
who, in June 1917, started publishing a series of devastating
articles defending Donald Grant, gaoled for activities connected
with the I.W.W. Boote came to the conclusion that Grant and
several others who had been gaoled for lengthy periods were
victims of a police frame-up. They were, and most were ultimately
released, but not before the government of New South Wales
sought the opinion of the Crown Solicitor with a view to silencing
Boote and his cry for justice. The Crown Solicitor commented on
the issue of the *Worker* of 28 June 1917 that there was no way of
bringing Boote to trial; he went on to assert that Boote's words

were 'in the main the fanatical outpourings of the ill-balanced journalists who cater for certain of the lower classes; the average decent man does not read them.'[61]

The industrial troubles of 1917 disturbed the federal government, of course, and in August drew from Hughes a communication to Pearce concerning a report of a meeting of wharf labourers in Melbourne where people had been persuaded not to offer their services, and employees of the Colonial Sugar Refineries dissuaded from loading sugar. Hughes also drew attention to the sale in Sydney of the I.W.W. periodical *Direct Action* in the face of government prohibition, and instructed that the office of the paper be raided and the offending issue, with the printing plant, be seized.[62]

The I.W.W. was significant here because the attacks on it excited and increased suspicion in the industrial and labour movement concerning government methods against the workers. Basically, the ideas of the I.W.W. did not have the sympathy of labour men but, as did H. E. Boote, they became sympathetic because of the injustice handed out by the police and agents of the government. Ultimately the strikes of 1917 were defeated by the governments of the States and the Commonwealth using volunteer labour and taking over many forms of transport. Censorship was used to play down some aspects of the strike and Hughes even cabled to New Zealand suggesting suppression by censorship of references to the strikes in Australia. The Prime Minister noted that the *Manuka* was shortly due in New Zealand from Australia and expressed the fear that on her arrival the crew, passengers and newspaper files on board would give wide and undesirable publicity to the Australian situation and tend either to spread the trouble or seriously hamper New Zealand and Australian vessels. The New Zealand government refused to comply with Hughes's ideas, however, on the ground that this would cause strong resentment in the Dominion; Hughes was told that he would need to show more reasons than he had so far given if censorship was to cover Australia's troubles.[63]

Though the Prime Minister did not prevent news of the industrial troubles and disruption of the war effort in Australia from reaching New Zealand, firm steps had been taken in the Commonwealth to minimize the strikes, because in August instructions were issued to all censors to prevent the transmission of news concerning starvation or unemployment in Australia. By the same means instructions were given that statements of 'grievances' of returned men were to be suppressed.[64]

In the period beginning in January 1917 there was a very significant increase in the number of eighteen- and nineteen-year-olds who enlisted in the A.I.F.,[65] and this was noticed by the public. The Director-General commented that the enlistment of men who had previously been unable to get their parents' consent had undoubtedly helped to raise the number of recruits, but it was incorrect to say that this was solely due to 'baby boys'. He cited the week ended 4 May. In New South Wales 498 men had enlisted of whom 329 were single. The figures, broken down into age-groups, were eighteen to twenty-five, 212; twenty-five to thirty-five, 171; thirty-five to forty-five, 47. This did not satisfy Frank Brennan, federal Labor M.P. for Batman in Victoria, who asked a parliamentary question on the matter: was it a fact, as reported in the press, that Captain Burkett, a military officer, stated that the improved position as to enlistment arose from the enlistment of 'baby boys'? This was not allowed to pass before Labor members had got some political value from it; W. G. Higgs, Labor member for Capricornia, told the House that before the censors started to suppress the publication of letters from the front, he had read the statement of one correspondent that what pained him most was to hear wounded boys of eighteen crying for their mothers.[66]

One soldier turned out to be fourteen; he had the consent of his parents, who said he was eighteen, but the father had second thoughts and sought the lad's discharge. Later on a boy of ten offered his services.[67] This showed a gratifying sense of the urgency of the situation, but some people took a different view of permitting youths to go to the front, one lady demanding angrily of the Minister for Defence, 'Are they murderers? Are parents murderers for allowing them to go and get killed?'[68] Other people were not so concerned, the Australian Labour Federation in Perth sending to the Prime Minister's Department a copy of a letter from the Perth town clerk to employees on the City Council which was a notice (a) to submit for examination for the A.I.F., (b) produce a rejection certificate, (c) leave the service.[69]

It was all very well for some people to condemn the government, but if the quota was to be reached and kept up, what means other than conscription might be used that had not been tried already and found wanting? That was the question to which there remained hardly a feasible answer. There was a plan in September 1917 to impose a tax of £10 on single men not in the forces, and the House was told by Sir John Forrest that the government had two objects in imposing such a measure. One was that it would stimulate recruiting, not by people fearing to pay the impost on their bachelorhood, but by bringing to the stay-at-homes a powerful realization of their duty to their country and to themselves. The other reason was to provide funds towards the repatriation of soldiers. J. W. Leckie, M.P., supported this scheme, observing that the tax would be the easiest one in the world to avoid. All you had to do was to enlist. He went on to make the interesting comment that many farmers' sons received no wages, which was a bad thing and to be set right: there were cases where the sons were anxious to go to the front, but were threatened by parents that if they enlisted they would receive no benefits then or thereafter; because these youths received no wages, if the parents were so anxious to keep them home slaving away for nothing, they would have to pay the tax.[70]

James Mathews, Labor member for Melbourne Ports, disagreed with the projected £10 tax. Claiming that thousands of men had hurried into marriages to avoid the tax, he accused the government of ulterior motives in connection with the repatriation point: the tax was no more nor less than economic conscription, designed to force men into the ranks, and W. F. Finlayson, Labor member for Brisbane, expressed his disgust that the government could aim to reckon £10 a year as the equivalent of enlistment.[71]

What was to be done? Even the recruiters were breaking down. As W. M. Fleming, the member for Robertson, reported sadly, men who had been reliable when they went to the war had been quite 'ruined' on the Western Front: 'I have been on recruiting platforms with many of them who seem quite sane and normal under ordinary conditions, but who, when given the extra excitement which is engendered at public meetings, go over the edge, and one has to help them away.'[72]

On that Western Front, never out of the thoughts of tens of thousands of Australian parents, the A.I.F. suffered 55,000 casualties in the Third Battle of Ypres in September and October, and in the earlier battles of Messines and Bullecourt. The ravages of the front line in north-west France threatened the existence of the veteran 4th Division. Reports reached Australia that it would be broken up to reinforce the others—the shock troops which were the A.I.F. could only be kept together as a national force if adequate reinforcements came. They were not coming. In August 1916 New Zealand passed a conscription law which it enforced in November; Canada passed it in August 1917 and enforced it in October; the United States conscripted its army right from the start; in Australia, Sir William Irvine continued to urge the adoption of conscription.[73]

On 7 November 1917 W. M. Hughes announced to the Australian people that his government would conduct another conscription referendum. The date for the vote was set down for five days before Christmas.[74]

9

Conscription Again Divides
the Nation

At Bendigo on the night of Monday 12 November 1917, W. M. Hughes delivered one of the great speeches of his career. In asking the Australian people to support his government, he spoke with all the superb skill and conviction of which he was capable. He emphasized that, because of the grave nature of the war, the existing voluntary system of recruitment would have to be supplemented. Reinforcements at the rate of 7,000 men a month were needed; therefore to the extent that the voluntary system had failed to produce that number of soldiers, he now proposed that a ballot should be taken from among the single men alone, between the ages of twenty and forty-four, including divorcés and widowers without children dependent on them.

Certain exceptions were to be made, such as the physically unfit, judges, police magistrates, ministers of religion, people employed in essential industry, conscientious objectors and people whose calling up would involve them in undue hardship.

These proposals were put in one question, 'Are you in favour of the proposal of the Commonwealth government for reinforcing the Australian Imperial Force overseas?' Hughes on several occasions told his audiences that the government would not continue to run the country unless the referendum were answered in the affirmative. Because the word 'conscription' was not used in the question, the question was later condemned as improper because it assumed knowledge of the government's 'proposal' which some electors certainly did not have.[1]

Why did Hughes once again seek the approval of the people

by referendum? Why did he not use his majority in both Houses of Parliament to impose conscription under the War Precautions Act? Was it that he lacked the necessary support in Cabinet? It is hard to know. Certainly the consistent Sir William Irvine wanted a Conscription Bill and an election fought on it and, in a highly significant comment, the Labor Premier of Queensland, T. J. Ryan, commented that Irvine was the only logical candidate in the Nationalist Party in the recent election because he had said that the federal government should stand or fall on the issue of conscription.[2] Both Irvine and Ryan were right; Hughes was in a world of his own. For some reason, the Prime Minister really wanted the formal approval of the Australian people for his proposal. That approval may have been connected with—what? Did he still flirt with the Labor Party? Was this decision a compromise which the hard-line conscriptionists were compelled to adopt because they needed the leadership of Hughes? What real chance had a referendum now that opinion had hardened and war-weariness rendered the situation worse?

Hughes was reported as saying that he spoke as a member of the Imperial War Cabinet which had sent certain information to the Australian Prime Minister, meaning that he spoke with great authority in seeking 7,000 men a month as the maximum number required. W. G. Higgs, lately resigned from the Cabinet because of Hughes's attempts to subject voters in the 1916 referendum to invidious questions, took the opportunity offered to point out that no Imperial War Cabinet existed when Hughes was in England. When, asked Higgs in bitter innocence, had the Prime Minister been made a member of it?[3]

The anti-conscriptionists in this second campaign adopted much the same lines as they had in the first, but the clashes of opinion were now more violent, more emotional, more final. The break-up of the Labor Party aggravated the conscription conflict in the same way as did the sectarian savagery associated with the English armed occupation of Ireland and the record killing matches on the Western Front. Australia had gone into the war with great-heartedness and wide generosity and was now suffering an equal and opposite reaction as the war continued without any sign of victory which the people could accept. Every day meant an increase in the number of killed and wounded and brought home to yet another family the fact that next of kin would never be seen again. Calls for further sacrifice, peril and patriotism were beginning to ask for more from Australia than the Empire had ever deemed necessary from its people.

One obvious aspect of the anti-conscriptionists' campaign was instantly touched upon by the comments of F. G. Tudor, the federal Labor leader: Hughes could not be trusted, he said, because the Prime Minister had said earlier that no one would be sent outside Australia against his will. Could Hughes be depended upon when he said that married men would not be called up? The issue the people had to decide, claimed Tudor, was the same as the issue twelve months previously.[4]

It was a sickening measure of the state of the war that those opposing conscription now touched upon an aspect of soldiering not noticed by people who supported compulsory service. This was exemplified in *The Bucket*, a leaflet put out by those who detested war. It was an extract from an item often reprinted during the campaign by the anti-conscriptionists, either as a very short piece or else in much longer form, in which it appeared as *The Glories of War*, a Socialist Party leaflet dealing with 'the human fuel that feeds the engine of Armageddon'. Here there was a very grisly description of 'the Casualty Station'. It purported to describe the shambles at a dressing station; the longer version in fact was less repulsive than this extract seems to suggest:

The bucket outside contains hands and feet, pieces of jaw, and the rest. Have you seen a butcher after the day's killing? Well, that's how the surgeon appears. Their aprons are saturated with gore. In a field at the back the dead are lying. The first has no face, the next has bled to death. The corpses are pulled about as the slaughterman pulls his dead sheep. Intestines and pieces of lung are in a bucket outside the tent, so that the surgeon may get good practice.

This disgusting pamphlet suggests that strong anti-war feeling was displacing earlier pacifism and that the conscription campaign in 1917 may have been more emotional than the one in 1916. It seems so. In the nightmare world of 1917 it was difficult to detect reality, but the point which appealed to many supporters of conscription was the argument that reinforcements were undoubtedly needed after the huge casualties of the 1917 campaigns in France, that not only was the man in the street not in a position to know the complete truth, but that the lack of reinforcements must surely lead to more and more deaths and the destruction of the A.I.F. Much was made of the 'Will they never come?' plea, epitomized by the imprimatur of the Returned Sailors' and Soldiers' Imperial League in Sydney and Melbourne which was quoted on a poster as an organization which knew the facts:

Our men who have fought at Gallipoli, France and in Palestine, know the desperate straits of their comrades. They know what it is to look with anxious eyes for the reinforcements which mean so much to them. With full knowledge of the position at the front and in Australia, the Returned Sailors' and Soldiers' Imperial League in Melbourne and Sydney have given their undivided support to the efforts of the government to gain reinforcements.

And the reader was told to vote 'Yes'.

One of the anti-conscriptionists' replies to this was to show that not all returned soldiers were prepared to vote 'Yes'. There existed a Returned Soldiers' No-Conscription League of Australia, and the New South Wales branch, in a pamphlet issued under the auspices of the Anti-Conscription League of Australia, 43 Wentworth Avenue, Sydney, opposed a government decision to share with capitalists all profits over 10 per cent, asserting that even in tory England the government exacted at least 60 per cent of excess war profits and that the Australian government should do the same.

Sarcasm was used to drive home the anti-conscriptionists' picture of a war profiteer quite happily sending off other people, but not budging himself. In a poster of this type, W. A. Watt was quoted under the heading of 'The Nobility of Sacrifice' as saying (rather confusingly) that there were numbers of willing people in the community who saw other men more eligible for service and with less responsibility and who desired that they should take their due place with the colours. This was followed by a quotation from Artemus Ward, the American humorist, 'Yes, Sir, we've got a war, and the true patriot has to make sacrifices, you bet. I have already given two cousins to the war, and I stand ready to sacrifice my wife's brother rather than not see the rebellion crushed. And if

worse comes to worse, I'll shed every drop of blood my able-bodied
relations have got to prosecute the war.'

The anti-conscriptionists were also able to turn a poster circulated by their opponents against the conscriptionists by answering
the question, 'How would the Kaiser like you to vote?' with 'How
would Christ like you to vote?' The indomitable labour publicist
H. E. Boote warned against what was termed the unjustifiable
optimism with which many labour people were contemplating
the 1917 vote and its outcome, and he told labour supporters to
stop flattering themselves simply because in 1916 there had been
a 'No' majority of 72,000. That majority, said the publicist, had
been wiped out before the voting by what he described as 'a piece
of treachery so vile that only base-minded creatures could have
been guilty of it'. He alluded to disfranchisement of 'tens of
thousands' of people because of the speed with which electoral
rolls had been closed. And the reason? The government knew that
large numbers of workers, especially those with nomadic occupations, had lost their registration as a result of unemployment; that
fact, together with the changing of polling day from a Saturday
to a Thursday would lead to an enormous loss of labour votes.
The writer concluded grimly that another majority would have to
be won by eloquence and force of argument.

The most important of the arguments brought forward concerned the actual numbers of men needed for reinforcements.
What seemed conclusive details were cited on a poster headed,
'Has the voluntary system failed?' Here it was affirmed by a series
of figures that whereas 3,503 men a month were being put out of
action, enlistments for the period of about the preceding twelve
months were 4,637 a month, leading to the conclusion that voluntary enlistments exceeded the casualties by 1,134 men a month.
This, claimed the poster, was a powerful reason to vote 'No' and
not be misled by Australia's traducers.[5]

Certainly Hughes's figure of 7,000 recruits a month was difficult
to understand. In August 1917 Foster, the Australian Chief of the
General Staff, estimated from the rate of casualties that from
6,340 to 7,340 men a month were needed for the A.I.F. But
General Birdwood put the figure at 5,500, the same as an estimate
made by the Army Council. On 3 November the Minister for

Defence, Senator Pearce, accepted this figure and, allowing for 10 per cent wastage in Australia, put it up to 6,000.[6]

The problem of making an estimate was not an easy one, of course, and Hughes may be too readily criticized when his experts had shown they could not agree. Presumably he wanted to be on the safe side, but the fact was that no one from Field-Marshal Haig downwards knew what casualties might be incurred in the conflict at any given time, and nor could anyone forecast deaths from disease.

Those who favoured conscription invoked the ideals of the Empire and the high-minded motives for which the Empire had gone to war. In 'Reasons why true Australians must vote "Yes" on 20 December 1917', the conscriptionists implied chicken-heartedness and lack of character and manliness to those who ran away when the going got tough. Those reasons included recognition that Australia was in deadly peril, that the fate of the Empire hung in the balance, and that unless people pulled themselves together for the mightiest effort in history, the war might drag on into 1920 and beyond. Australia must vote 'Yes', it was argued, because the rest of civilization looked in hope to the Empire and to Mother England as she played the role of consoler, comforter and sustainer of the weak; Australia must vote in favour of the government's proposals because by supporting members of the A.I.F. at the front their risks would be halved and their rests doubled; because Australia's honour was involved in keeping the Commonwealth's five divisions at the front; because the Nationalist government was honour-bound to supply reinforcements; because no man could discharge his obligations to the men at the front simply by buying a button and because no woman could simply do her duty by knitting socks. They should vote 'Yes' because an affirmative vote would show how deeply the loyal Australians resented the audacious attempts being made to do the enemy a service by sowing the seeds of sedition, conspiracy and rebellion in Australia, and because the time had passed for the fatuous belief that it would all somehow come right in the long run.

Not all the cases for and against were written in prose. There was produced a publication called *Labour's Volunteer Army Song Book*. The 3rd edition included a piece entitled 'The Anti-Conscriptionist' which had such lines as 'Are you fooled and muddled by the press?/ By the Age and Argus and Hughes? . . .' and 'Kaiser Hughes I'll tell—/ "I'll see you rot in hell/ Before you make a willing slave of me".'

On the other hand, the appeal to vote 'No' against compulsory recruitment could be framed just as crudely in cartoon: one such showed a fat capitalist turning a screw labelled 'profit' on a woman and her little baby as he says to the soldier standing near by, 'You go back to the front, I'll look after your women and children.' This pamphlet advertised a meeting on the Yarra Bank to oppose the 'Prussianizing' of Australia.

Not only 'Labour' and 'Capital' stereotypes appeared in the campaign of 1917. The sectarian animosity and suspicion which had been a feature of the recent general election also emerged, accompanied by their inveterate associates, rumour and paranoia; in Melbourne, for instance, rumours had been circulated among Catholics that the Christian Brothers would have to go to war if the referendum were carried.[7] With his customary directness, Dr Mannix expressed his views[8] with something approaching the relish of a man whose people had been embattled for centuries. Daniel Mannix in some curious way was home at last as with ridicule and invective he attacked the government's arguments, turned his withering words on Hughes, and made himself the centre of anti-conscriptionist feeling to the extent of putting into words and polarizing the issues of the referendum.

For the government, the Prime Minister travelled up and down the country putting the case for a 'Yes' vote with all the energy and conviction of a man who is leader of his country at a time of war never before known or imagined. Hughes's nerves were laid bare, those of Dr Mannix were not and did not have to be, though the Broken Hill Methodist Synod wanted the Commonwealth power which made the I.W.W. illegal invoked also to prevent further disloyal utterances from Mannix.[9] It was not so much that Mannix chose to attack Hughes but that Hughes, whether for genuine or propagandist purposes, elevated Mannix to the role of arch-villain. Hughes turned his personal attacks on to Mannix, the I.W.W. and socialist riff-raff, and therefore Mannix became an outstanding figure not only because of his own exertions but also because the press and the Prime Minister and others chose him as the focus for their attacks, a different situation from the first campaign.

As the pamphlets rained down[10] and the men to whom W. M. Hughes had once been 'Billy' recalled how the little man had torn apart the political party he had helped to build, there occurred an application of Commonwealth censorship to the proceedings of a State Parliament, thereby revealing either the crude authoritarianism of the government or the critical nature of the war, or both. On 19 November 1917 T. J. Ryan spoke to a public meeting in Brisbane; the Premier of Queensland expressed opposition to the Commonwealth's plans for conscription, and J. J. Stable, censor of the 1st (Queensland) Military District, stopped publication of part of Ryan's speech in Queensland newspapers. On 20 November the Prime Minister's Department sent to leading dailies a circular setting out the rules to be observed in censoring material connected with the referendum. The next day, 21 November, Ryan lodged a complaint with the Prime Minister protesting against the censor's actions in mutilating his remarks. On 22 November the Prime Minister's Department in Melbourne heard that there was a motion in the Queensland Parliament to discuss censorship, and it was asked whether anything could be done to prevent the distribution of Hansard, because Ryan was repeating the censored material within the precincts of the Queensland Lower House, in the belief that the censor would hesitate to cut a record of the proceedings of a lawfully and democratically elected Parliament.

The Defence Department said that no instructions had been issued to censor Ryan's observations, and asked to see examples of what had been excised. In the Queensland *Parliamentary Debates* (no. 37, of 22 November 1917) appeared the statements which had offended Stable the censor. They were printed in thick black type, and it was further learnt that Ryan, so it was said, had issued instructions for 10,000 copies of his speech to be reprinted in the form of pamphlets so that they might be distributed to the public.

The situation was becoming interesting. Stable on 24 November served a notice on the Queensland Government Printer ordering him to submit the report of the debate in the Legislative Assembly before publication. The printer did not do so.

Two days later there arrived on the scene none other than the

Prime Minister. He told the censor to seize all copies of no. 37 and the projected pamphlet. This was done, whereupon Ryan, in the *Queensland Government Gazette*, informed the electorate that their *Parliamentary Debates* had been denied transmission through the post by the Commonwealth government.

Ryan and Hughes then met, and after a time Ryan observed that he supposed Hughes would have martial law invoked next time. Hughes's reaction was to draw up, in his role of Attorney-General, a warrant of doubtful legality to send Stable, in the company of government officials, to the printing office. They could not get in and, in a moment fraught with ridiculous drama, the censor was about to jump down from the fence into the court-yard of the printery and into the arms of a body of State police, when the Government Printer arrived on the scene and admitted Stable. He reported that no copies of *Parliamentary Debates* no. 37 were on the premises.

So ended one chapter of a transaction which made Hughes appear to some to be acting like a thwarted dictator and militarist. The next began when Ryan issued a writ against the Common-wealth to test the legality of the federal government's actions. The Commonwealth then summonsed Ryan, but the magistrate dis-missed the case. Ryan's action against the Commonwealth was settled out of court, after an application in March 1918 to the High Court to commit William Morris Hughes to gaol for con-tempt of court. The matter was stood over till 1 April. The Chief Justice: 'I would suggest adjournment to the Greek kalends or Day of Judgement.' To the accompaniment of this rich wit the case of Ryan versus Hughes, with all its grave constitutional implications, was judicially laid to rest.[11]

At what point in this business the over-mighty subject Ryan might have started to laugh is uncertain; perhaps he did not, and certainly the Prime Minister gave no sign of being amused. Hughes had even less reason to feel tickled two days later when, on 29 November 1917 at 2.59 p.m., he arrived in Warwick, on the Darling Downs, on a train which also bore a party of his supporters. He left the train and was escorted to an adjacent platform so that he might address a crowd on the issues involved in the current referendum. What happened during the next thirteen minutes is confused and the subject of various descriptions and distortions.

At its most dramatic it was alleged that among the threatening crowd awaiting the Prime Minister were men armed with hammers and spanners, that when eggs were thrown at the Prime Minister of Australia he, though fearing for his life at the hands of a wild mob, leapt courageously into the brawl and came out of it with bleeding knuckles when the local police refused to arrest his assailant.

The whole incident was over in minutes, according to an extensive enquiry made by the Queensland police. Their account of an episode which received headlines all over the nation was that when Hughes went to speak, someone undoubtedly threw an egg towards him; it missed the Prime Minister, after which another was thrown which either splashed on to Hughes or struck his back or hat; a sergeant of police in plain clothes caught hold of him to look after him but it appeared likely that Hughes, in an excited state, thought the man in plain clothes was a civilian perhaps bent on mischief. A police-constable then singled out one of two brothers named Brosnan, who had evidently hurled the offending missile, drew him away and warned him. Brosnan's brother, however, then made his appearance in front of the Prime Minister as he returned to his carriage. The police enquiry raised the point that Hughes may have thought that the second Brosnan was the egg-thrower, and asked angrily why he had not been arrested. There was a scuffle. The sergeant of police refused to arrest the man. Hughes spoke to the crowd in an emotional way about Sinn Feiners, and at 3.12 p.m. the train pulled out of Warwick station.

In his report on all this, the Chief Inspector of Police in Queensland concluded that the men with hammers and spanners were well-known and reputable railway employees on duty, that it was a pity that the plain-clothes man (Sergeant Kenny) had not been in uniform when he caught hold of Hughes, that the egg which had struck the Prime Minister had probably been thrown by Barty Brosnan, and that Police Constable Tong had been remiss in not arresting Patrick Brosnan. The Inspector added that the blood alleged to have been seen on the Prime Minister's hand could not be accounted for by those present. The blood had been mentioned in one statement, that of C. E. McDougall, a member of the National Political Council. The Inspector came to the conclusion that the Prime Minister was undoubtedly excited but that the only blows struck were aimed at Barty Brosnan and that there was no evidence that he did anything to provoke the men who set upon him.[12]

As one result of this fuss, Ryan refused to offer State help to the Commonwealth officer who was told to investigate the incident, and Hughes, it was said, created the Commonwealth police force. Perhaps he did not really; a joke of the time had it that the Commonwealth had one policeman, but if it did the *Commonwealth Year Book* for 1919 and 1920 omitted him from mention. Others did not disregard him: early in December a telegram from Hughes to the Victorian Premier denied press reports that the federal government intended to appoint special Commonwealth police in both loyal and disloyal States of Australia. This was absolutely incorrect, said Hughes, because the government intended to appoint special police in the State which was disloyal and not in the loyal States. Melbourne was to be the centre of such a force who would move about the Commonwealth irrespective of State boundaries.

Holman in New South Wales had his doubts about Hughes's motives, and in a circular letter sent to all States a week before Christmas 1917 he speculated that the move might be a campaigning one under the stress of the referendum, but that Commonwealth-State relations should not be the sport of political vicissitudes. Holman emphasized a subject he always had in mind: the prospect of the central authority gaining power at the expense of the States. He concluded that there was no justification for the establishment of a Commonwealth police, either at Warwick or anywhere else.[13]

The political atmosphere was neurotic. The Prime Minister's Department heard from a firm of Adelaide solicitors who brought under notice the actions of a German who had left his employer because the employer stated his intention of voting 'Yes'. The German was said to be spreading rumours that he had been dismissed because he was opposed to conscription. The Ship-Building Trades Federation of Victoria, on the other hand, sought the prosecution by the Commonwealth of the authors of a pamphlet entitled *The Anti's Creed*. This was authorized by the Reinforcements Referendum Council and said that those who voted 'No' believed that it was right to sacrifice men at the front, right that the

Lusitania was sunk, that the murder of women and baby-killing were good, that treachery was a virtue, that Nurse Cavell had got her deserts, and that Australia should be handed over to Germany.

The Prime Minister's Department was also sent a copy of a pamphlet entitled *Leg Irons for Australian Soldiers*. This evocation of Australia's origins was 'reprinted from the *Sydney Morning Herald* 22 March 1917', and read: 'Six men had been sent into the desert in Egypt with three days supply of water to build a railway. They finished the water in a day and a half, and when they could not get water for the balance of the three days they ceased work. They were court-martialled and sentenced to terms ranging from two to five years. After being landed in Long Bay gaol, Sydney, the soldiers were removed to Goulburn gaol, shackled by a blacksmith.' If this happened to volunteers, demanded the poster, what would happen to conscripts? It wanted everybody to vote 'No' on 20 December.[14]

The No-Conscription Campaign Committee also wanted people to vote 'No', and produced among other leaflets one entitled *The Death Ballot*, a cartoon by Claude Marquet. It showed Hughes seated on a high stool next to a filing cabinet of war census cards. He writes while Death, equipped with a skull for a head and grasping a scythe, pulls cards out of a hat. On the reverse of the leaflet was another cartoon of a terrified woman gazing at a piece of paper with 'Yes' and 'No' on it. In the background is a vision of her baby in a cradle; next to her Death, with dice cup and scythe, tempts her now-grown boy. Four stanzas of verse conclude:

Mothers we wait your answer—you of the travail-breed;
You who suffer in silence, you have paid indeed!
The life that you brought to being—the life that was half your own
How will you treat it?—answer before the dice are thrown!

There had been confusion in 1916 about whether the hotels were to be open or shut on polling day, and in what manner and at what time of day or night the results were to be posted. Now Hughes, two weeks before the people voted, informed States that they were to have control over how and when the results of the referendum were to be revealed. But nothing was said about the hotel hours on that Thursday until the day immediately before the vote was taken, when the Prime Minister invoked the War Precautions Act and ruled that no liquor was to be sold on polling day, that all hotels were to be closed all day, and that no referendum figures were to be published or announced.[15] This latter direction arrived by telegram but too late in Queensland to be acted upon; Ryan was able nevertheless to reassure Hughes that Queensland, on its own, had shut the hotels anyway, in a timely fashion, and that nothing of note had happened during a quiet polling day.[16]

Not all Australian adults were permitted to vote freely; a letter from a man in Ruby Vale, Queensland, who said he was of Dutch descent, was sent to Ryan for comment. This man complained that his vote had been enclosed in a special envelope and that the votes of his married sister and many other people besides had been singled out in the same way by the scrutineer. He forwarded the form he had been given. It read:

In connection with the Referendum held on 20 December 1917, the Ballot-paper issued to you was endorsed 'Regulation 25' and placed in the prescribed envelope (which was fastened) and has been forwarded to me in such (fastened) envelope for the purpose of scrutiny. In order that I may be in a position to satisfy myself as to whether your Ballot-paper is to be accepted for further scrutiny, or rejected, I hereby require you to furnish information so as to reach me before 22 January 1918 as to whether or not (a) you are a naturalized British subject who was born in an enemy country within the meaning of the War Precautions (Military Service Referendum) Regulations 1917; and (b) your father was born in an enemy country within the meaning of the aforesaid regulations. If you fail to furnish me with information as aforesaid on or before the said date, the Ballot-paper may be rejected.

(Signed) Divisional Returning Officer.

The Queensland Chief Secretary replied that the case was one of many similar injustices perpetrated during the referendum.[17]

Other people expressed sympathy with the government and recognized the supreme importance of getting more men to the front. One, for instance, informed on a man whose seven sons had not enlisted; a few days before the referendum a resident of Prahran also recognized the plight of the country and suggested it send off physically fit men who were serving terms in gaol, and this

The First A.I.F.

TABLE 4

Voting in Conscription Referendum 1917
(inclusive of soldiers' votes)

| | | | Soldiers' votes | |
State	Yes	No	Yes	No
N.S.W.	341,256	487,774	36,138	35,316
Vic.	329,772	332,490	29,576	25,778
Qld	132,771	168,875	13,866	12,924
S.A.	86,663	106,364	9,701	8,087
W.A.	84,116	46,522	11,006	8,374
Tas.	38,881	38,502	3,502	3,431
Federal	1,700	1,220	—	—
Total	1,015,159	1,181,747	103,789	93,910

SOURCES: *P.P.* (Cwlth), 1917-19, vol. 4, p. 1469; *Official History*, vol. 11, pp. 427-8.

idea was repeated by another correspondent, an archdeacon, who wanted the formation of a draft of men from Bathurst Gaol.[18]

If such correspondents feared that the referendum might not be approved, they were correct. The 'No' vote increased and Victoria turned 'No', but the margin of defeat for the government was still very slight (see Table 4).

The Prime Minister of course was disappointed but he was not joined by the secretary of the Anti-Conscription League, Innisfail, who wrote to offer his hearty congratulations to T. J. Ryan. Flushed with victory, he suggested that the Queensland Premier should proclaim 20 December an annual 'Liberty Day' holiday, and prayed that T. J. Ryan live long to right all wrong.[19] From far away in Caulfield, Melbourne, a man living in Kambrook Road asked Ryan if he could please have a copy of the famous confiscated Hansard, now out of print. He urged Ryan to give Hughes another knock-out blow, and drew the Premier's attention to what was going on in the south of the continent where 'the Press and parasites of Victoria are trying to reinstate Hughes'.[20] The no-conscription campaign headquarters at 321 Pitt Street, Sydney, decided to arrange the publication of a souvenir volume to commemorate their victory.[21]

The Prime Minister had not been knocked out, but whatever remained of a whole-hearted common desire to go forward together to win the war certainly had. Though he had repeatedly said that his government would decline to take responsibility for the conduct of public affairs unless the referendum were passed, on 3 January 1918 a meeting of the parliamentary Nationalists expressed confidence in Hughes. Shortly afterwards Hughes side-stepped the earlier undertaking with its implication of going to the country by saying that Labor could not be trusted with the government of the Commonwealth. The Governor-General then interviewed a number of apparently prospective prime ministers but the upshot of this was that the same ministry as before was reinstated under the name of the second Nationalist government. When Tudor in the House of Representatives moved a vote of no confidence on the ground that Hughes had pledged not to govern unless the conscription referendum were approved, the Prime Minister answered that he had fulfilled his pledge by handing in his resignation to the Governor-General, and said that what he had really meant by his promise was a choice between him and Tudor.[22] And that was that.

10

The Final Year of the War

Hughes was a devious man, but his deviousness could not lead to the raising of 7,000 men a month to reinforce and maintain the A.I.F. Mackinnon, the Director-General of Recruiting, had an impossible task. In New South Wales the Recruiting Committee wanted more definite knowledge of how many reinforcements were needed, and demanded that the pay for dependents be increased; on 14 February 1918 only twenty-eight men were enlisted for the whole of the State of Victoria, and a conference of various metropolitan recruiting committees in Melbourne produced only the usual pious platitudes and hopes.[1]

Various reasons continued to be offered to explain why there was no sudden increase in the numbers of men coming forward, and some people asked whether earlier standards of fitness had not perhaps been too high, thus leading to a greater current demand for men than should have been necessary. He was appalled, said the Director-General of Recruiting, when he heard that no less than 27,450 men had been rejected in Victoria during the preceding two and a half years. Surely there was something radically wrong with a system which rejected 50 per cent of the volunteers who offered? He had helped some of the young rejected to go to England, pursued Mackinnon, and they had there been received with open arms. Indeed, some of them had been fighting for two years and he had not heard anything about them coming back as physical rejects.[2]

In other words, there was a tendency to blame someone for the fact that not enough recruits could be found, and who else to blame but the Defence Department?

This blame took a number of forms. In one case, Senator Mc-
Dougall reported that inadequate family allowances had in New
South Wales alone led to 1,600 families of soldiers being in need
of food and clothes;[3] and other individuals engaged in or interested
in recruiting criticized the Minister for Defence for announcing
that the future policy of his Department would be to send enlisted
men out of Australia as soon as ships were ready for them. This
sort of thing, it was said, would prejudice recruiting because men
trusted the authorities to see that they were properly trained before
being sent into the firing line. Some took the view that under the
new policy the men would be shipped away before the unfit could
be divided from their stronger comrades. The result would be loss
of efficiency and financial loss to the Commonwealth.[4]

One of the most interesting ways in which recruits were sought
in 1918 was particularly divisive. The idea was for a newspaper
to examine a district and then comment on whether or not it had
done its bit. Bendigo was selected for this treatment, the 'Special
Correspondent' of the *Argus* reporting that though 3,150 soldiers
had been provided by Bendigo electorate, there were still 6,500
eligibles. Ballarat, her rival, was well ahead, went on the report,
which then did a breakdown by districts and proceeded to mention
many families with numbers of sons away at the front. In Huntly
shire the names of Mew, Holmberg, Anderson, Burgoyne and
Youla were praised but three other families criticized because they
had not provided one recruit. Did all these families meet on equal
terms at Huntly social gatherings, asked the correspondent? A
fortnight later the Echuca area was looked into along the same
lines, and veiled complaints made about the apparent lack of
patriotism of certain families.[5]

Various complaints were also made about the treatment of
members of the A.I.F. who were under age, namely, that when
their true age was discovered they were packed off back home to
Australia, even when they had been in the firing line. This discouraged recruiting, claimed the Director-General, as did the
return of men who had undergone operations for hernias and
similar relatively minor physical defects. He cited cases of youths
who had fought for lengthy periods of time and who were brought
home and discharged but were refused their deferred pay and
discharged soldier's badge. Mackinnon complained that the

N

despatch of large numbers of these lads created the impression that recruits were not wanted. Some of these under-age soldiers had been found out by the last referendum, and one was taken out of the front line and compelled to scrub floors in a base hospital in France. His parents had been told all this in an indignant letter, said Mackinnon, and he drew attention to a total of more than 20,000 men who had returned to Australia in the third and fourth quarters of 1917.

These were serious accusations and were answered by the Adjutant-General, Major-General V. C. M. Sellheim. He replied that under-age soldiers were not refused returned soldiers' badges unless they had been sent back home for misconduct. He went on to say that the Defence Department did not ask for the return of soldiers who were over eighteen, but confined its attention to those under eighteen, who were of no use for fighting purposes till they reached the age of nineteen years. Sellheim added sharply that Mackinnon should urge his recruiting officials to realize that the recruitment of under-age soldiers led to waste of public funds. What usually happened in these cases, he went on, was that the soldier or his relatives remained quiet until he was about to go to the front, and then protested. It also happened that the youth paraded before his commanding officer and demanded to be returned or kept out of the firing line because he was under age. If it were discovered that the offender was under eighteen, his return to Australia was ordered for discharge; if over eighteen he was usually kept in England till he was nineteen. The whole matter, concluded the Adjutant-General, was a gross waste of public money and the individuals concerned deserved severe treatment, not sympathy. With regard to Mackinnon's complaint about men who had had operations, the Director-General of Medical Services reported that the doctors knew what they were doing.[6]

The fact was that the recruiters could not have it both ways; if they let through the under-aged, or a doctor disregarded a minor physical defect of recruits, then the numbers enlisted were increased but also more men were sent back because conditions on the Western Front were such that trench life, which varied from the uncomfortable to the nightmarish, sometimes forced the fittest men out of action, let alone someone who was already not up to the mark. In April 1918 Senator Pearce admitted in the Senate

that 10,000 members of the A.I.F. had been returned from England to Australia as unfit for active service.[7] (Whether this included
wounded men is not clear.)

Some such ex-soldiers were reported to be begging in the streets
of Newcastle. Such a sight certainly did not say much for the way
returned men were treated, which in turn was held to be a powerful
deterrent to recruiting. Blame was again laid at the door of the
Defence Department. An investigation was ordered into the case
of the begging soldiers and revealed that one of them, late 13th
Battalion, had been discharged medically unfit after 347 days'
service of which 291 had been served abroad. He had been sent
home suffering from chronic rheumatism and had never been in
the firing line. He had no pension because he had made a false
attestation concerning his rheumatism. He played an organ to
support himself and had displayed on the instrument a notice
which read, 'Kindly assist A Returned Soldier. Unable to work.
Receiving no Pension.' The second man who had been reported
as soliciting alms had joined the army in England, it was disclosed,
and had been discharged as 'unlikely to become an efficient soldier'.
After the police made their enquiries, both returned soldiers
disappeared.[8]

War-weary as it was, disillusioned and nervy, Australia thought
that the inevitable relatively minor matters which followed a war
in which hundreds of thousands of its men were involved were
bound to have a disastrous effect on recruiting: a correspondent
from Corryong advised that returned soldiers could be heard
complaining about the food and conditions in France: such talk
could only militate against recruiting.[9] Indeed it might, though
whether in mid-1918 such stories really had any effect is another
matter.

As the year dragged on and the supply of men levelled out at
around 2,500 a month, there continued the recriminations brought
about by the conscription campaigns and their political aftermath.
Though less virulent than in 1917, the forces of bitterness were not
wholly spent by war-weariness: in the House, a member commented sourly that if recruiting were a failure, then the blame lay
at the door of those men who had angered the people, divided
families against themselves, and in every way thwarted the voluntary system.[10]

Anger, disgust and disillusion characterized some statements by the Labor M.P. Frank Brennan at the end of January. He was reported in the *Age* on 29 January 1918, and a printer felt it his duty to write a memorandum to the Defence Department drawing attention to Brennan's outcries, and asking that enquiries be made so that the charge could be refuted or confirmed, because such comments by prominent men ruined recruiting.

The extract concerned was: 'Mr. Brennan averred that we were now fighting against old men, women and infants-in-arms in the heart of Germany. A voice: What about the Lusitania? Mr. Brennan replied that the Lusitania was on a par with the recent reported callous shooting of men in Ceylon by British officers.'

Lieutenant-Colonel J. G. Legge, the Chief of the General Staff, minuted that Brennan was probably referring to some natives who were shot during riots in Ceylon. Pearce then asked for the *Age* reporter's notes to be obtained and referred the matter to the Crown Solicitor for advice. The reporter's notes were:

Brennan (referring to war jingoes): The inflexible determination of these patriots to carry the war to a finish is very cheap indeed— the determination of full stomachs and full purses. But the war is being carried out by the soldiers and by the women and children of every one of the belligerent countries. Let us starve them into submission! says the patriot with his *inflexible determination*. And so, with inflexible determination ladies and gentlemen, we are *fighting* against the old men, the women and the little infants-in-arms in the heart of Germany. A voice: What about the Lusitania? Brennan (angrily): That is about on a par, my friend, with the reported callous shooting of men by British officers in Ceylon. It was all part of the rotten system of war.

(The reporter noted that the italicized words were used ironically rather than literally.)

The Crown Solicitor found that the extract quoted was likely to prejudice recruiting, but Pearce decided not to press charges. He thought that to do so would create the impression of persecution and, because the case was not really very strong, would lend weight to the arguments that the government was using its power to interfere with free speech.[11]

The government had been using its power to curb the reporting of free speech. At least three Premiers—Holman, Ryan and Lee—

had complained at the mutilation of news reports, but not everyone criticized the government on this use of its power: indeed, the Victorian Protestant Federation and the Women's Reform League of New South Wales thought the government had not gone far enough in stifling the reports of Dr Mannix's comments; the Congregational Union of Victoria asked the government to make Sinn Fein an illegal society, and the British Empire Union advised the Prime Minister's Department of a meeting conducted by Dr Mannix at the opening of a school in Manning Road, East Caulfield, the nature of that meeting being distinctly anti-British, in the view of the Union. The same society asked the federal government not to permit proposed meetings of Irish organizations. Dr Mannix was under observation, reported the Defence Department, but shorthand notes of his speech revealed nothing disloyal enough to warrant action by the Commonwealth.[12]

The Irish were a problem to a government worried that sectarianism and the problems of Ireland's relationship with England were diverting attention from the business of the moment, which was the speedy defeat of Germany to be made speedier by a healthy increase in recruitment. But how could this be accomplished when Irish-Australians persisted in drawing attention to the ills of Ireland? Attention was drawn really well on St Patrick's Day 1918 when a 'monster meeting' at the Melbourne Town Hall, at which Dr Leeper was chief speaker, protested at the carrying of 'Sinn Fein flags and other disloyal emblems' in the annual Melbourne procession. Protestant Melbourne was particularly affronted by the appearance of a tableau to the memory of the heroes of Easter week in Dublin.[13]

Especially were the Irish under suspicion in a State with an elected leader called Ryan. In March 1918 that Premier had occasion to correspond with the Prime Minister when he reported that his office in Brisbane had just received letters from a Thomas Fitzgerald who had stated that his business premises at 65 Melbourne Street, his home, and the rooms of the Irish National Association of Queensland in Queen Street, Brisbane, had been visited by officials of the Commonwealth who examined and removed certain documents. Fitzgerald was secretary of the Association under notice. Two other men at no. 65 also lodged similar complaints. Ryan was shortly informed by the Prime Minister that the searches had been made under the powers of the War Precautions Act.[14]

It was characteristic of the strain of the war and the rancour caused by the defection from the Labor Party of Hughes and his followers that members could not forgo introducing political bitterness into a simple motion that the House of Representatives record its unbounded admiration of the heroic efforts of the Allied armies on the Western Front, its pride in the valour and achievements of the Australian troops, and its firm intention to fight on to secure a victorious peace and the freedom of the world. In the Senate this resolution was resolved in the affirmative, honourable Senators rising to sing the National Anthem, but in the people's House a long discussion followed the same motion.

In the course of this debate Frank Brennan was moved to state that he did not propose to concur in any more fatuous expressions on the part of the government in regard to what they were pleased to term a victorious peace. The adjective 'victorious' did not suit J. H. Catts, Labor member for Cook in New South Wales, who suggested it be replaced with 'equitable', and he moved an amendment to that effect, to replace 'victorious' with 'equitable'. This was defeated by sixteen votes to forty. Finally the original motion was resolved in the affirmative, honourable members rising to sing the National Anthem. Perhaps some did not; a rumour was started that some members stood up but did not open their mouths to sing, but this was warmly repudiated by one of the accused, Patrick Considine, a Labor man who represented some of the inhabitants of Broken Hill. Dr W. R. N. Maloney, Labor member for Melbourne and possessor of a sense of humour, was heard to observe, 'We might as well have the whole song; what is the good of singing only one verse?'[15]

What was the position concerning recruitment in April 1918? There had been efforts made to increase the number of recruits, but those efforts had failed miserably. Some of them were more realistic than others but all reflected a nation at the end of its tether so far as voluntary recruiting went.

An effective revival of recruiting supposed that the remaining eligibles in Australia could be talked into joining the A.I.F. in droves. They could not; except for those turning eighteen or nineteen or those whose circumstances suddenly changed, it was unlikely that any inducement would bring men to the army in the numbers said to be needed. But the cash consideration was publicized and the scales of payment to wives and children set out in the newspapers.[16]

Over and above that it was emphasized that the soldier in training in 1918 led a healthy open-air life in company with others of his kind amongst whom he would visit places which otherwise he would never see. Certainly the recruit's life had its risks but there was no necessity to exaggerate them: tens of thousands of men had gone unharmed through all the fighting of the preceding years and tens of thousands of others who had stayed home had been run over in the capital cities or died from despised complaints, observed the *Argus*. Those who had enlisted and returned had had an experience that none of their ancestors had ever had and that none of their descendants might ever have. Who had not thrilled at the recital of daring deeds that won for some obscure Australian bush boy or city lad the prized Victoria Cross?[17]

But talk and friendly persuasion were not going to win the war, asserted some people, and a lady from Prahran desperately and angrily told the Defence Department to round up the stalwart men she saw wandering about Melbourne, and fling them all into camps.[18] The government could not very well do that, but the fact that eligibles remained in cosy billets always rankled with the conscriptionists. It also annoyed others, the Premier of Queensland receiving a petition from twelve original Anzacs who considered that they had done their share for the present. They were on furlough, they asserted, and were unwilling to go back to the front. Wistfully, wearily, angrily or cunningly, they pointed out that there were in Queensland many officers and other ranks holding good positions who had not yet left Australia, some of whom had held such appointments for upwards of three years. The Prime Minister rejected their plea on the ground that granting it would involve a possible breach of faith with the military command.[19]

Another person considered that enlistment would be increased if the wealthy men of Australia took up mortgages on the houses of prospective recruits.[20] The government did not take any action in regard to mortgages either, but a fresh and systematic attempt[21] was made to raise the numbers needed for reinforcements. A scheme launched by Hughes on 25 February 1918 involved an estimate by the Chief Electoral Officer of the Commonwealth and the Commonwealth Statistician of the probable number of people in the various electorates and subdivisions. The government wanted 5,400 recruits a month and tables were prepared showing the estimated number of males between the ages of nineteen and forty-four at the end of 1917 together with the annual quota for each electorate and subdivision which would raise that number. This table was issued to all recruiting authorities throughout the Commonwealth in regard to a voluntary ballot, and signed by Pearce, the Minister for Defence. The annual quota of males aged between nineteen and forty-four was based, then, on the total number of electors enrolled in each electorate and subdivision. This figure turned out to be 7.8 per cent of that total (see Table 5).

TABLE 5

State Recruiting Quotas in February 1918

State	No. of electors	Quota
N.S.W.	325,510	25,227
Vic.	220,920	17,120
Qld	123,620	9,581
S.A.	67,985	5,268
W.A.	66,183	5,130
Tas.	31,921	2,474
Total	836,139	64,800

SOURCE: Defence Dept, MP 367 582/2/542, 14 March 1918.

Table 5 is based on the assumption that the percentage of persons not less than nineteen years nor more than forty-four appearing on the federal electoral rolls was:

N.S.W.	60.2	S.A.	52.6
Vic.	57.6	W.A.	75.1
Qld	61.0	Tas.	60.2

The regulations concerning recruitment were altered: those aged under nineteen might not enlist without parental consent; the remaining member of a family the other sons of which were in the A.I.F. might not enlist under twenty-one without parental consent; parents might lodge objections if their children enlisted. On the other hand, the *Argus* of 7 May 1918 quoted Pearce saying that parental consent was no longer necessary for the enlistment of soldiers aged under twenty-one, on the understanding they would not be drafted into the firing line until they were nineteen.[22]

It was also decided in the month following the Governor-General's recruiting conference that volunteers who were slightly under the minimum chest measurement, or who were suffering from some minor defects at the time of volunteering which would normally cause their rejection, might be accepted provided that the examining medical officers considered that a special course of training and gymnastics, combined with the open-air life of camp, would remove their disability within three months.[23]

Many other efforts were made to increase reinforcements, but it was no good; still the recruitment remained well below the required numbers. Then in April the Governor-General, at the suggestion of Captain A. C. Carmichael, stepped in and called a conference of representatives of Australian employers and employees, together with parliamentary representatives from all States, to discuss the recruiting problem. It was the last effort during the war to re-invoke the feelings of solidarity expressed in 1914 when the Australian people reacted in one of those rare heady moments of unanimity and enthusiasm.

The invitations were sent out all over Australia at the same time as the great German offensive beginning in March rolled across the old Somme battlefield and threatened to break through where the French and British armies joined. Indeed, Munro Ferguson sent out his invitation the day after Field-Marshal Haig issued his famous 'Backs to the wall' appeal to his army. This was a crisis. Would not all Australians of good will sink their differences in the face of the German threat and strive as one to defeat the enemy? They would not. Some would not even come to the Governor-General's conference. The Tasmanian Labor caucus replied that it opposed any more men being sent out of Australia, and Munro Ferguson feared that such a sentiment was very widespread. But there were few such point-blank refusals to attend at Government House, Melbourne, and there duly appeared some forty representative men in a body which the Governor-General wryly likened to a '*sovyet*' (Hughes was absent ill when the conference

started). Ryan and Holman were the leading figures in the preliminary sparring.

The federal government, however, had prepared no definite
proposals for the opening of the meeting, which started on Friday
12 April and lasted for a week. It went off on to a fruitless contro-
versy which continued during the second day, when the Minister
for Recruiting, R. B. Orchard, Nationalist member for Nepean in
New South Wales, tabled a very weak suggestion for a ballot. The
number of reinforcements needed each month having been decided, it was agreed to distribute cards to all men aged between
nineteen and forty-four, asking for information about age, occupation and enlistment, and asking as well a definite question: Are
you prepared, provided . . . (number) of men in your (town,
district, division) agree to submit their names to a ballot, to submit
your name to a ballot to enlist, if and when the ballot results in
your being chosen in the quota for any month?[24] This ballot was
planned to be conducted by means of numbered marbles, stated
the Minister; Australian lads, he announced, were prepared to
take a sporting risk and there was an element of chance about the
ballot which would appeal to them. (Early in October it was reported that the draw for the first 100 men had occurred in Sydney
before a large crowd.)

On the Monday, Hughes arrived, having shaken off the flu, and
at once the sparks began to fly. The old bitterness emerged, the
conference turned into another boots-and-all conscription campaign, and when Hughes produced what he described as secret
cables from the Secretary of State, someone interjected, 'We've
'ad enough of them forgeries of yours!' At this, Hughes stormed
out of the room and, ordering the Military Secretary's office to be
cleared, stayed there with some kindred spirits till the storm died
down. The conference was not a success, though the Governor-
General concluded after the muttering representatives had gone
home that there had been one conspicuous success gained, and
that was closer relations between employers and employees.[25]

Perhaps there had, and certainly the recruiting figures increased
in May by more than 50 per cent over April (in part due to the
increased German threat on the Western Front and the lowering
of the age limit?).[26] But thereafter it was once again clear that a
maximum level in recruiting had been reached. It was claimed

that industrial strife in New South Wales had caused the figures to decline there, but the drop was Australia-wide and particularly marked in Western Australia which in 1918 was recruiting fewer men than Tasmania which had less than half its population. A sense of frustration had been fed by the cooked news featured in the papers for four years and by the self-defeatingly cheerful cables from the Western Front. There was a recognition of this in the baffled cry of D. C. McGrath, Labor member for Ballarat, for the return of basic freedoms when he said in the House that if the government would only abolish half the war regulations, sack half the censors and return to the liberty and the conditions operating in 1914, there would be no lack of recruits.[27] But there was never to be a return.

Recruiting agencies were faced with the task of invoking a spirit of optimism after four years of misleading news, the refusal of a few thousand Australians to support conscription on two occasions, and the creation of warring and bitter political and religious groups. The year of 1918 is the story of further withering away of enthusiasm for winning the war and, as a reaction, a series of desperate steps to make up the numbers of men said to be necessary to reinforce the A.I.F. The Minister for Recruiting admitted that it was quite impossible to expect to raise the 30,000 men needed to bring the Australian divisions up to full strength, so all efforts were made to raise a quota of 5,400 a month.[28] It was a wonder that enthusiasm for the war effort lasted as long as it did.

At the very time the Governor-General's conference was being held, the man who had suggested it, Captain Carmichael, was trying in Sydney to recapture the earlier zeal and raise 'Carmichael's Thousand'. In 1915–16 he had helped to recruit the 36th Battalion,[29] and on 13 April 1918 there were scenes of great enthusiasm in Martin Place when 120 men responded to his appeal in little more than an hour. It was a remarkable revival as men came forward in half-dozens and did not wait to enter the stand by the steps of the recruiting area. Captain Carmichael appealed to them to 'be sports and hop in'; they did hop in—over the front of the stand, frequently landing on the other side in a confused heap. So did the Captain raise his thousand men and prepare to enter camp with them, it was reported.

This was all very heartening; perhaps it was too good to be

true, because E. Riley, Labor member for South Sydney, chose to repeat a story that when the recruiting in Sydney was opened for Carmichael's Thousand, more than one hundred men in Liverpool Camp were marched in civilian clothes to the railway station with orders to go to Martin Place and 'when the recruiting meeting started, to jump up on the platform and enlist.' On 29 April the Commandant of the 2nd Military District (New South Wales), Major-General Ramaciotti, reported that some sixty-four men at Liverpool Camp had been given civilian clothes to respond to Captain Carmichael's appeal and come forward as volunteers.[30]

That was one way flagging efforts were rallied. Another concerned medical students at the University of Melbourne, but they did not exactly try to revive the feelings of 1914; they attempted to shame some of their fellows into joining the army by excluding all 'slackers' from membership of the Medical Students' Society. By more than a two-thirds majority, the voting being 170 to 65, it was decided that no one should be allowed to become or remain a member of the Society unless he could give satisfactory reasons why he was not in khaki to a committee composed of a medical man, a lawyer and a business man. It was further decided that the medical member of the committee should be an outside practitioner not associated with the university staff. The announcement of the voting figures was greeted with loud cheers.[31]

This was severe social pressure but others protested that naked economic pressure was being used to fill the ranks of the A.I.F. In the House of Representatives, S. R. Nicholls, Labor member for Macquarie in New South Wales, announced that Massey-Harris, the machinery manufacturers, had issued a letter to ten single eligible men in its employ saying that their services would no longer be needed. Regretting that this was so, the firm said that it must release all single men for the service of the Empire, and had come to the conclusion that every man who was of military age and medically fit and who could be of service to the country should be available in the crisis. The firm announced that it would not like to think that any action taken by it would withhold one single man from service. Nicholls went on to say that Anthony Hordern and Son had adopted the same policy; on every pay-day their young single men received a pay-docket on which were the words, 'Your country needs you; we do not.'[32]

Others, too, were accused of compelling their employees to join up; at the Governor-General's recruiting conference it was said by the leader of the opposition in Tasmania, J. A. Lyons, later to be a member of the federal Parliament and Prime Minister of Australia, that local government authorities and other such bodies in Tasmania were practising economic conscription. In response to this accusation, the State Premier, W. H. Lee, sent a circular to all such authorities pointing out that the conference had concluded that economic conscription should not be used, and calling upon them for a policy of harmony.

Most of the replies he received were in agreement and many of those canvassed angrily denied they were using economic conscription. Hamilton municipality in the Derwent Valley, however, passed a motion regretting that the Premier should have seen fit to send such a letter when the Empire was fighting for its life, and deplored the policy of pandering to men disloyal to the Empire, Australia, and the Australians at the front; the Circular Head Marine Board answered that it had never had the chance to practise economic conscription but, if it ever did, it would use its own discretion; the Leven Harbour Trust replied that it had no eligibles in its employ but if it had it would deem it their duty to be helping at the front.[33]

There were other indications that men were, in effect, having intolerable pressure put on them to join the forces. In April the Melbourne Trades Hall Council asked the Prime Minister to receive a deputation to present a resolution protesting against what it termed economic conscription, and it sent in particulars of three cases where single men in the Clerks' Union had been discharged from employment because they were eligible for active service. The arrival home of returned soldiers may have been behind some such moves, because the Defence Department stated that the three cases involved making way for returned men, to whom first preference in employment was given.[34]

This was one way of getting men into the A.I.F., and it was also suggested that girls be employed to interview eligibles in the government departments and business premises and try to coax them to enter the army.[35] This was evidently not done but another method involved the use of recruiting teams sent on tour through the country districts. They were enthusiastically received and their concerts were great attractions. Each team was accompanied by a medical officer who examined each recruit on the spot. If he were passed, he was sworn in and his measurements taken before being sent down to Melbourne. In a day or two a full set of uniform was sent to him; this the new recruit was expected to wear during his period of leave when not working at his civilian occupation. Every man was expected to be a recruiting agent.[36]

In Melbourne recruiting marches were still bravely conducted in 1918, and at the old G.P.O. in Bourke Street and at the Town Hall, 'Skipper' Francis, the man who composed the songs 'Australia Will be There' and 'Keep Smiling, Mother', and who had swum the Bristol Channel, sang those pieces to the crowd. Francis had been rejected from the A.I.F. because of a deformed foot.[37]

All these different efforts, then, were tried, and certainly in May 1918 the numbers of recruits increased to 4,888 from 2,781 in April; thereafter they dropped back to around the 2,500 mark and remained there, although the insurance of soldiers was taken on by four companies, reported the Queensland Public Curator. The companies were willing to insure the lives of soldiers, the numbers ranging in the different companies from fifty men up to five hundred. Each company was prepared to issue policies up to an amount of £200 each, at a premium of £10 per cent.[38]

The appeals for reinforcements were so ineffective during the autumn and winter of 1918 that even news of famous Australian battalions being disbanded one after the other on the Western Front for lack of reinforcements did not produce any increase in recruits. In June the 36th, 47th and 52nd battalions were so scrapped to provide men for other units. The Acting Prime Minister, W. A. Watt, took the opportunity to say that the only way this sort of thing might be checked would be for recruiting figures to rise; those battalions had earned names that would live in history, he declared, and to lose their identity was one of the keenest punishments that could be inflicted on them. (One of them, the 36th, had been raised by Captain Carmichael, and that officer considered that such a fate was 'simply hellish' for the 36th.)[39] But no matter what the news was in 1918, it failed to bring forward the required numbers of men. It was not simply due to the bitterness left by the conscription referendums or what a member of Parliament termed 'the abuse and everlasting scandalizing of members' of the Labor Party by the press and the anti-labourites. To all intents and purposes, Australia had run out of men who were prepared to recruit in any quantity.

Still the slaughter of Australia's soldiers continued with undiminished regularity on the Western Front: some 25 per cent of all Australian casualties occurred in 1918.[40] It was against this background that in mid-June the triennial conference of the Labor Party was held in Perth; on 25 June it was announced that, in a resolution concerning recruiting, the party had decided that the Allies should assert their readiness to enter into peace negotiations. Other resolutions also showed that the conference had moved away from wholehearted endorsement of the voluntary system of recruiting. Up to a point, the Labor Party was in danger of splitting yet again; although no full account of the proceedings was published at the time, it was clear that there was a deep division of opinion.[41] Was it realistic to expect the Germans to come to an agreement? What was to be said for an 'unconditional surrender' line? Too many nations had lost too many men.

Certainly the Director-General of Recruiting thought it was not realistic to expect the Germans to make terms with the Allies, and issued a pamphlet entitled *Germany's Twelve Commandments*. This was a 'Warning to those Australians who would slacken their effort in carrying through the war to a successful conclusion', that is, a warning to those who were prepared to settle for less than unconditional surrender. This pamphlet was a list of conditions said to have been voiced by Count von Roon, of the Prussian Upper House, in July 1918, and those Australians who were considering peace by negotiation were likened by the Director-General to sheep seeking mercy from the butcher. Among these 'twelve commandments' were: no armistice till the British left France and Belgium, and the Germans were in Paris; the annexation of most of Belgium; the return of the German colonies; the surrender of the British navy to Germany; and the payment of an indemnity of £9,000 m. by America, England and France.[42]

If the Germans were so determined to fight it out, then, as some Australians had seen for a long time, strikes and disloyal activity should not be permitted under any circumstances. Perhaps they were right; it all depended on how immediate the danger was, whether from the I.W.W., pacifists or anyone else who hampered full-scale defence of the nation. At the end of June it was reported that at a Sydney meeting of returned soldiers, Brigadier-General Alexander Jobson said that there were sundry influences working against recruiting, but that disloyal speech was perhaps the most important. The time had not arrived, he declared, when returned soldiers should resort to force, but that time might come. The meeting decided to ask the federal ministry to take drastic action against all disloyalists,[43] and in July the secretary of the Returned Sailors' and Soldiers' Imperial League informed the Defence Department of a motion that immediate action be taken to stop seditious utterances, otherwise the League would take the law into its own hands.[44]

This unhealthy tendency by some to threaten and, at times, actually to usurp the powers of the government had been present throughout most of the war and regardless of the rights and wrongs of ex-soldiers' feelings, their conduct could not be expected to lead to more recruits coming forward. The existence of ex-soldiers' organizations may have provided an institutionalized channel for that minority of such bodies which went in for violence. In May the Returned Soldiers' Association at Townsville had protested against continued disloyal utterances by the socialists and members of the I.W.W. in Queensland, and at the same time the Brisbane branch also asked the government to prevent recurrence of disloyal speech by anyone. Some utterances were reckoned to be more disloyal than others, because the town clerk of Adamstown sent to the Prime Minister's Department declarations by two men of a Patriotic Committee concerning disloyal remarks made by a man when asked to buy some tickets.[45]

At least some of the more outspoken disloyal statements were associated with the I.W.W. In 1918 the Defence Department was told that there had been found stuck on a verandah post a slip bearing the legend, 'Don't enlist while the Twelve are in gaol.'[46] This was a reference to the trial and imprisonment for long periods of a dozen men; accused of being associated with the I.W.W., most of them were ultimately freed after it was admitted that justice had miscarried.[47] This travesty shocked many members of the labour movement: the government's crack-down on the I.W.W. was seen by some as a grim example of what happened to minority movements under Hughes's administration and further showed how the police might be used as agents of the government. Unquestionably the name of the I.W.W. struck terror into the hearts of some Australians. Its influence in deterring men from enlisting cannot be assessed, but certainly it was thought to have that effect. In mid-1918 a Sydney detective stated that an organized attempt was being made by extremists to capture trade unions by securing positions on the New South Wales State executive. Former members of the I.W.W. were being absorbed into the 'Industrial Labour Party', he claimed; especially was the I.W.W. active in the Amalgamated Society of Engineers, and the propaganda appeared to be capturing unionists who had no material interests in New South Wales, or who lacked British patriotism.[48] In the same spirit, J. M. Chanter, Nationalist member for the Riverina in the House, sent in to the Prime Minister's Department two booklets which he wanted suppressed. These were *Guilty or Not Guilty?* and *The Case of Grant* (the latter presumably H. E. Boote's work regarding Donald Grant's fifteen-year gaol sentence as one of 'the Twelve').[49]

But what was disloyalty and what were disloyal utterances? To whom or what was one disloyal? Was it worth being loyal to? One could be loyal and yet be punished instead of being rewarded or let alone. The manager of the *Barrier Miner* at Broken Hill, for instance, set out the circumstances of a series of violent attacks on his office, such attacks being in the nature of revolutionary acts directed against public policy, order and government, he suggested, and not the outcome of private enmity or desire for revenge for private grievance. It sounded as if the manager had seen a lawyer, and it was a nice legal point. The opinion of the Crown Solicitor of New South Wales was sought and, in an opinion citing extensive precedent, he found that there was at common law no obligation on the government of New South Wales to pay compensation for injury to property caused by rioting.[50]

The sense of frustration and carelessness, combined with a victory fixation, took forms other than seeking revenge on people who sounded as if they might be disloyal in 1918. Under the heading 'Supply of Socks Falls Off', the *Argus* in May reported a reference by the Minister for Recruiting, who said that in Sydney it was particularly noticeable that girls no longer knitted socks in the trams and trains. The loss of enthusiasm might have been due to the high price of wool, said the Minister, but he regarded knitting-wool as a war necessity; there was no doubt that hand-knitted socks were far better for marching troops than the machine-made articles.[51] Again, a man in Western Australia said that because he conducted recruiting meetings near the Perth Post Office he had received a summons to appear in the police court. This would not help the recruiting campaign, he said with injury, and in Melbourne the leader of the Labor Party reported another sort of injury when he twice complained that recruiting bandsmen at Maldon had blown up the 'Vote No' sign there.[52] Then there was the curious charge of the British Empire Union: it wanted the Director-General of Recruiting, Donald Mackinnon, removed because of some offensive remarks he was said to have made. The Prime Minister was in England in September 1918 and informed his government that Captain Bruce Bairnsfather, cartoonist and creator of the soldier 'Old Bill', had now placed his services at the disposal of Australia,[53] and 'Soldier's Widow' suggested in a letter to the *Argus* on 11 October 1918 that all the widows and children belonging to fallen soldiers have a procession, either through the city some lunch hour, or at some race meeting, to impress the gravity of the situation on the people, 'and if that appeal does not touch their hearts, nothing will. Myself, I think, their hearts are past touching.'

In this confusion of self-analysis and breast-beating, the hatred of the enemy had not been quite dulled. There was still a cutting edge to it because in July 1918 a resident of South Perth, Western Australia, advised the Defence Department that he had seen a photograph of a club used by the Germans for finishing off their prisoners of war, and suggested that posters depicting this and other instruments be exhibited to the public. In the same spirit, the Director-General issued a recruiting poster which featured something called the 'German Monster'.[54] This inducement to enlist led to a question in the House, J. W. Leckie, Nationalist member for Indi, New South Wales, asking the Minister for Recruiting whether he really thought that the placarding of cities and towns with a horrible picture of a gorilla dripping blood everywhere was likely to have a good effect in inducing eligibles to enlist? He also sought to know from the Minister if forthcoming posters were to be of the same nature, and concluded by asking whether, in view of the shortage of paper, there was not a waste of hundreds of tons of it. R. B. Orchard, replying to a similar question asked by Frank Brennan, said that he was considering withdrawing the poster, but added sharply that if the position were less favourable than it was on the Western Front, it was possible that the poster in question might have brought home to eligibles the methods of the enemy.[55]

But Brigadier-General L. C. Wilson had ideas other than poetry, platitudes, terror or outworn appeals: he wanted the exploits of the Australian Light Horse written up, and was convinced that this would bring in the recruits with a rush. Hot-blooded incidents of expeditions could be truthfully described and would form admirable recruiting propaganda: no young, lusty and romantic Australian could resist enlisting immediately after reading how Sergeant Julian, using his bayonet as a sword in the mêlée in the streets of Es Salt, ran through two Turkish cavalry-men, or how Lieutenant Foulkes-Taylor galloped up to a German officer, snatched his Mauser pistol from him, emptied the contents thereof into the Turkish cavalry, and then smashed the butt on the skull of another Turk.[56]

But no matter what was done, the number of recruits did not increase in any significant way. What increase there was could be accounted for by the lowering of the age limit, stated Senator J. Newland of South Australia,[57] and this was the conclusion reached by his State Recruiting Committee. It reported that the quota had been reached only in the seven-day period ending 18 May, when 121 men enlisted. This had been during the period when the need for consent to enlistment was temporarily withdrawn, and scores of recruits described as 'mere boys', but 'fine big brave boys', flocked to the recruiting offices.

Describing this effort by South Australia, the Committee recorded that open-air appeals had been conducted, and large crowds attracted to Rundle Street, opposite Allans Ltd, by the sweet singing of the members of six ladies' choirs, at first daily and then three days a week during the lunch hour. These were known as Adelaide Business House Choirs. On many occasions the crowds attracted were so thick that vehicular traffic had to be diverted, with the Mayor's permission, from Rundle Street. Recruits were obtained from every meeting.

Another South Australian enterprise during 1918 was the distribution by the Women's Recruiting Committee of 'crosses of honour' to soldiers' dependents. The scheme was given a start at a great recruiting drive held in the Town Hall on 28 May; the idea was to get the crosses placed in the window of every house from which a man had been enlisted for active service in the A.I.F., thereby bringing into prominence the residence from which no representative was fighting for the Empire, home and humanity. These crosses were a white Geneva cross hanging from a gilt clasp and blue ribbon on a crimson background. A purple bar across the centre of it indicated that a hero from that house had made the supreme sacrifice. The words 'For King and Country' in blue letters were printed on each cross. There had been an immediate rush for these, reported the Committee, and on the first day of the issue more than 5,000 were handed out. All told, about 20,000 were distributed.[58]

In the same state, Lieutenant-Colonel C. P. Butler, invalided home after commanding the 43rd Battalion, undertook to raise 1,000 men to return with him to France, and the State Recruiting Committee recommended to the Defence Department that such permission be granted. Senator Newland's view that 150 men was a reasonable target was rejected, and ultimately Colonel Butler was given approval to try to raise 500 soldiers and to go with them as transport officer. That was in June; by September it was reported that he had got together 130 men, by the end of the month the number was given as 101 and in October 117 men were in camp; ultimately only thirty-seven recruits were enlisted in Butler's Five Hundred.[59]

It was a sad and discouraging difference from the ease with which men had been recruited in the early part of the war. Fortunately Australia's agony was about to end because, after a number of false alarms, on 11 November 1918 there came news of the official armistice; the rattle of the machine-guns and the roar of the artillery ceased, and the recruitment of the A.I.F. came to an end.

Approximately 417,000 men had enlisted in the force: of the 330,000 who served in theatres of war, 60,000 were dead and

160,000 wounded and maimed. Approximately 40 per cent of all Australian men aged between eighteen and forty-five had enlisted in the A.I.F.

The cost of the victory in which that superb force of infantry and other units participated has yet to be calculated, but so has the meaning of 'victory' in World War I.

Abbreviations

A.A.	Army Archives (Albert Park Barracks, Melbourne)
A.A.N.S.W.	Archives Authority of New South Wales (Public Library Building, Sydney)
A.W.M.	Australian War Memorial, Canberra
C.A.O.	Commonwealth Archives Office, Canberra and Melbourne
C.H.B.E.	*Cambridge History of the British Empire*
L.B.W.A.	Libraries Board of Western Australia (Battye Library, Perth)
N.L.A.	National Library of Australia, Canberra
N.S.W.	New South Wales
Parl. Deb.	*Parliamentary Debates*
P.M.	Prime Minister
P.P.	*Parliamentary Papers*
Q.S.A.	Queensland State Archives (Public Library of Queensland, Brisbane)
S.A.A.	South Australian State Archives (Public Library of South Australia, Adelaide)
S.M.H.	*Sydney Morning Herald*
T.S.A.	Tasmanian State Archives (State Library of Tasmania, Hobart)
Vic.	Victoria
V.S.A.	Victorian State Archives (State Library of Victoria, Melbourne)

Notes

I AUSTRALIA ON THE EVE
OF THE WAR

1 *Age, Argus, S.M.H.*, 2 January 1901; A. G. Austin, *The Webbs' Australian Diary 1898*, p. 113; Patrick Ford, *Cardinal Moran and the A.L.P.*, pp. 242-3. For a general account, see L. L. Robson, *Australia and the Great War, 1914-1918.*

2 W. K. Hancock, *Australia*, chapter 10; R. N. Ebbels, *The Australian Labor Movement 1850-1907*, p. 221.

3 Austin, op. cit., pp. 24-6.

4 J. A. La Nauze, *Alfred Deakin*, chapter 3; Alfred Deakin (ed. La Nauze), *Federated Australia*, introduction; C. M. H. Clark, *Short History of Australia*, p. 180.

5 Vance Palmer, *The Legend of the Nineties*, p. 10.

6 *C.H.B.E.*, vol. 7, p. 502.

7 Ibid., pp. 509-10; Clark, op. cit., p. 186.

8 La Nauze, op. cit., p. 569.

9 *The Statesman's Year Book 1914*, p. 307.

10 D. C. Gordon, *The Dominion Partnership*, pp. 78, 204-5.

11 *Parl. Deb.* (Cwlth), vol. 3, p. 3292, 31 July 1901; L. F. Fitzhardinge, *William Morris Hughes*, pp. 137-49.

12 Gordon, op. cit., pp. 91-6.

13 Ibid., pp. 189-90; Fitzhardinge, op. cit., p. 142.

14 Fitzhardinge, op. cit., pp. 142-7; *Parl. Deb.* (Cwlth), vol. 14, pp.

1793-4, 7 July 1903.

15 *Round Table*, vol. 1, no. 2 (February 1911), p. 192.

16 H. L. Hall, *Australia and England*, p. 255.

17 M. P. A. H. Hankey, *The Supreme Command*, vol. 1, pp. 126-7.

18 *Call*, August 1906, p. 2; Fitzhardinge, op. cit., p. 221.

19 *Call*, August 1907.   20 Ibid.

21 Ibid., February 1907.

22 Ibid., May 1907.

23 Emil Ludwig, *Kaiser Wilhelm II*, p. 241.

24 Fitzhardinge, op. cit., p. 136.

25 *Call*, May 1907.

26 Ibid., August 1907.

27 Ibid., November 1907.

28 Ibid., February 1908, February 1909.

29 *P.P.* (Cwlth), 1910, vol. 2, pp. 83-104; *The Statesman's Year Book 1914*, pp. 307-8; J. E. Lee, *Duntroon, passim.*

30 *Official Year Book of the Commonwealth of Australia 1901-1914*, no. 8 (Melbourne, 1915), p. 951.

31 Gordon, op. cit., p. 188; Barbara Penny, 'Australia's reactions to the Boer War', *Journal of British Studies*, vol. 7, no. 1 (November 1967).

32 *C.H.B.E.*, vol. 3, p. 416.

33 Hankey, op. cit., vol. 1, p. 129.

34 G .F. Pearce, *Carpenter to Cabinet*, pp. 81-2.

35 I. R. Hancock, 'The 1911 Imperial Conference', *Historical Studies, Australia and New Zealand*, vol. 12, no. 47.

[36] *C.H.B.E.*, vol. 3, p. 399.
[37] Grey of Fallodon, *Twenty-five Years*, vol. 1, p. 81.
[38] C. W. Dilke, *Greater Britain*, p. 395.
[39] Jethro Brown, 'Australia and the war', *Political Quarterly*, no. 5 (February 1915).
[40] C. E. W. Bean (ed.), *Official History of Australia in the War of 1914-18*, vol. 1, p. 15.
[41] *Round Table*, vol. 1, no. 4 (August 1911), pp. 497-9.
[42] *United Empire*, vol. 1, no. 1 (January 1910), p. 2.
[43] *Official Year Book of the Commonwealth of Australia*, no. 8, pp. 100-1.
[44] Penny, op. cit., p. 97.
[45] A. R. Trethewey, 'The teaching of history in state-supported elementary schools in Victoria 1852-1954', unpubl. M. Ed. thesis, University of Melbourne, 1965.
[46] *Citizen Reader* (Melbourne, 1906), p. 212. (I owe the above references to M. Migus, 'Assumptions about, and reactions to, Australia's entry into World War I', unpubl. B.A. thesis, Department of History, University of Melbourne, 1967.)
[47] C. E. W. Bean, *Anzac to Amiens*, chapter 1.
[48] Charles Grimshaw, 'Australian nationalism', *Australian Journal of Politics and History*, vol. 3, no. 1 (1957), pp. 120-1.
[49] J. F. Fraser, *Australia*, p. 18.
[50] C. P. Cuttriss, *Over the Top*, pp. 120-1.

2 FORMATION OF THE A.I.F.

[1] P.M. Dept, A 77 'General file', C.A.O., Canberra.
[2] C. E. W. Bean (ed.), *Official History*, vol. 11, pp. 6-13.
[3] Ibid., vol. 1, p. 16.
[4] *Argus*, 3 August 1914.
[5] *S.M.H.*, 3 August 1914.
[6] *Argus*, 5 August 1914.
[7] *Argus*, *Age*, 6 August 1914; *Age*, 4, 5 August 1964.
[8] MS 696/10, 19 December 1914; MS 696/377, 12 February 1915, Novar Papers, N.L.A.
[9] *Argus*, 18 August 1914; *Official History*, vol. 11, pp. 206-7.

[10] *Official History*, vol. 10, *passim*; vol. 11, p. 205.
[11] *Argus*, 11, 14 August 1914; *Official History*, vol. 11, p. 208; *S.M.H.*, 11 August 1914; A. G. Butler (ed.), *The Official History of the Australian Army Medical Services in the War of 1914-1918*, vol. 1, p. 21n.; *Parl. Deb.* (Cwlth), vol. 76, p. 1970, 16 December 1914.
[12] *Official History*, vol. 11, p. v.
[13] *Age*, 4 August 1914; M. Migus, 'Assumptions about, and reactions to, Australia's entry into World War I', unpubl. B.A. thesis, University of Melbourne, 1967.
[14] *Argus*, 9, 15 September 1914.
[15] Ibid., 15 August 1914; *Age*, 10 August 1914.
[16] *Spectator*, 7 August 1914; *S.M.H.*, 12 September 1914.
[17] *Age*, 10 August 1914; *S.M.H.*, 13 August 1914.
[18] *Daily Standard*, 26 September 1914; *Official History*, vol. 11, p. 155.
[19] *Worker*, 6 August 1914, cited Ian Turner, *Industrial Labour and Politics*, p. 70.
[20] *Labor Call*, 13 August 1914.
[21] Turner, op. cit., p. 71.
[22] Premier's Dept, 16/2870, 15 March 1916, Q.S.A.
[23] P.M. Dept, A 77, 'Miss Adela Pankhurst', 30 November 1915, C.A.O., Canberra.
[24] *Daily Telegraph*, 20 December 1915.
[25] Premier's Dept, 15/1863, V.S.A.
[26] Turner, op. cit., p. 71.
[27] *Argus*, 12 August 1914.
[28] Ibid., 8 September 1914; *S.M.H.*, 10 August 1914; Roger Pocock (ed.), *The Frontiersman's Pocketbook*, preface.
[29] *Argus*, 18 August 1914; *S.M.H.*, 6 August 1914; Defence Dept, WAR Series 245/1/13, 'Miscellaneous matters', 16 August 1914, A.A., Melbourne.
[30] *S.M.H.*, 4, 11 August 1914.
[31] *Argus*, 31, 26, 28 August 1914.
[32] *Official History*, vol. 11, p. 286; vol. 1, p. 41.
[33] Chief Sec., GRG 24/29/7, 1914/345, 11 August 1914, S.A.A.
[34] *S.M.H.*, 12 August 1914.
[35] *Argus*, 5 August 1914.

36 Ibid., 5, 14 August, 4, 2 September, 12 August 1914.
37 Defence Dept, WAR Series 245/ 1/117, 204, 228, 'Miscellaneous matters', 23 September 1914, 11 December, 9 March 1915.
38 Premier's Dept, 14/8171, 10 December 1914, A.A.N.S.W.
39 Ibid., 14/8212, 12 December 1914; 15/2200, 14 September 1914.
40 *S.M.H.*, 12 August 1914.
41 Defence Dept, ABDE Series 38/4/ 82, 'Aviation inventions', A.A., Melbourne.
42 Defence Dept, MP 133, Series 2, Box 6, 45/1/28, 4 January 1916, C.A.O., Melbourne.
43 Ibid., 45/1/24, 29 June 1915.
44 Ibid., 45/1/8, 19 January 1914.
45 MS 696/599, 8 September 1914, Novar Papers, N.L.A.
46 *Official History*, vol. 11, pp. 38-41.
47 Ibid., pp. 225-6.
48 *S.M.H.*, 4, 5 September 1914.
49 MS 696/10, 19 December 1914, Novar Papers, N.L.A.
50 *S.M.H.*, 15 September 1914.
51 Ibid., 29 September 1914.
52 Ibid., 2 October 1914.
53 *Argus*, 9, 15, 17 September, 8 October 1914.
54 Jethro Brown, 'Australia and the war', *Political Quarterly*, no. 5 (February 1915), p. 42; *Argus*, 26 September 1914; *Australasian*, 3 October 1914; *Leader*, 3 October 1914; C. E. W. Bean, *Anzac to Amiens*, p. 46; *Age*, 26 September 1914.
55 *Official History*, vol. 9, chapter 7.
56 P.M. Dept, A 77, 'Congratulations', 10 November 1914, C.A.O., Canberra.
57 *Argus*, 21 November 1914.
58 *S.M.H.*, 10 September 1914.
59 Ibid., 16 November 1914, 3 June 1915.
60 Ibid., 23 November, 10 December 1914.
61 Premier's Dept, 15/4475, 5754, A.A.N.S.W.
62 *S.M.H.*, 28, 29 January 1915.
63 Ibid., 28 December 1914.
64 Ibid., 11 January 1915.
65 Ibid., 15 January 1915.
66 *Argus*, 21 December 1914.
67 Ibid., 2, 26 January 1915.
68 Ibid., 4 February 1915.

69 *Official History*, vol. 11, p. 871; *Argus*, 27 March 1915.
70 *Argus*, 3 February 1915.
71 Ibid., 17 March 1915.
72 Ibid.
73 *Official History*, vols 1 and 2.
74 MS 696/14, 1 March 1915, Novar Papers, N.L.A.; *Argus*, 10 March 1915; *Parl. Deb.* (Cwlth), vol. 76, p. 2695, 29 April 1915.
75 P.M. Dept, A 77, 'Congratulations', 29, 30 April 1915, C.A.O., Canberra.
76 Ibid., 29 April 1915.
77 Ibid., 29, 30 April 1915.
78 See Premier's Dept, PRE 38, 44/ 27, Q.S.A. (correspondence relating to World War I) and 15/ 4720, 4873.
79 *Argus*, 10 September 1915.
80 Ibid., 10 May 1915.
81 Ibid., 11 May 1915.
82 *Official History*, vol. 11, p. 871.
83 *Argus*, 1 July 1915.

3 RECRUITING DRIVES OF 1915

1 C. E. W. Bean (ed.), *Official History of Australia in the War of 1914-18*, vol. 11, p. 292.
2 *Argus*, 23 June 1915.
3 Chief Sec., GRG 24/34, 15/862, 14 July 1915, S.A.A.; *Argus*, 24 June 1915.
4 *Argus*, 1 July 1915.
5 *S.M.H.*, 3 July 1915.
6 *Argus*, 2 July 1915.
7 Premier's Dept, 15/2863, 19 July, 18 August 1915, V.S.A.; *S.M.H.*, 9 August 1915.
8 *Parl. Deb.* (L.A. Vic.), vol. 140, p. 1324, 20 July 1915.
9 6-10 July 1915.
10 *Argus*, 6, 13 July 1915.
11 Ibid., 4 June 1915.
12 Premier's Dept, 15/2608, 2686, 4, 14 July 1915, V.S.A.; *Official History*, vol. 11, p. 871.
13 *Argus*, 3, 5, 22 July, 14 August, 24 November, 7 December 1915.
14 *Parl. Deb.* (Cwlth), vol. 77, p. 4770, 9 July 1915.
15 Defence Dept, MP 133/1, 112/5/ 611, 8 July 1915—23 February 1916, C.A.O., Melbourne; *Argus*, 9 October, 26 November 1915; *Official History*, vol. 11, p. 871.
16 *S.M.H.*, 2 August, 8 July 1915.

17 Premier's Dept, 18/2430, A.A.
N.S.W.
18 Ibid., 15/6042, 10 August 1915.
19 *S.M.H.*, 23 August 1915.
20 Ibid., 14 October 1915.
21 *Parl. Deb.* (Cwlth), vol. 78, p. 6337,
31 August 1915.
22 Premier's Dept, 16/1042, 14
March 1916, A.A.N.S.W.
23 Chief Sec., GRG 24/34, 15/862,
S.A.A.
24 Premier's Dept, 43/80/15; Chief
Sec. 65/17, 22/183, T.S.A.
25 *Official History*, vol. 11, p. 871.
26 Defence Dept, AIF series 144/2/
131, 20 July 1915, A.A., Melbourne.
27 *Argus*, 12 April 1916.
28 Ibid., 10 September 1915.
29 Premier's Dept, 16/1859, V.S.A.
30 *S.M.H.*, 24 September 1915.
31 *Argus*, 4 February 1916.
32 Premier's Dept, 15/9254, 3 August
1915; 15/12204, 16 August 1915,
Q.S.A.
33 *Argus*, 8 November 1915; MS
696/811, 7 February 1916, Novar
Papers, N.L.A.
34 *Official History*, vol. 11, p. 317;
Premier's Dept, 16/3759, 26 May,
7 July 1916, A.A.N.S.W.
35 *Parl. Deb.* (Cwlth), vol. 76, p. 2435,
21 April 1915.
36 *S.M.H.*, 13 November 1915;
Official History, vol. 11, p. 315.
37 Premier's Dept, 19/122, A.A.
N.S.W.; *S.M.H.*, 13 November
1915. See also *Daily Telegraph*, 14
October 1915; *Parl. Deb.* (L.A.
N.S.W.), 1915-16, vol. 60, pp.
2528-9, 12 October 1915; ibid., pp.
2913-14, 26 October 1915; vol. 62,
p. 4488, 10 December 1915.
38 MS 658/1/6, Catts Papers, N.L.A.;
Official History, vol. 11, p. 316.
39 Premier's Dept, 15/5834, 1 August
1915, A.A.N.S.W.
40 Ibid., 15/5858, 31 July 1915.
41 MS 696/192, 25 November 1915;
696/785, 13 December 1915, Novar Papers, N.L.A.
42 Defence Dept, MP 133/6, 144/2/
920, 23 December 1915, C.A.O.,
Melbourne.
43 *Argus*, 22 December 1915.
44 *S.M.H.*, 18 November 1915.
45 Chief Sec., GRG 24/34, 15/862,
9 August 1915, S.A.A.

46 *Argus*, 23 December 1915.
47 Ibid., 26 November 1915.
48 G. H. Knibbs, *The Private Wealth
of Australia, passim.*

4 DECLINE OF THE VOLUNTARY
SYSTEM

1 Geoffrey Sawer, *Australian Federal
Politics and Law 1901-1929*, p.
128; Ian Turner, *Industrial
Labour and Politics*, pp. 77-8.
2 Turner, op. cit., pp. 79-81.
3 *Worker*, 11 November 1915.
4 Arthur Marwick, *The Deluge*, p.
64.
5 C. E. W. Bean (ed.), *Official History*, vol. 11, p. 310; G. H. Knibbs,
*The Private Wealth of Australia,
passim.*
6 *Argus*, 15 July 1915; *Parl. Deb.*
(Cwlth), vol. 77, pp. 4833-8, 14
July 1915.
7 *Argus*, 6 September 1915.
8 Ibid., 15 December 1915; Knibbs,
op. cit., pp. 13-16; *Official History*,
vol. 11, p. 310.
9 F. B. Smith, *The Conscription
Plebiscites*, p. 6; Turner, op. cit.,
p. 98.
10 *Official History*, vol. 11, pp. 312-
13; Defence Dept, AIF Series 133/
1/260-431, 22 December 1915—
17 February 1916, A.A., Melbourne; 'Political' folder, 17 December 1915, Hughes Papers 1915,
N.L.A.
11 *Argus*, 18 December 1915.
12 Ibid., 14 January 1916.
13 Defence Dept, MP 133/6, 144/2/
1118, 10 February 1916, C.A.O.,
Melbourne.
14 P.M. Dept, A 77, '(State) census of
males in New South Wales', 30
July 1915, C.A.O., Canberra.
15 Defence Dept, MP 133/6, 144/2/
118, 1147, January-March 1916,
C.A.O., Melbourne; MCC 1/61/9,
1/32, Correspondence, Letter-
book, Register concerning Beaconsfield recruiting, T.S.A.
16 Knibbs, op. cit., p. 14.
17 *Parl. Deb.* (Cwlth), vol. 79, p.
7743, 10 May 1916.
18 *Argus*, 11 January 1916.
19 Defence Dept, AIF Series 226/1/
558, 27 November 1915, A.A.,
Melbourne; *Official History*, vol.

11, p. 230; P.M. Dept, A 77, '(Royal) Commission re Liverpool encampment', 12 July 1915, C.A.O., Canberra; *Parl. Deb.* (Cwlth), vol. 77, pp. 4513-16, 1 July 1915.

20 *Daily Telegraph*, 15 February 1916; *Argus*, 21 February 1916; *S.M.H.*, 1 March 1916; *Official History*, vol. 11, p. 230.

21 *Parl. Deb.* (Cwlth), vol. 76, pp. 2642-53, 28 April 1915; ibid., p. 3397, 26 April 1915.

22 *S.M.H.*, 20 August 1915.

23 *Daily Telegraph*, 11 September 1915.

24 *Argus*, 7 June 1916, 5 August 1914.

25 *Parl. Deb.* (Cwlth), vol. 77, 9 June 1915.

26 Defence Dept, MP 113/1-2, 112/4/841, 26 August—25 September 1915, C.A.O., Melbourne.

27 *Parl. Deb.* (Cwlth), vol. 77, p. 4577, 2 July 1915.

28 Defence Dept, WAR Series 281/4/22, 'Official war correspondents' messages', 1 June 1916, A.A., Melbourne.

29 Premier's Dept, 16/363, 20 January 1916, V.S.A.

30 Defence Dept, MP 133/6, 144/2/1148, 16 March-10 May 1916, C.A.O., Melbourne.

31 Premier's Dept, 16/4153, 29 May 1916, A.A.N.S.W.

32 P.M. Dept, CP 447/3, SC 15, 'A.I.F., recruiting for, financial', 28 October 1916, C.A.O., Canberra.

33 *Argus*, 7 February 1916.

34 Premier's Dept, 16/4027, V.S.A.

35 658/1/6, 21 June 1916, Catts Papers, N.L.A.

36 Premier's Dept, 16/2528, 2 August 1916, A.A.N.S.W.

37 Defence Dept, MP 369/1/152, 17-20 March 1917, C.A.O., Melbourne.

38 J. P. Fletcher and J. F. Hills, *Conscription under Camouflage*, p. 7; H. E. Holland, *The Crime of Conscription*, chapter 3.

39 *Parl. Deb.* (Cwlth), vol. 77, p. 5066, 16 July 1915.

40 Ibid., vol. 79, p. 7467, 11 November 1915.

41 MS 696/2441, 7 January 1916, Novar Papers, N.L.A.

42 *Parl. Deb.* (Cwlth), vol. 79, p. 7745, 10 May 1916, cited by Senator Millen.

43 Smith, op. cit., pp. 7-8.

44 Premier's Dept, 16/840, 29 August 1916, A.A.N.S.W.

45 *Argus*, 31 January, 2 May 1916.

46 Ibid., 13 March 1916.

47 Ibid., 2, 9 May 1916.

48 Ibid., 9 May, 26 July, 26 June, 2 August 1916.

49 Australian Labor Party, *Official History of the Reconstruction of the Labor Party*, p. 4.

50 *Parl. Deb.* (Cwlth), vol. 79, pp. 8212-13, 22 May 1916.

51 Ibid., p. 8387, 23 May 1916.

52 *Argus*, 9 June 1916.

53 *Sun* (Sydney), 7 June 1916.

54 Defence Dept, ABDE Series 125/1/26, 8 June 1916; AIF Series 172/1/17, 7 March 1916; 144/2/278, 1 September 1915, A.A., Melbourne.

5 OPPOSITION TO CONSCRIPTION IN 1916

1 Defence Dept, WAR Series 281/3/1243, 31 January 1917, A.A., Melbourne.

2 *Argus*, 9 August 1916. For the effect of the Gallipoli campaign, see L. L. Robson, *Australia and the Great War, 1914-1918*, pp. 59-61.

3 See C. E. W. Bean (ed.), *Official History*, vol. 3; John Terraine, *Douglas Haig*, chapter 8; A. J. P. Taylor, *The First World War*, pp. 132-4.

4 F. B. Smith, *The Conscription Plebiscites*, p. 9.

5 C. E. W. Bean, *Two Men I Knew*, p. 144.

6 Defence Dept, MP 133/1, 112/5/611, 16 August-17 November 1916, C.A.O., Melbourne; *Official History*, vol. 11, pp. 338-9. ('Stralis' was A.I.F. headquarters, London.)

7 *Parl. Deb.* (Cwlth), vol. 79, pp. 8402-3, 30 August 1916; ibid., p. 8424, 1 September 1916.

8 Australian Labor Party, *Official History of the Reconstruction of the Labor Party*, p. 5.

9 MS 696/825, 20 September 1916, Novar Papers, N.L.A.

10 Defence Dept, MP 112/5/611, 6 October 1916, C.A.O., Melbourne.

11 Geoffrey Sawer, *Australian Federal Politics and Law 1901-1929*, p. 153; *Parl. Deb.* (Cwlth), vol. 79, p. 8557, 14 September 1916.

12 *Parl. Deb.* (Cwlth), vol. 70, pp. 8808-11, 21 September 1916.

13 *Advocate*, 6 May 1916.

14 *Argus*, 16 May 1916.

15 I conclude this from an analysis of the attestation papers (see Acknowledgments).

16 *Argus*, 13 July 1916.

17 *Parl. Deb.* (L.A. Vic.), vol. 143, pp. 900-5, 22 August 1916.

18 MS 696/1025, 22 April 1918, Novar Papers, N.L.A.

19 *Argus*, 21 August 1916.

20 Defence Dept, WAR Series 281/3/889, 'Press censorship', 29 August 1916, A.A., Melbourne.

21 Niall Brennan, *Dr Mannix*, p. 126.

22 Defence Dept, WAR Series, 'Press censorship', 29 August 1916.

23 See, e.g., *Argus*, 24 October 1917.

24 P.M. Dept, A 77, 'Irish rebellion', 22 August 1916, C.A.O., Canberra.

25 Premier's Dept, 16/6406, 24 September 1916, A.A.N.S.W.

26 *S.M.H.*, 5 September 1916.

27 Premier's Dept, 16/6406, A.A. N.S.W.

28 Riley Collection, N.L.A.

29 Ibid.

30 Maurice Blackburn, *The Conscription Referendum, 1916*, p. 13.

31 *Official History*, vol. 11, p. 354.

32 Defence Dept, WAR Series 281/3/1062, 31 October 1916, A.A., Melbourne.

33 Premier's Dept, 66/7/16, 26 October 1916, T.S.A.

34 *Official History*, vol. 11, p. 354.

35 Chief Sec., GRG 24/29/8, 1916/95, 19 September 1916, S.A.A.

36 Conscription Collection, La Trobe Library, Melbourne.

37 'A.C.T.U.' folder, ibid.

38 Conscription Collection, folder no. 2, 'Trade unionism and conscription', N.L.A.

39 Defence Dept, ABDE Series 299/10/13, 13 November 1916, A.A., Melbourne.

40 P.M. Dept, A 77, 'Meetings calculated to provoke breaches of the peace', C.A.O., Canberra; *Herald*, 22 December 1961.

41 Defence Dept, AIF Series 133/1/285-628, 6 January-22 May 1916, A.A., Melbourne.

42 Ibid., 133/1/457, 596, 8 May 1916.

43 Premier's Dept, 15/1094, 17 August, 23 November 1915, S.A.A.

44 Material cited above is held in the La Trobe Library, Melbourne, and the National Library of Australia, Canberra. It was lodged by F. J. Riley and the Hon. Sam Merrifield respectively.

6 CONSCRIPTION REJECTED

1 Premier's Dept, 16/17176, Q.S.A.

2 P.M. Dept, A 77, 'Raemaekers' cartoons', C.A.O., Canberra; Premier's Dept, 16/2569, 'Raemaekers' cartoons', V.S.A.

3 Conscription Collection, N.L.A.

4 *Argus*, 3 October 1916.

5 Ibid.

6 C. E. W. Bean (ed.), *Official History*, vol. 11, p. 349; Premier's Dept, 16/228, 25 September 1916, L.B.W.A.

7 Conscription Collection, N.L.A.

8 *Argus*, 4 October 1916.

9 Ibid., 26, 27 October 1916.

10 Ibid., 27 October 1916.

11 'Conscription' folder, 15 October 1916, Hughes Papers, N.L.A.

12 Premier's Dept, 16/228, 13 December 1916, L.B.W.A.

13 MS 696/823, 31 August 1916, Novar Papers, N.L.A.

14 *Commonwealth Gazette*, no. 134, 29 September 1916.

15 Premier's Dept, 17/1174, 13 December 1916, A.A.N.S.W.

16 *Official History*, vol. 11, p. 351.

17 *Argus*, 2 October 1916.

18 Premier's Dept, 16/16012, 3, 8 November 1916, Q.S.A.

19 Defence Dept, MP 133/2, 150/6/377, C.A.O., Melbourne.

20 *Courier* (Brisbane), 21 October 1916; 17/4644, 6 December 1916, Q.S.A.

21 *Argus*, 18 October 1916; Defence Dept, MP 133/2, 150/6/377, 'Exemptions', C.A.O., Melbourne.

22 Defence Dept, MP 133/2, 150/6/

415, 13/14, 'Exemptions', C.A.O., Melbourne.
23 P.M. Dept, A 77, 'Compulsory military service', C.A.O., Canberra; Premier's Dept, 66/7/16, T.S.A.; Premier's Dept, 16/228, L.B.W.A.
24 *Argus*, 28 October 1916; 17/1174, 13 December 1916, A.A.N.S.W.
25 *S.M.H.*, *Age*, *Argus*, 30 October 1916.
26 MS 696/834, 29, 30 October 1916, Novar Papers, N.L.A.; *Argus*, 28, 30 October 1916.
27 MS 696/64, 8 December 1916, Novar Papers, N.L.A.
28 P.M. Dept, A 77, 'Compulsory military service', 5 January 1917, C.A.O., Canberra.
29 Defence Dept, ABDE Series 299/10/68, 87, 1, 12 December 1916, A.A., Melbourne; *Parl. Deb.* (Cwlth), vol. 80, p. 9538, 7 December 1916.
30 *Official History*, vol. 11, p. 362.
31 *Worker*, *Labor Call*, 2 November 1916.
32 Australian Labor Party, *Official History of the Reconstruction of the Labor Party*, p. 7.
33 F. B. Smith, *The Conscription Plebiscites*, pp. 11-12; *Official History*, vol. 11, p. 352.
34 P.M. Dept, A 77, 'Compulsory military service', 18 November 1916, C.A.O., Canberra.
35 B. H. Liddell Hart, *The Real War 1914-1918*, pp. 263-4; E/4/2/12, 23 October, E/2/17/3, 20 November, E/1/2/5, 22 November 1916, Lloyd George Papers, Beaverbrook Library, London.
36 *Parl. Deb.* (Cwlth), vol. 82, p. 1133, 16 August 1917.
37 P.M. Dept, A 77, 'Censorship', 31 May 1917, C.A.O., Canberra; *Official History*, vol. 11, p. 352.
38 *Official History . . . Labor Party*, p. 8; *Official History*, vol. 11, pp. 363-5; Smith, op. cit., p. 13.
39 MS 696/64, 8 December 1916, Novar Papers, N.L.A.
40 Smith, op. cit., p. 14; *Official History*, vol. 11, chapter 10; *Official History . . . Labor Party*, p. 9.
41 MS 696/883-6, 14 February 1917, Novar Papers, N.L.A.

7 RECRUITING CAMPAIGNS OF 1917
1 *Parl. Deb.* (Cwlth), vol. 81, p. 11661, 16 March 1917; C. E. W. Bean (ed.), *Official History*, vol. 11, p. 871.
2 *Argus*, 7 February 1917, cited in *Parl. Deb.* (Cwlth), vol. 81, p. 10420, 13 February 1917.
3 *Official History*, vol. 11, p. 405.
4 *Argus*, 30 November 1916.
5 Premier's Dept, 16/16817, Q.S.A. (Circular on recruiting issued by Director-General of Recruiting, dated Melbourne, 6 December 1916).
6 J. K. Jensen, 'Department of Defence war activities 1914-1917', p. 581. (Conscription Collection, Troedel Collection, La Trobe Library, Melbourne.)
7 Director-General of Recruiting, *The Speaker's Companion*.
8 *Argus*, 30 November, 28 December 1916.
9 Ibid., 19 January 1917.
10 Ibid., 9 February 1917.
11 Ibid., 16 February 1917.
12 Ibid., 6 December 1916.
13 Ibid., 30 January 1917.
14 Defence Dept, AIF Series 142/4/1921, 7 February 1917, A.A., Melbourne.
15 See posters in Troedel Collection, La Trobe Library, Melbourne.
16 Defence Dept, AIF Series 142/4/2194, 2422, 9 March—16 April 1917, A.A., Melbourne.
17 *Argus*, 7 April 1917.
18 Defence Dept, AIF Series 142/4/2698, 5 June 1917, A.A., Melbourne.
19 Ibid., 278/2/52, 61, 23 March, 4 April 1917.
20 'The sportsmen's recruiting committee', p. 1. 533, 17/10/63, 1121 DRL, A.W.M. Library.
21 'Enlistment of over-age men', p. 6, 533.2, 5 April 1917, A.W.M. Library.
22 Defence Dept, WAR Series 363/1/1565, 25 June 1917, A.A., Melbourne.
23 Defence Dept. AIF Series 278/2, A.A., Melbourne.
24 *Argus*, 16 July 1915.
25 Defence Dept, MP 133/5, AIF

Series 144/1/274A, 29 January 1915.

[26] Defence Dept, '1917-29 Military system', PB 582/1/14, 6 August 1917, A.A., Melbourne.

[27] Ibid., 582/1/18, 8 August 1917.

[28] Ibid., 581/1/164, 191, 21 November, 12 December 1917.

[29] MS 696/76, 10 July 1917, Novar Papers, N.L.A.

[30] P.M. Dept, A 77, 'Censorship', 12 June 1917, C.A.O., Canberra.

[31] Defence Dept, MP 133/1, 112/4/2193, 22 May 1917, C.A.O., Melbourne.

[32] Ibid., MP 367, 582/1/162, 19 October 1917.

[33] Premier's Dept, 17/2302, 19 February 1917, Q.S.A.

[34] Ibid., MS 658/1/6, 31 May 1917, Catts Papers, N.L.A.

[35] Defence Dept, MP 367, 582/1/252, 22 January 1918, C.A.O., Melbourne.

[36] 1917 S.A. State Recruiting Committee, Miscellaneous papers, 620/1-90, especially 620/57, 30 June 1917, S.A.A.

[37] Defence Dept, '1917-29 Military system, Recruiting, general', PB 582/1/14, 6 August 1917, A.A., Melbourne.

[38] 1917 S.A. State Recruiting Committee, Miscellaneous papers, 620/1-90, S.A.A.

8 PATRIOTISM AND PARANOIA

[1] Premier's Dept, 17/13853, 12 November 1917, Q.S.A.

[2] MS 236/61, 7 June 1917, Groom Papers, N.L.A.; *Argus*, 5 June 1917.

[3] *Argus*, 18 June 1917.

[4] Conscription Collection, N.L.A.

[5] *Argus*, 9 June 1917.

[6] 'The sportsmen's recruiting committee', 533, 17/10/63, 1121 DRL, A.W.M. Library; Defence Dept, MP 367, Box 147, 582/1/296, 5 February 1918, C.A.O., Melbourne.

[7] *Argus*, 20 February 1917.

[8] Defence Dept, WAR Series 245/1/599, 2 May 1917, A.A., Melbourne.

[9] Defence Dept, MP 367, Box 83, 526/2/13, C.A.O., Melbourne.

[10] *Argus*, 3 July 1917.

[11] Ibid., 21 July 1917.

[12] P.M. Dept, CP 477/1, SC 307, 'Expeditionary force', 17 May, 26 October 1917, C.A.O., Canberra.

[13] MS 696/959, 23 September 1917, Novar Papers, N.L.A.

[14] *Argus*, 16 July 1917.

[15] Ibid., 2 August 1917.

[16] *Age*, 2 July, 8 August 1917; *Sun* (Sydney), 20 July 1917; *Daily Telegraph*, 13, 18 September 1917.

[17] *Argus*, 22, 27 April 1915.

[18] *Parl. Deb.* (L.A. Vic.), vol. 147, p. 1258, 30 August 1917.

[19] Maurice Blackburn, *The Conscription Referendum, 1916*, p. 13; D. W. Rawson, *Labor in Vain?*, p. 16.

[20] Defence Dept, MP 367, 582/1/218, C.A.O., Melbourne.

[21] MS 696/877, 2 February 1917, Novar Papers, N.L.A.; *Argus*, 6 March 1917.

[22] *Argus*, 2 February 1917.

[23] Premier's Dept, 17/1686, 17 March 1917, A.A.N.S.W.

[24] MS 696/877, 2 February 1917, MS 696/82, 4 November 1917, Novar Papers, N.L.A.

[25] 1917 'Political' folder, 19 January 1917, Hughes Papers, N.L.A.; F/32/4/22, 18 January 1917, Lloyd George Papers, Beaverbrook Library, London.

[26] I conclude this from an analysis of the attestation papers. *Parl. Deb.* (Cwlth), vol. 82, p. 526, 26 July 1917, statement by J. H. Catts.

[27] P.M. Dept, A 77, 'Irish rebellion', C.A.O., Canberra.

[28] 'Offensive remarks by individuals', ibid.

[29] 'Critchley Parker', ibid.

[30] Defence Dept, MP 367, Box 147, 582/2/56, C.A.O., Melbourne.

[31] 'The sportsmen's recruiting committee', p. 2, 18 October 1917, 533, 17/10/63, 1121 DRL, A.W.M. Library.

[32] *Argus*, 8 November 1916.

[33] Defence Dept, MP 367, Box 66, 512/1/64, 26 March 1917, C.A.O., Melbourne.

[34] C. E. W. Bean (ed.), *Official History*, p. 144.

[35] *Parl. Deb.* (Cwlth), vol. 76, p. 4570, 2 July 1915; Defence Dept, MP

133/2, 112/2/759, 2 July 1915; *Argus*, 2 July 1915.

36 J. K. Jensen, 'Department of Defence war activities 1914-1917', p. 287. (Conscription Collection, Troedel Collection, La Trobe Library, Melbourne.)

37 Defence Dept, WAR Series 216/1/50, 4 September 1914, A.A., Melbourne.

38 Premier's Dept, 14/6278, 28 September, 8 October 1914, A.A. N.S.W.

39 Defence Dept, WAR Series 363/1/1238, 1245, 6, 10 February 1917; 124/4/1861, 1891, 1, 5 February 1917; 216/1/240, 9 November 1914; 216/1/290, 16 November 1914; 216/4/480, 588, 10 December 1914; 216/4/45, 7 July 1915, A.A., Melbourne.

40 G. F. Pearce, *Carpenter to Cabinet*, p. 134.

41 Defence Dept, WAR Series 216/1/224, 134, 579, 5 November 1914, 8 January 1915.

42 These examples are drawn from Defence Dept, WAR Series 175, 216, 245 and 298, '1917-29 Military system', PB 512/1/64, A.A., Melbourne.

43 Premier's Dept, 14/10948, 26-28 October 1914, Q.S.A.

44 Ibid., 15/7318, 17 July 1915.

45 Ibid., 15/8240, 3 July 1915.

46 *Parl. Deb.* (Cwlth), vol. 83, p. 2712, 26 September 1917.

47 P.M. Dept, A 77, 'Censorship', 22 October 1917, C.A.O., Canberra.

48 *Argus*, 3 November 1917.

49 P.M. Dept, A 77 'Censorship', 1 March 1917, C.A.O., Canberra.

50 Defence Dept, MP 133/3, 281/3/1269, 17 February 1917, C.A.O., Melbourne.

51 *Argus*, 7 August 1917.

52 *Argus*, *Age*, 29 December 1916.

53 Premier's Dept, 17/7514, Q.S.A.

54 *Parl. Deb.* (Cwlth), vol. 82, p. 54, 11 July 1917.

55 Ibid., pp. 65-6, 11 July 1917; *Age*, 10 July 1917.

56 *Argus*, 23 March 1917.

57 'The sportsmen's recruiting committee', 533 17/10/63, 1121 DRL, A.W.M. Library.

58 Ian Turner, *Industrial Labour and Politics*, pp. 144-6; *Age*, 6 September 1917; *Labor Call*, 6 September 1917.

59 *Argus*, 24, 25 September 1917.

60 Ibid., 1 September 1917.

61 *Official History*, vol. 11, p. 424; *Worker*, 28, 21 June 1917; Premier's Dept, 17/4160, A.A.N.S.W.

62 P.M. Dept, CP 447/1, SC 110, 'Labour difficulties', 20 August 1917, C.A.O., Canberra.

63 P.M. Dept, CP 447/3, SC 6, 'Censorship', 5-7 September 1917, C.A.O., Canberra.

64 Defence Dept, '1917-29 Military system', 430/2/12, 205, 8 August, 17 October 1917, A.A., Melbourne.

65 I have concluded this from an analysis of the attestation papers.

66 'Enlistment of over-age men', p. 6, 533.2, A.W.M. Library; *Parl. Deb.* (Cwlth), vol. 84, p. 4759, 16 May 1918; ibid., vol. 83, pp. 4968-9, 22 May 1918, pp. 5749-50, 12 June 1918.

67 Defence Dept, '1917-29 Military system', 461/9/525, 15 May 1918, A.A., Melbourne.

68 Defence Dept, WAR Series 216/1/2154, 25 May 1917, A.A., Melbourne.

69 P.M. Dept, A 77, 'Economic conscription', 30 July 1917, C.A.O., Canberra.

70 *Parl. Deb.* (Cwlth), vol. 83, p. 2174, 18 September 1917, p. 2278, 19 September 1917; 'Enlistment of over-age men', p. 6, 533.2, A.W.M. Library.

71 *Parl. Deb.* (Cwlth), vol. 83, pp. 2279-80, 19 September 1918.

72 Ibid., p. 2565, 24 September 1917.

73 F. B. Smith, *The Conscription Plebiscites*, p. 15; *Official History*, vol. 11, pp. 410-12.

74 *Argus*, 13 November 1917; *Official History*, vol. 11, pp. 412-14.

9 CONSCRIPTION DIVIDES THE NATION

1 *Argus*, 13 November 1917.

2 Ibid., 8 November 1917.

3 Ibid., 13, 16 November 1917.

4 Ibid., 16 November 1917.

5 Conscription Collection, La Trobe Library, Melbourne.

6 C. E. W. Bean (ed.), *Official History*, vol. 11, p. 414n.

7 Defence Dept, '1917-29 Military system', 467/2/69, 24 November 1917.

8 *Advocate*, 8 December 1917.

9 P.M. Dept, A 77, 'Offensive remarks by individuals', 8 November 1917, C.A.O., Canberra.

10 The conscription pamphlets referred to in this chapter are in the La Trobe Library, Melbourne, and the Australian National Library, Canberra (see chapter 5, n. 44).

11 *Official History*, vol. 11, pp. 95-8; P.M. Dept, A 77, 'Censorship—referendum campaign 1917', 21 November—19 December 1917, C.A.O., Canberra; *Argus*, 1 March 1918.

12 *Argus*, 30 November 1917; *Worker*, 6 December 1917; Premier's Dept, 17/15010, Q.S.A.

13 Premier's Dept, 17/8293, 4-17 December 1917, V.S.A.; *Official History*, vol. 11, p. 416.

14 P.M. Dept, A 77, 'Military service referendum 1917—miscellaneous', 17/4471, C.A.O., Canberra.

15 Premier's Dept, 17/8033, 19 December 1917, A.A.N.S.W.

16 Premier's Dept, 17/15506, Q.S.A.

17 Ibid., 18/793, 26 January 1918.

18 Defence Dept, '1917-29 Military system', 582/1/173, 6 December 1917; 582/2/81, 17 December 1917; 461/9/303, 3 January 1918, A.A., Melbourne.

19 Premier's Dept, 18/449, 9 January 1918, Q.S.A.

20 Ibid., 18/463, 4 January 1918.

21 Ibid., 18/790, 17 January 1918.

22 *Official History*, vol. 11, pp. 431-7.

10 THE FINAL YEAR OF THE WAR

1 *Argus*, 25 January, 15 February 1918.

2 Ibid., 31 January 1918.

3 *Parl. Deb.* (Cwlth), vol. 84, p. 3452, 24 January 1918.

4 *Argus*, 20 February 1918.

5 Ibid., 1, 15 March 1918.

6 Defence Dept, MP 367, Box 147, 582/2/196, 13 March, 9 April 1918.

7 *Parl. Deb.* (Cwlth), vol. 84, p. 3702, 10 April 1918.

8 Premier's Dept, 18/1384, 8 June 1918, A.A.N.S.W.

9 Defence Dept, '1917-29 Military system', 582/1/769, 8 July 1918, A.A., Melbourne.

10 *Parl. Deb.* (Cwlth), vol. 84, p. 3214, 18 January 1918.

11 Defence Dept, MP 367, Box 69, 512/3/105, 29 January, 21 March 1918, C.A.O., Melbourne. For the Ceylon incident, see *Argus*, 8 July 1915.

12 P.M. Dept, A 77, 'Protests against Dr. Mannix', 10 July 1915, C.A.O., Canberra.

13 *Argus*, 22 March 1918.

14 Premier's Dept, 18/4095, 27 March, 17 April 1918, Q.S.A.

15 *Parl. Deb.* (Cwlth), vol. 84, pp. 3585-6, 3595-3646, 4 April 1918.

16 Defence Dept, '1917-29 Military system', 407/29/32, 27 February 1918, A.A., Melbourne.

17 *Argus*, 23 February 1918.

18 Defence Dept, '1917-29 Military system', 582/1/290, 11 March 1918, A.A., Melbourne.

19 Premier's Dept, 18/8723, 18 July 1918, Q.S.A.

20 Defence Dept, '1917-29 Military system', 582/2/226, 28 March 1918, A.A., Melbourne.

21 Ibid., 582/1/719, 28 June 1918; Defence Dept, MP 367, 582/2/542, 14 March 1918, C.A.O., Melbourne.

22 *Parl. Deb.* (Cwlth), vol. 85, p. 4979, 23 May 1918; *Argus*, 7 May 1918.

23 *Argus*, 23 May 1918.

24 Defence Dept, MP 367, Box 147, 582/2/173, C.A.O., Melbourne.

25 C. E. W. Bean (ed.), *Official History*, vol. 11, pp. 446-58; MS 696/1024-5, 9, 22 April 1918; MS 696/310, 30 April 1918, Novar Papers, N.L.A.; *P.P.* (N.S.W.), 1918, no. 3.

26 *Argus*, 5 June, 7 May 1918.

27 *Parl. Deb.* (Cwlth), vol. 85, p. 5332, 30 May 1918.

28 *Official History*, vol. 11, pp. 451-2.

29 Ibid., p. 446.

30 *Argus*, 13, 29 April 1918; *Parl. Deb.* (Cwlth), vol. 84, p. 4177, 25 April 1918; Defence Dept, '1917-29 Military system', 461/9/474, 29 April 1918, A.A., Melbourne.

31 *Parl. Deb.* (Cwlth), vol. 84, p. 4067, 19 April 1918.

32 Ibid., pp. 4138-9, 24 April 1918; ibid., vol. 79, p. 54, 11 July 1917.
33 Premier's Dept, 66/4/18, 5 June 1918, T.S.A.
34 P.M. Dept, A 77, 'Economic conscription', 13 June 1918, C.A.O., Canberra.
35 Defence Dept, '1917-29 Military system', 582/2/348, 17 April 1918, A.A., Melbourne.
36 *Argus*, 13 April 1918.
37 *Official History*, vol. 11, p. 218.
38 Ibid., p. 872; Premier's Dept, 18/13235, 18 November 1918, Q.S.A.
39 *Argus*, 5, 6 June 1918.
40 I have concluded this from an analysis of the attestation papers and files.
41 *Official History*, vol. 11, pp. 465-9.
42 Pamphlet in the Battye Library, Perth.
43 *Anzac Bulletin*, 18 October 1918.
44 Defence Dept, '1917-29 Military system', PB 512/1/486, 2 July 1918, A.A., Melbourne.
45 P.M. Dept, A 77, 'Offensive remarks by individuals', 4 May 1918, C.A.O., Canberra.
46 Defence Dept, '1917-29 Military system', 582/2/702, 20 June 1918, A.A., Melbourne.
47 Ian Turner, *Sydney's Burning*, pp. 240-2.
48 Premier's Dept, 18/2579, 19 June 1918, A.A.N.S.W.
49 P.M. Dept, A 77, 'Censorship', 7 August 1918, C.A.O., Canberra.
50 Premier's Dept, 18/3654, 12 March 1918, A.A.N.S.W.
51 *Argus*, 23 May 1918.
52 Defence Dept, '1917-29 Military system', 582/1/390, 1 May 1918; 582/1/611, 712, 13, 27 June 1918, A.A., Melbourne.
53 P.M. Dept, A 77, 'Offensive remarks by individuals', 2 July 1918, C.A.O., Canberra; Defence Dept, '1917-29 Military system', 609/30/465, 11 July 1918, 582/1/1139, 12 September 1918, A.A., Melbourne.
54 Ibid., 582/2/538, 10 July 1918; 582/1/1223, 16 October 1918.
55 *Parl. Deb.* (Cwlth), vol. 86, p. 6847, 11 October 1918, p. 6935, 16 October 1918.
56 'Correspondence from Brig.-Gen. L. C. Wilson', p. 7, 533, VB 3/9/40, A.W.M. Library.
57 *Parl. Deb.* (Cwlth), vol. 84, pp. 6016-17, 14 June 1918.
58 Defence Dept, MP 367, Box 147, 582/1/1458, 'South Australian State Recruiting Committee', p. 8, C.A.O., Melbourne.
59 Defence Dept, '1917-29 Military system', 582/2/391-461, A.A., Melbourne; *Official History*, vol. 11, p. 461 (Butler is credited with 'barely 101' men).

Bibliography

UNPUBLISHED SOURCES

Army Archives, Melbourne: records of the Defence Department.
Australian National War Memorial Library, Canberra: miscellaneous papers on recruiting.
Beaverbrook Library, London: Lloyd George Papers.
Commonwealth Archives Office, Canberra: records of the Prime Minister's Department.
Commonwealth Archives Office, Melbourne: records of the Defence Department.
La Trobe Library, Melbourne: J. K. Jensen, 'Department of Defence war activities 1914-1917'. 2 vols, in proof. 1918.
National Library of Australia, Canberra: Catts Papers, Groom Papers, Hughes Papers, Novar Papers.
State Archives of New South Wales, Queensland, South Australia, Tasmania, Victoria, and Libraries Board of Western Australia: records of the Premiers' and Chief Secretaries' Departments.

THESES

Migus, M., 'Assumptions about, and reactions to, Australia's entry into World War I', B.A. thesis, Department of History, University of Melbourne, 1967.
Trethewey, A. R., 'The teaching of history in state-supported elementary schools in Victoria 1852-1954', M.Ed. thesis, University of Melbourne, 1965.

NEWSPAPERS

Advocate (Melbourne)	*Call* (Sydney)
Age (Melbourne)	*Courier* (Brisbane)
Anzac Bulletin (London)	*Daily Standard* (Brisbane)
Argus (Melbourne)	*Daily Telegraph* (Sydney)
Australasian (Melbourne)	*Herald* (Melbourne)

Labor Call (Melbourne)
Leader (Melbourne)
Round Table (London)
Socialist (Melbourne)
Spectator (Melbourne)

Sun (Sydney)
Sydney Morning Herald
United Empire (London)
Worker (Brisbane)

BOOKS AND ARTICLES

Austin, A. G. (ed.), *The Webbs' Australian Diary 1898*. Melbourne, 1965.

Australian Labor Party, New South Wales Executive, *Official History of the Reconstruction of the Labor Party 1916*. Sydney, [1917].

Bean, C. E. W., *Anzac to Amiens: A shorter history of the Australian fighting services in the First World War*. Canberra, 1946.

———, *Two Men I Knew: William Bridges and Brudenell White, founders of the A.I.F.* Sydney, 1957.

——— (ed.), *Official History of Australia in the War of 1914-1918*. 12 vols. Sydney, 1921-37.

Blackburn, Maurice, *The Conscription Referendum, 1916*. Melbourne, 1936.

Brennan, Niall, *Dr. Mannix*. Adelaide, 1964.

Brown, W. Jethro, 'Australia and the war', *Political Quarterly*, no. 5 (February 1915).

Butler, A. G. (ed.), *The Official History of the Australian Army Medical Services in the War of 1914-1918*, vol. 1. Melbourne, 1930.

Cambridge History of the British Empire, vols 3 and 7. London, 1959, 1933.

Clark, C. M. H., *Short History of Australia*. New York, 1963.

Cuttriss, G. P., *'Over the Top' with the Third Australian Division*. London, [1918].

Deakin, Alfred (ed. J. A. La Nauze), *Federated Australia: Selections from letters to the 'Morning Post' 1900-1910*. Melbourne, 1968.

Dilke, C. W., *Greater Britain: A record of travel in English-speaking countries during 1866 and 1867*. London, 1872.

Director-General of Recruiting, *The Speaker's Companion: For speakers, organizers and recruiters*. Melbourne, 1917.

Ebbels, R. N., *The Australian Labor Movement 1850-1907*. Melbourne, 1965.

Fitzhardinge, L. F., *William Morris Hughes: A political biography*, vol. 1. Sydney, 1964.

Fletcher, J. P. and Hills, J. F., *Conscription under Camouflage: An account of compulsory military training in Australia down to the outbreak of the Great War*. Adelaide, [1919].

Ford, Patrick, *Cardinal Moran and the A.L.P.* Melbourne, 1966.

Fraser, John Foster, *Australia: The making of a nation.* London, 1910.

Gordon, Donald C., *The Dominion Partnership in Imperial Defence 1870-1914.* Baltimore, 1965.

Grey of Fallodon, *Twenty-five Years: 1892-1916.* 2 vols. London, 1926.

Grimshaw, Charles, 'Australian nationalism and the imperial connection 1900-1914', *Australian Journal of Politics and History,* vol. 3, no. 1 (1957).

Hall, Henry L., *Australia and England: A study in imperial relations.* London, 1934.

Hancock, I. R., 'The 1911 Imperial Conference', *Historical Studies, Australia and New Zealand,* vol. 12, no. 47 (1966).

Hancock, W. K., *Australia.* Brisbane, 1961.

Hankey, M. P. A. H., *The Supreme Command 1914-1918.* 2 vols. London, 1961.

Holland, H. E., *The Crime of Conscription.* Sydney, 1912.

Jauncey, L. C., *The Story of Conscription in Australia.* Melbourne, 1968.

Knibbs, G. H., *The Private Wealth of Australia and its Growth as Ascertained by Various Methods: Together with a report of the war census of 1915.* Melbourne, 1918.

La Nauze, J. A., *Alfred Deakin: A biography.* 2 vols. Melbourne, 1965.

Lee, J. E., *Duntroon: The Royal Military College of Australia 1911-1946.* Canberra, 1952.

Liddell Hart, B. H., *The Real War 1914-1918.* London, 1930.

Ludwig, Emil, *Kaiser Wilhelm II.* London, 1926.

Marwick, Arthur, *The Deluge: British society and the First World War.* London, 1967.

Palmer, Vance, *The Legend of the Nineties.* Melbourne, 1966.

Pearce, G. F., *Carpenter to Cabinet: Thirty-seven years of Parliament.* London, 1951.

Penny, Barbara R., 'The age of empire: An Australian episode', *Historical Studies, Australia and New Zealand,* vol. 11, no. 41 (1963).

———, 'Australia's reactions to the Boer War: A study in colonial imperialism', *Journal of British Studies,* vol. 7, no. 1 (November 1967).

Pocock, Roger (ed.), *The Frontiersman's Pocket-book.* London, 1909.

Raemaekers, Louis, *Cartoons.* London, [1923].

Rawson, D. W., *Labor in Vain?: A survey of the Australian Labor Party.* Melbourne, 1966.

Robson, L. L., *Australia and the Great War, 1914-1918.* Melbourne, 1969.

Sawer, Geoffrey, *Australian Federal Politics and Law 1901-1929.* Melbourne, 1956.

Smith, F. B., *The Conscription Plebiscites in Australia 1916-1917.* Melbourne, 1965.

The Statesman's Year Book 1914. London, 1914.

Taylor, A. J. P., *The First World War: An illustrated history.* London, 1966.

Terraine, John, *Douglas Haig: The educated soldier.* London, 1963.

Turner, Ian, *Industrial Labour and Politics.* Canberra, 1965.

———, *Sydney's Burning.* Sydney, 1969.

Pamphlets and posters are to be found in the Conscription Collection and the Troedel Collection, La Trobe Library, Melbourne, and in the Conscription Collection, National Library of Australia, Canberra.

Index

Adams, A. H., 14
Adelaide, 177
Adelaide Business House Choirs, 201
Adelaide Recruiting Committee, 132
Advertiser (Adelaide), 98
Age: outbreak of war, 24; censorship, 159-60
Alcohol, 69, 146, 157-8
Allans Ltd, Adelaide, 201
All British Association, W.A., 114
Amalgamated Society of Engineers, 112, 199
Anderson family, Bendigo, 183
Angliss, W. H., 162
Anthony Horden and Son, 194
Anti-Conscription League, 170, 180
Anti's Creed, 177-8
Anzacs, 41-2, 84
Argus, 18, 149, 155-6, 199-200; advantages of enlistment, 189; censorship, 160; compulsory call-up, 107-8; conscription, 70-1, 107; recruiting, 48, 191
Armed Australia, 13
Ashmead-Bartlett, Ellis, 43, 79
Asquith, H. H., 61, 78, 91
Associated Chambers of Commerce, 111
Austin, Alfred, 17
Australian Freedom League, 102
Australian Industries Preservation Acts, 8
Australian Labor Party: associated with Liberals, 7; and conscription, 73-4, 81, 85-6, 173, 185; emergence, 6; general election (1914) 21, 32-3, 62, (1917) 146-7; industrial strife, 161; in opposition, 9; split, 79, 115-22, 188; war problems, 60, 62, 197; *see also* Brennan, Frank; Hughes, W. M.; *Labor Call*; Ryan, T. J.; Tudor, F. G.; *Worker*

Australian Labour Federation, W.A., 164
Australian National Defence League, 11-14
Australian Natives' Association, 36, 41, 79-80
Australian Naval and Military Expeditionary Force occupies New Guinea, 22-3
Australian Peace Alliance, 80, 98-9
Australian Trade Union Congress, 96-7
Australian Women's Association, 145
Australian Workers' Union, 55

Bairnsfather, Capt. B., 200
Bakhap, T. J. K., 57
Ball, Sergt A., 79
Ballarat, Vic., 34, 98, 104, 183
Ballendella, Vic., 55
Balmain, N.S.W., 68-9
Bannockburn, Qld, 153
Baptist Church, 158
Barossa District, S.A., 151
Barrett, R. J., 109
Barrier Miner, Broken Hill, 199
Barton, Edmund, 6, 10
Batchelor, E. L., 16
Bathurst gaol, 179-80
Battalions of A.I.F.: 1st-12th, 22; 6th, 44; 11th, 43; 13th, 185; 24th, 50; 36th, 193, 196; 40th, 75-6; 43rd, 202; 47th, 196; 52nd, 196
Baulkham Hills, N.S.W., 53
Beaconsfield, Tas., 68
Bean, C. E. W., 17, 123
Bellchambers, Gunner, 28
Bendigo, Vic., 156, 167, 183
Bijou Theatre, Melbourne, 26, 98
Billson, J. W., 46
Binjour, Qld, 156
Birdwood, Field-Marshal Sir William, 49-50, 83, 119-20, 171